TECHNIQUES FOR THE COUPLE THERAPIST

Techniques for the Couple Therapist features many of the most prominent psycho-therapists today, presenting their most effective couple therapy interventions. This book provides clinicians with a user-friendly quick reference and an array of techniques that can be quickly read and immediately used in session. The book includes over 50 chapters by experts in the field on the fundamental principles and techniques for effective couple therapy. Many of the techniques focus on common couple therapy processes such as enactments, communication, and reframing. Others focus on specific presenting problems, such as trauma, sexual issues, infidelity, intimate partner violence, and high conflict. Students, beginning therapists, and seasoned clinicians will find this pragmatic resource invaluable in their work with couples.

Gerald R. Weeks, PhD, is a professor in the Marriage and Family Therapy Program at the University of Nevada, Las Vegas.

Stephen T. Fife, PhD, is an associate professor in the Marriage and Family Therapy Program at the University of Nevada, Las Vegas.

Colleen M. Peterson, PhD, is the director of the Center for Individual, Couple and Family Counseling and an associate professor-in-residence in the Marriage and Family Therapy Program at the University of Nevada, Las Vegas.

TECHNIQUES FOR THE COUPLE THERAPIST

Essential Interventions
From the Experts

Edited by Gerald R. Weeks,
Stephen T. Fife, and Colleen M. Peterson

Routledge
Taylor & Francis Group
NEW YORK AND LONDON

First published 2016
by Routledge
711 Third Avenue, New York, NY 10017

and by Routledge
2 Park Square, Milton Park, Abingdon, Oxon, OX14 4RN

Routledge is an imprint of the Taylor & Francis Group, an informa business

© 2016 Taylor & Francis

Library of Congress Cataloging-in-Publication Data
Names: Weeks, Gerald R., 1948– , editor. | Fife, Stephen T., editor. |
   Peterson, Colleen M., editor.
Title: Techniques for the couple therapist : essential interventions
   from the experts / edited by Gerald R. Weeks, Stephen T. Fife, and
   Colleen M. Peterson.
Description: New York, NY : Routledge, 2016. Includes bibliographical
   references and index.
Identifiers: LCCN 2015040238 | ISBN 9781138814608
   (hardback : alk. paper) | ISBN 9781138814615 (pbk. : alk. paper) |
   ISBN 9781315747330 (ebook)
Subjects: | MESH: Couples Therapy—methods.
Classification: LCC RC488.5 | NLM WM 430.5.M3 |
   DDC 616.89/1562—dc23
LC record available at http://lccn.loc.gov/2015040238

ISBN: 978-1-138-81460-8 (hbk)
ISBN: 978-1-138-81461-5 (pbk)
ISBN: 978-1-315-74733-0 (ebk)

Typeset in Bembo
by Apex CoVantage, LLC

To Nancy Love
—GW

To April Fife
—SF

In memory of my best friend, Kathleen Briggs
—CP

CONTENTS

PREFACE

Working with couples can be challenging and requires specialized clinical knowledge and skills. This book grew out of the needs expressed by many of the graduate students and new professionals we (the Editors) have supervised. As faculty who train beginning clinicians, one of the most common questions we are asked is, "What technique should I use for this particular client with this particular problem?" Over the years, we have been able to offer numerous techniques based on our own experience and our knowledge of couple therapy models. With over 75 years of supervision experience, we find that clinicians often benefit from having a roadmap or guide to help them navigate the challenges associated with couple therapy. The purpose of this book, however, is not to provide an overview of couple therapy—this is addressed thoroughly in the book *Couples in Treatment* (3rd ed.) (Weeks & Fife, 2014). Rather, our objective is to present some of the key interventions used by experts in couple therapy.

With this book, we wanted to provide the reader with a user-friendly quick reference to an array of techniques designed specifically for use with couples. We identified several areas of concern and presenting problems by couples coming to therapy. Once these areas had been identified, our strategy was to invite the top figures in the field of couple therapy to submit one or two short chapters. To our delight, almost everyone we invited accepted the invitation. Thus, the contributors represent many of the Who's Who in the field of couple therapy.

How This Book Is Organized

This book is divided into two main sections. Section I addresses fundamental principles for effective couple therapy and includes chapters on the foundations of successful practice with couples, building a strong therapeutic alliance, developing clinical mastery, and improving couple therapy outcomes. We begin with a chapter that places clinical techniques in the context of the central common factors that undergird their effectiveness. We believe that previous debates in the field about whether techniques or common factors are the mechanisms of change are unhelpful, as these disputes are based on either/or thinking rather than both/and thinking. The dialectical position proposed in this volume is that both are important—a technique(s) will probably not be effective unless the therapist has attended to various common factors (Fife, Whiting, Davis, & Bradford, 2014; Weeks & Fife, 2014), and common factors alone, without the substance of technique, will not be effective. In short, effective couple therapy is facilitated through a combination of common factors *and* techniques, which together provide the structure to generate meaningful change in couples' relationships. Another way one of the editors (G. W.) teaches this idea is that, "Techniques can help to mend a broken relationship, but only a relationship can mend the broken hearts within the relationship."

Section I of the book also includes three chapters that discuss ways to achieve clinical excellence and form a therapeutic alliance with couples. Research on how to achieve clinical excellence is a relatively new and under-discussed area, and two of these chapters provide the clinician with practical, easy-to-use research-based ideas that will help readers become more effective therapists and achieve clinical excellence. There is also a chapter in this section that addresses fundamental principles of forming a therapeutic alliance with couples. Although this is considered by some to be a technique, the alliance is an essential common factor that is necessary for the successful implementation of the techniques.

Section II constitutes the majority of the book and consists of 46 techniques contributed by experts within the field. The goal was to offer clinicians a variety of creative and effective techniques that could be quickly read, absorbed, and immediately used in session. The chapters are intentionally very short and concise. Each contributor was asked to follow a standard outline (see below) and keep their technique to roughly five double-spaced pages in length.

Descriptive Title of Technique
  Purpose Statement
    Introduction
    Purpose of the technique
    Description and implementation of the technique
    Contraindications (if pertinent)
    A brief case example illustrating the technique

We intentionally constructed the book so that it does not emphasize one specific theory or couple therapy model, and we purposefully invited authors with expertise in a variety of theoretical backgrounds to contribute to the book. We see many books that discuss theory without clear discussion of how to implement the theory through techniques. Therefore, one important purpose of the book was to provide clinicians with a pragmatic resource of effective interventions to use with couples.

The techniques in Section II are organized by topic and/or purpose. The reader will note that the Table of Contents is a bit unusual. In addition to presenting the title of the chapter (i.e., the name of the technique) and the author's or authors' name(s), we also include the purpose of the technique. The clinician will be able to consult the Table of Contents when preparing for a session in order to quickly find an appropriate technique, and within a few minutes of reading be prepared to use the technique. In some cases, a variety of techniques are available that serve the same goal or purpose. The clinician can choose the technique they think is best suited to their couple. The techniques are grouped according to the following topics and purposes (Parts A through H):

- Enactments
- Couple Communication
- Reframing
- Anger and Conflict
- Intimacy, Growth, and Change
- Health and Wellness
- Intimate Partner Violence
- Addressing Childhood Sexual Abuse in Couple Therapy

Many of the techniques address general couple therapy processes such as enactments, couple communication, and reframing. Others focus on specific presenting problems such as couple conflict, dyadic stress, and intimate partner violence. Additionally, there are a number of chapters devoted to promoting intimacy and growth in couples.

Not only does the book include interventions that target specific couple therapy process and presenting problems, but some chapters also describe techniques that are grounded in specific therapy models. Therapists who are applying a specific model with a couple may benefit from the straightforward descriptions of techniques that are associated with the following models:

- Cognitive-behavioral couple therapy (Chapters 9, 10, 17, and 22)
- Contextual therapy (Chapter 14)
- Emotion-focused couple therapy (Chapters 18 and 31)
- Internal family systems therapy (Chapter 27)
- Narrative therapy (Chapters 19, 20, 21, and 32)
- Object relations couple therapy (Chapters 24 and 25)
- Solution focused brief therapy (Chapters 33 and 34)
- Structural couple therapy (Chapters 15 and 23)

Nevertheless, the large majority of the techniques may be applied across theoretical orientations and couple therapy approaches.

Due to the book's purpose and organization, it is not expected that this book will be read from cover to cover. However, we suggest you begin with the chapters in Section I, which provide a solid foundation for using the interventions presented in the subsequent chapters. The remainder of the book contains techniques you are likely to use when needed, and the choice of interventions will likely be directed by your clinical judgment and sensitivity to the clients' needs. We encourage you to take advantage of the opportunity to learn from the experts in couple therapy who generously shared their clinical knowledge and experience in the chapters that follow.

Gerald R. Weeks
Stephen T. Fife
Colleen M. Peterson

References

Fife, S. T., Whiting, J. B., Davis, S., & Bradford, K. (2014). The therapeutic pyramid: A common factors synthesis of techniques, alliance, and way of being. *Journal of Marital and Family Therapy, 40*(1), 20–33.

Weeks, G. R., & Fife, S. T. (2014). *Couples in treatment: Techniques and approaches for effective practice* (3rd ed.). New York: Routledge.

ACKNOWLEDGMENTS

There have been many people who have helped us bring our ideas for this book to fruition. First, we express our deep gratitude to each of the contributing authors. They represent some of the finest couple therapy scholars and clinicians in the world. Their clinical experience and theoretical expertise provide a valuable resource for new professionals and veteran therapists alike. We consider ourselves blessed to work with such an amazing group of authors. We also express our sincere appreciation for the support of our family and friends throughout the process of developing this book from conception to publication. We would not have successfully completed this project without them cheering us on.

We also thank the staff at Routledge/Taylor & Francis for their assistance with this project, especially the support of associate editors Marta Moldvai and Elizabeth Graber. Finally, we acknowledge the diligent efforts of our graduate students in the preparation of this text. Given that graduate students and new professionals are important audiences for this book, their feedback on the chapters was invaluable in developing a resource that is user-friendly, with clear practical application for therapists in their work with couples. Specifically, we thank Jeana Alvarado, Diana Caldas, Dawn Canty, Zachary Card, Amanda Flores, Hannah Goodman, Chey'Anne Harris, Lawrence Jackson, Sherri Kehoe, Nedka Klimas, Lauren McCoy, Kiera McGillivray, Triston Neeson, Cherelle Ola, Milagros Severin-Ruiz, and Raelara Tilden.

ABOUT THE EDITORS

Gerald R. Weeks, PhD, is a Professor in the Marriage and Family Therapy Program at the University of Nevada, Las Vegas. For over 30 years, he has published, conducted research, practiced, taught, and supervised sex, couple, and family therapy. Dr. Weeks is a licensed psychologist, Approved Supervisor, and Clinical Fellow of the American Association of Marriage and Family Therapy; a Diplomate and Senior Examiner of the American Board of Family Psychology; and a member of the American Board of Sexology. He has published 24 books, including one or more classic texts in the fields of individual, sex, couple, and family therapy. Several of his texts are widely used in Marriage and Family Therapy Programs. In 2009, he was the 16th member to receive the "Outstanding Contribution the Marriage and Family Therapy" award from the American Association of Marriage and Family therapy. In 2010, the American Psychological Association awarded "Family Psychologist of the Year" to Dr. Weeks. One of his major contributions to the field of couple and sex therapy is the development of a new paradigm of therapy known as the Intersystem Approach. In fact, he founded the Intersystem Approach to therapy and the systemic approach to sex therapy. Dr. Weeks has lectured and conducted intensive training in couple and sex therapy throughout North America, Europe, and Australia.

Stephen T. Fife, PhD, is an Associate Professor in the Marriage and Family Therapy Program at the University of Nevada, Las Vegas. He is a Clinical Fellow of the American Association of Marriage and Family Therapy and a member of the National Council on Family Relations with over 15 years of experience teaching, supervising, and practicing individual, couple, and family therapy. He has published and presented his research nationally and internationally on couple therapy, the treatment and healing of infidelity, therapeutic change processes, and the foundations of effective clinical practice. Dr. Fife recently published *Couples in*

Treatment with Dr. Weeks, and was the lead author of an innovative meta-model of psychotherapy called the Therapeutic Pyramid, for which he and his co-authors were awarded the "Best Article of 2014" by the Editorial Council of the *Journal of Marital and Family Therapy*. Dr. Fife also has a private practice and lectures extensively in the community on topics related to couple and family relationships. He is happily married and is the father of two sons.

Colleen M. Peterson, PhD, is the Director of the Center for Individual, Couple and Family Counseling and an Associate Professor-in-Residence in the Marriage and Family Therapy Program at the University of Nevada, Las Vegas. She is a licensed marriage and family therapist and Clinical Fellow and Approved Supervisor with the American Association for Marriage and Family Therapy with over 25 years of experience as a marriage and family therapist. Dr. Peterson is the President of the Nevada Board of Examiners for Marriage and Family Therapists and Clinical Professional Counselors and served as a Commissioner, including chair, for the Commission on Accreditation for Marriage and Family Therapy Education. She has published and presented her research on marriage and family therapy ethics, medical family therapy, clinical supervision, and the treatment of sexual abuse/trauma.

CONTRIBUTORS

Harry J. Aponte, MSW, LCSW, LMFT, HPhD, Clinical Associate Professor, Couple and Family Therapy Department, Drexel University; private practice, Philadelphia, PA.

Guy Bodenmann, PhD, Professor of Clinical Psychology, Director of Couple Therapy Program, Director of Psychotherapy for Children Program, Department of Psychology, University of Zurich, Switzerland.

Lorrie Brubacher, MEd, LMFT, Director of Greensboro Charlotte Center for Emotionally Focused Therapy, Greensboro, NC.

Jon Carlson, EdD, PsyD, ABPP, Professor, Counselor Education and Supervision Program, Governors State University, University Park, IL.

Gene Combs, MD, Associate Clinical Professor of Psychiatry and Family Medicine at the University of Chicago-affiliated NorthShore University HealthSystem residency program in Family Medicine, Glenview, IL; volunteer faculty at Evanston Family Therapy Center, Evanston, IL, and the Chicago Center for Family Health, Chicago, IL.

Sean D. Davis, PhD, Professor, Couple and Family Therapy Program, California School of Professional Psychology, Alliant International University, Sacramento, CA.

Rachel M. Diamond, PhD, Postdoctoral Fellow, The Family Institute at Northwestern University, Evanston, IL.

Barry Duncan, PsyD, Director, Heart and Soul of Change Project (heartandsoulofchange.com) and CEO of BetterOutcomesNow.com, Jensen Beach, FL.

Norman B. Epstein, PhD, Professor, Director, Couple and Family Therapy Program, Department of Family Science, School of Public Health, University of Maryland, College Park, MD.

Sandra A. Espinoza, MA, Couple and Family Therapy Program, Alliant International University, Los Angeles, CA.

Stephen T. Fife, PhD, Associate Professor, Marriage and Family Therapy Program, University of Nevada, Las Vegas, NV.

Jill Freedman, MSW, Director of Evanston Family Therapy Center, Evanston, IL; International Faculty of Dulwich Centre, Adelaide, Australia; Faculty of Chicago Center for Family Health, Chicago, IL, and Hincks Delcrest Centre Brief Therapy Year-Long Extern Training Program, Toronto, Canada.

Nancy Gambescia, PhD, Director, Postgraduate Sex Therapy Program, Council for Relationships, Philadelphia, PA; Clinical Associate Professor, Center for Couples and Adult Families, Department of Psychiatry, University of Pennsylvania, Philadelphia, PA.

Shelley A. Haddock, PhD, LMFT, Associate Professor, Marriage and Family Therapy Program, Human Development and Family Studies Department, Colorado State University, Fort Collins, CO.

Miyoung Yoon Hammer, PhD, Assistant Professor of Marriage and Family Therapy, Fuller Theological Seminary, Pasadena, CA.

Terry D. Hargrave, PhD, Professor, Marriage and Family Therapy, Fuller Theological Seminary, Pasadena, CA.

Toni Herbine-Blank, MS, RN, CS-P, Senior Trainer for The Center for Self-Leadership, Developer of Intimacy from the Inside Out©; integrating the intrapsychic and interpersonal in couple therapy, Durango, CO.

Katherine M. Hertlein, PhD, Program Director, Marriage and Family Therapy Program, University of Nevada, Las Vegas, NV.

Jennifer L. Hodgson, PhD, LMFT, Professor, Departments of Child Development and Family Relations and Family Medicine, Marriage and Medical Family Therapy Programs, East Carolina University, Greenville, NC.

Mark A. Hubble, PhD, International Center for Clinical Excellence, Chicago, IL.

Sue Johnson, EdD, Founding Director of the International Centre for Excellence in Emotionally Focused Therapy, Ottawa, Canada; Distinguished Research Professor at Alliant University, San Diego, CA; Professor of Clinical Psychology at the University of Ottawa, Canada.

Sara Smock Jordan, PhD, LMFT, Associate Professor, Marriage and Family Therapy Program, Texas Tech University, Lubbock, TX.

Irina Kolobova, MA, CCRP, Doctoral Candidate, Medical Family Therapy Program, East Carolina University, Greenville, NC.

Daniel Kort, BA, Duke University, Durham, NC.

Luciano L'Abate, PhD, ABEPP, Professor Emeritus of Psychology, Georgia State University, Atlanta, GA.

Angela L. Lamson, PhD, LMFT, CFLE, Professor, Departments of Child Development and Family Relations; Program Director, Medical Family Therapy Doctoral Program; Director, Redditt House, Medical Family Therapy Research Academy, East Carolina University, Greenville, NC.

Jeffry H. Larson, PhD, Alumni Professor of Marriage and Family Therapy, School of Family Life, Brigham Young University, Provo, UT.

Jay L. Lebow, PhD, ABPP, Professor, The Family Institute at Northwestern University, Evanston, IL.

Janie K. Long, PhD, LMFT, Director, Center for Sexual and Gender Diversity, Duke University, Durham, NC.

Sonya Lorelle, PhD, LPC, Assistant Professor, Counselor Education and Supervision Program, Governors State University, University Park, IL.

Howard J. Markman, PhD, Professor, Department of Psychology, Co-Director of the Center for Marital and Family Studies, University of Denver, CO.

Anne Milek, PhD, Senior Researcher and Couple Therapist, Department of Psychology—Clinical Psychology for Children/Adolescents & Couples/Families, University of Zurich, Switzerland.

Scott D. Miller, PhD, Director, International Center for Clinical Excellence, Chiago, IL.

Amelia Muse, MS, LMFTA, Medical Family Therapy Program, East Carolina University, Greenville, NC.

Patricia L. Papernow, EdD, Psychologist in private practice, Hudson, MA; Instructor in Psychology, Department of Psychiatry, Harvard Medical School, Boston, MA; member, Senior Training Faculty and Experts Council, National Stepfamily Resource Center (www.stepfamilyrelationships.com), a division of Auburn University's Center for Children, Youth, and Families, Auburn, AL.

Aleja M. Parsons, MA, Center for Marital and Family Studies, Clinical Psychology PhD Program, Department of Psychology, University of Denver, Denver, CO.

Colleen M. Peterson, PhD, Director, Center for Individual, Couple and Family Counseling and Associate Professor in Residence, Marriage and Family Therapy Program, University of Nevada, Las Vegas, NV.

Lane L. Ritchie, MA, Center for Marital and Family Studies, Clinical Psychology Ph.D. Program, Department of Psychology, University of Denver, CO.

Judith P. Siegel, PhD, LCSW, Associate Professor, Coordinator, Certificate Program in Child & Family Therapy, Silver School of Social Work at New York University, New York, NY.

George M. Simon, MS, LMFT, Adjunct Assistant Professor, Department of Counseling and Mental Health Professions, Hofstra University, Hempstead, NY; Faculty, The Minuchin Center for the Family, New York, NY.

Laura S. Smedley, MS, Marriage and Family Therapist, Kayenta Therapy Center, Las Vegas, NV.

Douglas B. Smith, PhD, Associate Professor, Director, Marriage & Family Therapy Program, Department of Community, Family and Addiction Sciences, Texas Tech University, Lubbock, TX.

Jacqueline Sparks, PhD, Professor, Department of Human Development and Family Studies, Couple and Family Therapy Program, University of Rhode Island, Kingston, RI.

Gerald R. Weeks, PhD, ABPP, Professor, Marriage and Family Therapy Program, University of Nevada, Las Vegas, NV.

Jason B. Whiting, PhD, Professor, Marriage and Family Therapy Program, Department of Community, Family and Addiction Sciences, Texas Tech University, Lubbock, TX.

Toni Schindler Zimmerman, PhD, LMFT, Professor, Program Director for the COAMFTE Marriage and Family Therapy Program, Human Development and Family Studies Department, Colorado State University, Fort Collins, CO.

SECTION I

Fundamental Principles for Effective Couple Therapy

1

THE HEART AND SOUL OF COUPLE THERAPY

Stephen T. Fife

Purpose: To highlight the foundations of successful clinical practice with couples and to provide a framework for the effective use of interventions in couple therapy

Working with couples in therapy can be tremendously rewarding—and at times extremely challenging. Couple therapy is, perhaps, the most difficult modality of treatment, and many therapists receive little or no training specifically in couple therapy (Doherty, 2002). Although many mental health professionals take a class or two on family therapy in graduate school, therapists often struggle to apply what they learn in these classes with couples. Couple therapy requires that therapists be quick on their feet, join effectively with both partners, pay attention simultaneously to individual issues and interpersonal dynamics, and be able to tolerate and effectively manage emotional intensity in session, as interactions between partners can become volatile. Nevertheless, the majority of therapists end up working with couples at some point in their careers, and having a roadmap as a guide can be extremely helpful for clinicians.[1] The purpose of this chapter is to describe the foundations of effective work with couples and to provide a framework for the effective use of interventions in couple therapy.

What Makes Couple Therapy Effective?

Several decades of outcome research supports the effectiveness of couple therapy, with 84% of clients in marital therapy being better off than individuals receiving no treatment (Shadish & Baldwin, 2002). Furthermore, research and meta-analyses on the effectiveness of couple therapy find that it is generally effective regardless of the model being used (Shadish & Baldwin, 2009; Sprenkle & Blow, 2004a). In other words, no model is consistently more effective than others. The conclusion that all approaches of therapy are effective is famously known as the "dodo bird effect," arising from the dodo bird's observation in *Alice and Wonderland*: "At last the Dodo said, 'Everybody has won, and all must have prizes'" (Rosenzweig, 1936, p. 412).

Research findings indicating effectiveness across therapy models raise questions about what makes couple therapy effective and how we account for the change and positive outcomes that are experienced by couples. Many therapists and researchers claim it is the unique characteristics of couple therapy models that are primarily responsible for client change (Davis & Piercy, 2007a; Sexton, Ridley, & Kleiner, 2004; Sprenkle & Blow, 2004a). The history of couple and family therapy has been filled with an "arms race" of sorts, with different model developers promoting the unique (and purportedly superior) aspects of their respective approaches, followed by researchers intent on empirically determining the best model of therapy for couples (Sprenkle, Blow, & Dickey, 1999; Weeks & Fife, 2014). On the other side of the debate are those who argue there are important ingredients that are shared across models of therapy (i.e., common factors) that account for the effectiveness of couple therapy (Davis, Lebow, & Sprenkle, 2012; Davis & Piercy, 2007b; Fife, Whiting, Davis, & Bradford, 2014; Sprenkle, Davis, & Lebow, 2009).

Common Factors of Change

The research theoretical developments and on common factors of change represents one of the most significant developments in couple therapy of the 21st century. Although the debate regarding common factors associated with successful clinical outcomes first began in the individual psychotherapy literature, it picked up momentum among couple therapists with a series of articles published in the *Journal of Marital and Family Therapy* by Sprenkle and Blow (2004a, 2004b) and Sexton and Ridley (2004; see also Sexton et al., 2004).

Michael Lambert's seminal work on common factors led him to conclude that "different therapies embody common factors that are curative, though not emphasized by the theory of change central to any one school" (Asay & Lambert, 1999, p. 29). He determined that common factors of therapeutic change fall into four categories, each accounting for a portion of the outcome variance related to client change: extratherapeutic factors (40%), therapeutic relationship factors (30%), expectancy and placebo effects (15%), and therapy techniques and models (15%) (Asay & Lambert, 1999).

Of Lambert's four common factors, the therapeutic relationship is the therapist-influenced factor that has the greatest impact on change, and couple therapy models are consistently in agreement that the therapeutic relationship is a central aspect of effective therapy. The alliance between the clients and therapist is key to the process of therapy (Fife et al., 2014) and is strongly associated with positive clinical outcomes, regardless of the model a therapist uses (Horvath, 2001;

Wampold, 2001). A strong alliance is built through accurate empathy, positive regard, understanding, affirmation, congruence, and genuineness (Asay & Lambert, 1999). Gaston (1990, p. 145) determined that there are four dimensions to the therapist–client alliance:

1. The therapeutic alliance, or the patient's affective relationship to the therapist;
2. The working alliance, or the patient's capacity to purposefully work in therapy;
3. The therapist's empathic understanding and involvement; and
4. The patient–therapist agreement on the goals and tasks of treatment.

Common Factors in Couple Therapy

Guided by Lambert's four common factors, Sprenkle et al. (1999) reviewed the couple and family therapy literature to determine if there was congruence between Lambert's findings and research and theory in couple and family therapy. They found support for each of Lambert's factors of change, particularly in connection with the therapeutic relationship. Although Asay and Lambert (1999) estimated that relationship factors account for 30% of the outcome variance, Sprenkle et al. (1999) assert that this figure is probably much higher in couple therapy.

In addition to Lambert's factors, there are several unique common factors associated with couple therapy (Davis et al., 2012; Sprenkle et al., 2009). Through their review of the couple and family therapy literature, Sprenkle et al. (1999) identified additional common factors that are important to the practice of couple and family therapy:

1. *Relational conceptualization*: Conceptualizing or understanding client problems in relational terms. Couple therapists practice from a relational or systemic perspective and are aware of the systemic context of clients' individual and relationship challenges.
2. *Expanded direct treatment system*: Unlike individual therapy, couple therapists typically work with both partners simultaneously. Therapists also remain cognizant of individuals not present in therapy but who may be effected by therapy outcomes.
3. *Expanded therapeutic alliance*: Rather than focusing on an individual, couple therapy requires an expanded therapeutic alliance, as couple therapists work to join with both partners.
4. *Behavioral regulation*: Couple therapists attend to interpersonal dynamics, relationship patterns, and couple processes, rather than merely focusing on individual behavior. For example, clinicians may help couples modify existing patterns of interaction or develop new methods of communication or problem-solving.
5. *Cognitive mastery*: Therapists may help couples develop an understanding of their ineffective or destructive patterns of interaction by highlighting

interconnected sequences of thoughts, emotions, and behaviors between partners.

6. *Emotional experiencing*: Couple therapists often focus on the emotional connection (or lack of connection) between partners. Therapy may focus on enhancing emotional awareness, expression, and connection between partners.

Foundations of Successful Couple Therapy

Despite strong support and enthusiasm for common factors, some scholars have questioned their clinical relevance and application. For example, Sexton et al. (2004) argue that common factors do not provide sufficient guidance for successful treatment. On the other hand, Sprenkle and Blow (2004a, 2004b) assert that common factors do provide clinical direction and that they work through therapy models. In order to better convey the relationship between therapy models, techniques, and the alliance, Fife et al. (2014) developed an innovative meta-model of psychotherapy called the Therapeutic Pyramid. This model illustrates the functional relationship between three common factors: therapy models/techniques, therapeutic alliance, and the therapist's way of being, a construct introduced by the authors that is similar to self-of-the-therapist, with special attention given to a therapist's moral valuing of people. The model is organized hierarchically in a pyramid format, with models/techniques on top, the therapeutic alliance in the middle, and the way of being as the foundation. Fundamentally, the model asserts that the effective use of therapy models/techniques rests upon the quality of the therapist–client relationship, and the quality of the therapist–client relationship is grounded in the therapist's way of being (a construct grounded in Martin Buber's (1958) philosophy, which suggests that therapists can relate to clients either as objects or as people, with a person-to-person relationship providing the foundation for a truly *therapeutic* relationship).

Given the way that graduate education and licensing in couple and family therapy are structured, students and beginning therapists might naturally conclude that therapy models and techniques form the heart or foundation of couple therapy. Students likely take courses focused on couple and family therapy models and techniques; supervisors reinforce this by asking supervisees what models they are using; case note forms at university clinics may require student-therapists to document the interventions they use in session; and the national licensing exam for marriage and family therapists is heavily weighted toward a knowledge of marriage and family therapy (MFT) models. This emphasis sends an implicit message suggesting that the foundation of successful couple therapy is the correct application of therapy models and techniques. Thus, it should be no surprise that graduate students and beginning couple therapists devote significant time and energy to learning the major therapy models and their associated techniques.

Of course, the time spent learning to apply couple therapy models and techniques is not wasted. Models and techniques are essential to successful therapy, and good therapy requires talented, knowledgeable clinicians. Unfortunately, the robust support for the central importance of a strong therapeutic alliance is sometimes misinterpreted to mean that knowledge and skills related to therapy models and techniques are unimportant (Weeks & Fife, 2014). Recognizing that the effective couple therapy rests upon the foundations of the therapeutic alliance and the therapist's way of being is no excuse for laziness or lack of preparation. Therapists owe it to their clients to be knowledgeable and well-prepared. Models and techniques are essential, even if they are not the foundation of effective couple therapy. No effective therapy would take place without them. Davis and Piercy (2007a) concluded that therapy models have an important influence on therapy outcomes, in large part because "the client's chaos was replaced by the therapist's order (i.e., their model)" (p. 338). They suggest that models provide therapists with a structure that helps them know what to target for change and how to intervene.

Nevertheless, as the pyramid model suggests, the heart and soul of effective couple therapy is not the model or techniques a therapist uses, but a therapeutic alliance that is grounded in a person-to-person relationship (Fife et al., 2014). Most therapists intuitively understand this, in spite of couple therapy's historical obsession with models and contemporary trends suggesting that client problems can be fixed merely by the correct application of the right technique. Fortunately, in our work with clients we "are often guided in our professional roles more by our deep human responsiveness to people than by our theories. As a result, good things frequently happen" (Warner & Olson, 1981, p. 501). This principle reminds me of a saying I have heard a trusted MFT supervisor and friend repeat many times: "It's not the *arrow*; it's the *archer* that matters most." In other words, who the therapist is (their character and the way they regard their clients) is more fundamental than the techniques or model he or she is using. The pyramid model highlights the foundations of effective treatment and illustrates therapist characteristics that facilitate therapeutic relationships and successful outcomes in therapy. This meta-model is applicable across theoretical and professional orientations and can be a useful guide for a therapist's work with couples in treatment.

I learned about the relationship between these factors through an experience I had as a relatively new therapist. Lin was a woman in her early thirties who contacted me for marital therapy. She was a faculty member at a large university in the Midwest. Although her husband was not willing to attend therapy, she initiated therapy to learn what she could to do improve their relationship. She clearly loved her husband and wanted them to have a stronger marriage. She was careful to avoid criticizing her husband, choosing instead to focus therapy on what she was doing in the marriage that might be pushing him away or hurting their marriage. I was impressed at her humility and sincerity.

After a few sessions, her husband (Justin) decided to join her in therapy. After our first session together, he said he'd like to have an individual session with me. Based on Lin's description of Justin and from my first meeting with him, he seemed to be a capable, intelligent guy who was chronically under-employed and under-engaged in his marriage. I determined that solution-focused therapy would be the right approach to get him to step up and improve his situation and his marriage. I came to the individual session armed with my solution-focused techniques and game plan. However, the session ended up being a disaster. Despite my best efforts, I could not get him to go along with my plan, and the interventions I used fell flat.

I consulted with a colleague about the dreadful session and wondered what went wrong. He listened carefully and quickly recognized my fundamental error. "I know what you did wrong," he responded. "You tried to solution-focus him into submission!" He was right. I saw Justin as an object—a thing to be fixed—and decided on a strategy to fix him before I had built a relationship of trust with him. I put the therapy techniques *cart* ahead of the therapeutic alliance *horse*. I had turned the pyramid upside down on its point, and it had crashed. In the following appointment I abandoned my solution-focused agenda and tried to get to know him first as a person, which resulted in a much better outcome for the session.

Common Mistakes in Couple Therapy

In addition to remembering the importance of the alliance and way of being in their work with clients, couple therapists should be careful to avoid common pitfalls. Given the unique challenges of couple therapy, clinicians can very easily make unintended (although avoidable) mistakes when working with couples (Weeks, Odell, & Methven, 2005). Doherty (2002) suggests that beginning couple therapists often struggle to provide structure in sessions, fail to provide a plan for change in a couple's relationship, and give up on the couple's relationship because they (the therapists) feel overwhelmed by the couple's problems. Experienced therapists, on the other hand, may stumble in different ways when treating couples (Doherty, 2002). Rather than lacking clinical skill or techniques, they make mistakes with couples because of their own values, habits, and beliefs. For example, they may view all couples as equal and overlook the unique circumstances of couples' lives (e.g., working with a remarried couple in the same way one might work with a couple in their first marriage). Seasoned therapists may also unwittingly adopt prevailing cultural values of individualism and capitalism, which leads them to favor clients' commitment to individual well-being over their commitment to the relationship. They may even suggest to clients that if they are not happy with their partner or are dissatisfied with the relationship as it currently stands, perhaps they should consider separation or divorce (similar to suggesting to someone who is unhappy with his or her smart phone that they should trade it in for an upgraded model). Although there are times when separation and divorce may be warranted, Doherty (2002) argues that privileging clients' current satisfaction above all else is a lousy approach when it comes to working with marital and relationship commitment.

Sometimes I ask clients about the commitments they made when they got married or entered into their committed partnership. Most did not stand before friends and family and promise to stay together "until frustration do us part," or "as long as we both shall love" (Doherty, 2000, p. 18). Rather, they often pledged a lifetime commitment to their partner and the relationship, through both the good and not so good times. Rather than privileging the therapist's own value judgments, good couple therapy may include therapists helping clients learn to better keep the commitments they originally made when they began their partnership. High-quality couple therapy involves therapists who honor and respect clients' values while recognizing the impossibility of "therapist neutrality," and acknowledging the values that they hold and the ways in which these influence their work with clients (Fife & Whiting, 2007).

Conclusion

Couple therapy is an exciting, unpredictable, and often rewarding endeavor. This book presents a collection of very useful techniques from leading therapist-scholars in couple therapy. However, the use of any technique, no matter how well-conceived, is likely to fail in the absence of a solid therapeutic alliance and genuine regard for the humanity and well-being of the client. Therapists should dedicate themselves to expanding their knowledge and skills related to couple therapy approaches and techniques, while remaining mindful that the therapeutic alliance and their way of being with clients constitute the heart and soul of effective couple therapy.

Note

1. This book is not intended to provide a road map for couple therapy (for overviews of the practice of couple therapy, see Long & Young, 2007, and Weeks & Fife, 2014). Rather, it is to draw upon the collective wisdom of therapist-scholars who are experts in couple therapy and present some of the key interventions they use when working with couples.

References

Asay, T. P., & Lambert, M. J. (1999). The empirical case for the common factors in therapy: Quantitative findings. In M. A. Hubble, B. L. Duncan, & S. D. Miller (Eds.), *The heart and soul of change: What works in therapy* (pp. 23–55). Washington, DC: American Psychological Association.

Buber, M. (1958). *I and thou* (2nd ed.; R. G. Smith, Trans.). New York: Charles Scribner's Sons.

Davis, S. D., Lebow, J., & Sprenkle, D. H. (2012). Common factors of change in couple therapy. *Behavior Therapy, 43,* 36–48.

Davis, S. D., & Piercy, F. P. (2007a). What clients of couple therapy model developers and their former students say about change, Part I: Model-dependent common factors across three models. *Journal of Marital and Family Therapy, 33,* 318–343.

Davis, S. D., & Piercy, F. P. (2007b). What clients of MFT model developers and their former students say about change, Part II: Model independent common factors and an integrative framework. *Journal of Marital and Family Therapy, 33,* 344–363.

Doherty, W. J. (2000). Consumer and modern covenant marriage. *Marriages and Families, 3*(1), 16–22.

Doherty, W. J. (2002). Bad couples therapy: How to avoid it. *Psychotherapy Networker Magazine, 26*(2), 26–33.

Fife, S. T., & Whiting, J. B. (2007). Values in family therapy research and practice: An invitation for reflection. *Contemporary Family Therapy, 29*, 71–86.

Fife, S. T., Whiting, J. B., Davis, S., & Bradford, K. (2014). The Therapeutic Pyramid: A common factors synthesis of techniques, alliance, and way of being. *Journal of Marital and Family Therapy, 40*(1), 20–33.

Gaston, L. (1990). The concept of the alliance and its role in psychotherapy: Theoretical and empirical considerations. *Psychotherapy, 27*(2), 143–153.

Horvath, A. O. (2001). The alliance. *Psychotherapy, 38*(4), 365–372.

Long, L. L., & Young, M. E. (2007). *Counseling and therapy for couples* (2nd ed.). Belmont, CA: Thomson Brooks/Cole.

Rosenzweig, S. (1936). Some implicit common factors in diverse methods of psychotherapy. *American Journal of Orthopsychiatry, 6*, 412.

Sexton, T. L., & Ridley, C. R. (2004). Implications of a moderated common factors approach: Does it move the field forward? *Journal of Marital and Family Therapy, 30*, 159–164.

Sexton, T. L., Ridley, C. R., & Kleiner, A. J. (2004). Beyond common factors: Multilevel-process models of therapeutic change in marriage and family therapy. *Journal of Marital and Family Therapy, 30*, 131–149.

Shadish, W. R., & Baldwin, S. A. (2002). Meta-analysis of MFT interventions. In D. H. Sprenkle (Ed.), *Effectiveness research in marriage and family therapy* (pp. 339–370). Alexandria, VA: American Association of Marriage and Family Therapy.

Shadish, W. R., & Baldwin, S. A. (2009). Meta-analysis of MFT interventions. *Journal of Marital and Family Therapy, 29*, 547–570.

Sprenkle, D. H., & Blow, A. J. (2004a). Common factors and our sacred models. *Journal of Marital and Family Therapy, 30*, 113–130.

Sprenkle, D. H., & Blow, A. J. (2004b). Common factors are not islands-they work through models: A response to Sexton, Ridley, and Kleiner. *Journal of Marital and Family Therapy, 30*, 151–157.

Sprenkle, D. H., Blow, A., & Dickey, M. (1999). Common factors and other variables in marriage and family therapy. In M. Hubble, B. Duncan, & S. Miller (Eds.), *The heart and soul of change: What works in therapy* (pp. 329–360). Washington, DC: American Psychological Association.

Sprenkle, D. H., Davis, S. D., & Lebow, J. (2009). *Common factors in couple and family therapy: The overlooked foundation of effective practice*. New York: Guilford.

Wampold, B. E. (2001). *The great psychotherapy debate: Models, methods, and findings*. Mahwah, NJ: Erlbaum.

Warner, C. T., & Olson, T. D. (1981). Another view of family conflict and family wholeness. *Family Relations, 30*, 493–503.

Weeks, G. R., & Fife, S. T. (2014). *Couples in treatment: Techniques and approaches for effective practice* (3rd ed.). New York: Routledge.

Weeks, G., Odell, M., & Methven, S. (2005). *If only I had known: Avoiding common mistakes in couple therapy*. W. W. Norton: New York.

2

JOINING

From the Perspective of the Use of Self

Harry J. Aponte

Purpose: To gain the trust and partnership of the couple

Introduction

The first task of couple therapy is to gain the trust and partnership of the clients, the foundation of the therapeutic relationship. The work of therapy requires the active, two-way engagement of therapist and clients. The therapeutic relationship does not just imply the client(s) opening up to allow the therapist into his/her/their personal life struggles. It also involves the clients actively engaging with the therapist to understand and solve their "problem(s)." Something is broken, painful, and deeply personal—something the couple could not achieve a solution to alone. It will take the efforts of both the clients and the therapist to solve the issue. Neither one can do it on their own. These strangers, the couple and therapist, thus face the task of joining hands to meet this formidable challenge together, the therapeutic alliance.

The Purpose of Joining

The technique to accomplish this goal of the therapeutic alliance is commonly referred to as *joining.* There are many approaches to this technique, depending on the school of therapy. However, here I will focus on what therapists need to bring of their personal selves to successfully carry out this technique, regardless of therapeutic orientation. If we accept that the essential goal of joining is to gain a level of trust with the client that draws the client into partnering with the therapist, then joining implies a type of intimate personal connection between therapist and client within the boundaries of the therapeutic process.

To win the confidence of clients, therapists need to demonstrate competence. However, to gain a trust that allows clients to disclose their pain and failures—and to consent also to actively engage with the therapists in changing their lives—something very personally profound needs to happen between the therapist and client. At its core, that connection is a human connection, which means that on the part of the therapist there must be a depth of understanding and caring that says that the therapist is all in (Aponte & Kissil, 2014). Then clients can risk sharing their vulnerabilities and risk joining the therapist in the effort to change.

Description and Implementation

For therapists to be able to communicate their personal presence effectively in the relational process, the endeavor begins somewhere inside of themselves. First of all, they must *want* to make a connection with the client, whether it comes with little or great effort, because of who the client is and/or what the client's issue is. They must care, which means opening themselves in mind and emotion to the person(s) who is the client. This calls for finding something in themselves that they can identify personally with the client to the point of empathy, even as they remain well grounded in the differentiated self. No matter how different the clients are from them, therapists must be able to resonate with some aspect of their common humanity, enough to feel with and care about the clients' struggles. However, the deeper that emotional connection, the more vital is the need for therapists to be grounded in their own sense of self. This grounding is best achieved by therapists for their purposes as healers by connecting to their own personal struggles and vulnerabilities, and just as important, to be committed to and engaged in their own personal journey of healing and changing (Aponte & Kissil, 2014). This personal work will enable them to differentiate their experiences from those of their clients in the intimate engagement of therapy—all so necessary to be able to see their clients with some objective clarity and allow for the clients' responsibility and ability to contribute to their own efforts to change. Therapists look to join their clients in their journey—bearing with them their pain through empathy, and sharing with them their battle to overcome through their engaged presence and energy.

That connection, called joining, evolves not only through the commonality of the human experience, but also through the attributes that shape and define us—our gender, culture, race, social location, life experiences, and spirituality. These distinctive elements of our lives can serve as commonalities that help therapists connect with clients in their world views, personal sentiments, and resonating experiences. However, these distinctive characteristics can also present significant obstacles to communication and mutual understanding. From the perspective of the *use of self*, however, they can also serve as opportunities and challenges for therapists to stretch themselves beyond their comfort zones, and risk extending themselves to enter viewpoints and personal experiences that may not only be alien to them, but even disagreeable and distasteful. To join in these circumstances, therapists need not and likely should not try to force themselves to agree with or like what is presented to them, but they must open themselves to hear, see, and feel that other person's distinctiveness. Clients must feel *safe* to join the relationship from their side. They need to believe that their therapists can and will enter the swirling rapids with them, which means that therapists, when engaging with their clients, need to be aware of themselves, connected to what is going on in themselves, and have developed a degree of personal self-mastery within their professional roles to inspire confidence in clients. Joining is a deeply personal experience within a well-directed professional process.

Contraindications

There are no contraindications when therapists are able to put themselves consciously and purposefully into the therapeutic process. There are serious contraindications when they attempt to put their personal selves into the process without a self-awareness and self-discipline trained to work integrally with their professional training. The therapy's relationship must be personally intimate while professionally appropriate and therapeutically calibrated. The clinical assessment must be personally intuitive and professionally methodical. Therapeutic interventions must be personally meaningful and impactful while technically strategically fitting.

Case Example

In one case example (see also Aponte, 1988), the therapist was a Latino, married with children, from a relatively disadvantaged background. The client family was an upper middle-class Anglo-Saxon couple with three children. The family came complaining about their rebellious adolescent middle son, but with a strained marriage that clearly impaired their parenting. The therapist had to connect across an ethnic divide, although as a long-time professional he was now comfortable at this point in his career with this ethnic and socioeconomic segment of the population. However, he did not resonate easily with the emotionally inhibited, apologetic manner of the man, and the woman presented a controlled demeanor that initially distanced him. Their children, from pre-teen to college-age, were kids enough like his own that he had little trouble relating to them.

The wife had shut down to her husband, whom she felt abandoned her when it came to disciplining the children. The husband recognized he avoided confronting conflict in his family interactions. The therapist could see that in spite of their marital tension, this couple shared caring and commitment, which allowed the therapist to enter their relationship through his feelings about his own marriage. The therapist was reluctant to connect with his own failings as a husband, but he knew that this would be necessary if he were to identify with this man's pain in the relationship and the wife's frustrations with her husband. Reaching within himself, he drew from his own experience to speak to the husband in a way that touched the man about how difficult it was to want to do a better job relating to his wife. Connecting within himself to his own wife's frustrations with him, the therapist spoke with understanding to the wife about her frustrations with her husband. They each knew they were heard. The therapist could now reach to get them in touch with the affection they shared, allowing them to soften what was alienating each in the relationship. They could love even as they irritated and frustrated one another. They were ready to talk and work together. The therapist had been there and experienced these feelings himself, which he used to help him walk the journey with them.

References

Aponte, H. J. (1988). Love, the spiritual wellspring of forgiveness: An example of spirituality in our therapy. *Journal of Family Therapy, 20*(1), 37–58.

Aponte, H. J., & Kissil, K. (2014). "If I can grapple with this I can truly be of use in the therapy room": Using the therapist's own emotional struggles to facilitate effective therapy. *Journal of Marital & Family Therapy, 40*(2), 152–164.

3

THE ROAD TO MASTERY

Three Steps for Improving Performance as a Couples Therapist

Scott D. Miller and Mark A. Hubble

Purpose: To help practitioners improve engagement and outcomes in routine clinical practice

Introduction

Available research makes it clear: Couples therapy works (Miller & Bertolino, 2012). Across approaches, the average treated couple is better off than 80% of those receiving no treatment. While encouraging, other data show that the outcomes of individual clinicians vary widely. Put another way, some therapists are *more* (or less) helpful than others. In addition, instead of improving with experience, available evidence indicates that the effectiveness of the average practitioner plateaus early in their career and slowly deteriorates over time (Miller & Hubble, 2011).

The question naturally arises, "Where can a clinician go for instruction and guidance to become a better couples therapist?" As it is, the answer is not found in the field's traditions and methods. Although graduate training, supervision, and continuing education have all been shown to aid in skill acquisition, none have proven effective in enhancing individual clinician outcomes (Hill & Knox, 2013).

Fortunately, research outside of psychotherapy now provides a new direction for improving performance (Ericsson, Charness, Feltovich, & Hoffman, 2006). Drawn from many studies across a wide range of activities (including chess, sports, music, medicine, mathematics, teaching, and computer programming), these findings focus less on the specific behaviors unique to a particular domain than how mastery of any human endeavor is acquired. Informed by these results, Miller and Hubble (2011) reviewed three steps clinicians can follow to improve day-to-day performance. Working in tandem to create a "cycle of excellence," they include: (1) determining a baseline level of effectiveness; (2) obtaining systematic, ongoing, formal feedback; and (3) engaging in deliberate practice.

Purpose of the Three Steps

Therapists vary considerably in their effectiveness outcomes (Wampold & Imel, 2015). The average clinician is effective with some clients, somewhat helpful with others, and ineffective with the remaining. The purpose of this approach is to help therapists improve clinical outcomes in their work with couples. Following the three steps of the "cycle of excellence" will decrease variability in performance, thereby enabling the practitioner to deliver a more consistently effective service. Over time, the method enhances overall effectiveness by helping individual clinicians identify errors in their daily work and then develop and test remedial strategies.

Description and Implementation: Three Steps for Improving Performance

The first step for improving performance as a couples therapist is determining a baseline level of clinical effectiveness. Top performers are constantly comparing what they do to: (a) their own personal best; (b) the performance of others; and (c) existing standards or baselines (Ericsson et al., 2006). Numerous, well-established outcome measures are available to clinicians for determining their baseline (c.f., Corcoran & Fischer, 2013). Additionally, computerized systems exist that auto-mate calculations of individual clinician effect sizes and make real-time com-parisons of these overall results with national and international norms (PCOMS, 2013). Any of these tools or systems can be used to set a personal benchmark against which efforts aimed at improving outcomes can be assessed.

The second element in fostering superior performance is obtaining feed-back. Studies show that providing clinicians with real-time information about their clients' progress and engagement triples the success rate of couples ther-apy while significantly reducing deterioration and dropout (Miller, Hubble, Chow, & Seidel, 2013).

Only one proprietary system for providing feedback to couples therapists—the Partners for Change Outcome Management System (PCOMS)—has been desig-nated as "evidence-based" by the Substance and Mental Health Services Adminis-tration's (SAMHSA) National Registry of Evidence-based Programs and Practices (NREPP). It includes two brief, four-item measures that are completed by clients at every visit. The *Outcome Rating Scale* (ORS) is used to gauge improvement from session to session. The *Session Rating Scale* (SRS) taps the client's experience of the therapeutic relationship. Results from session to session are then compared to norms for expected progress to determine if the treatment is on track. If not, the therapist can initiate a discussion about modifying the service to better meet the couple's needs and ensure success.

As powerful an effect as feedback has on outcome, it is not enough for the development of superior performance. In effect, feedback functions like a GPS, pointing out when a driver is off track and even suggesting alternate routes while not necessarily improving overall navigation skills or knowledge of the territory (Miller et al., 2007; Miller & Hubble, 2011). To learn from feedback, deliberate practice is required. This, the third step, means setting aside time for reflecting on feedback received, identifying where one's performance falls short, seeking guidance from recognized experts, and then developing, rehearsing, executing, and evaluating a plan for improvement. Researchers be Chow, Miller, Seidel, Kane, Thornton, and Andrews (2015) found that therapists who improved the most in effectiveness spent four times as many hours outside of work engaged in deliberate efforts to improve their performance than their less-effective colleagues.

Contraindications

The three steps are purposefully designed to push practitioners beyond their current level of performance. In application, the process works by interrupting a therapist's customary approach to conducting therapy and the patterns they carry out automatically, often outside awareness. The risk is that therapeutic behaviors can be compromised at the same time unhelpful practices are being identified and changed.

According to the literature on expertise, the solution lies in pursuing small, incremental changes in performance that have been previously identified through feedback as problematic. Toward this end, having access to a teacher or coach to both determine appropriate targets for change and to help develop a remedial plan is critical. The process requires a long-term commitment, considerable motivation, and an ability to delay gratification. Owing to these demands, few succeed without support from a community of practice comprised of like-minded colleagues. Even if resources are not available locally, organizations now exist online for supporting this way of working. The International Center for Clinical Excellence (ICCE; www.centerforclinicalexcellence.com) is a good example. It's a free, web-based community for clinicians and researchers dedicated to helping individual practitioners achieve excellence in behavioral health via feedback and deliberate practice.

Case Example

Dr. Smith is a licensed marriage and family therapist working in a group practice. While her overall effectiveness rate as determined by routine application of the ORS is on par with national averages, a closer examination of her results reveals problems in some of the couples she treats. Within this group, outcomes are poorer and dropout rates are significantly higher. Further analysis shows that scores on the SRS assessing the client's engagement in treatment are frequently lower for the male partner in initial sessions. Looking carefully at her results, Dr. Smith discovers that male partners frequently score lower on the item related to understanding.

Dr. Smith seeks guidance from a colleague who specializes in work with men. Together, they begin reviewing audio recordings of sessions in which her male clients scored lower on engagement. The colleague identifies problematic exchanges, models alternate responses, and provides reading and exercises for Dr. Smith to complete between consultations.

Dr. Smith follows through on her commitment to the plan she and her colleague developed to help her male clients feel understood. Over time, the frequency of low scores among the subgroup of male clients begins to decrease. Dropout rates simultaneously improve. Overall, the number of couples Dr. Smith successfully helps increases. She returns to her data to identify the next, small target for performance improvement.

References

Chow, D., Miller, S., Seidel, J., Kane, R., Thornton, J. A., & Andrews, W. (2015). The role of deliberate practice in the development of highly effective psychotherapists. *Psychotherapy: Science, Research, and Practice, 52*(3), 337–345.

Corcoran, K., & Fischer, J. (2013). *Measures for clinical practice and research, Volume 1: Couples, families, and children* (5th ed.). New York: Oxford University Press.

Ericsson, K. A., Charness, N., Feltovich, P. J., & Hoffman, R. R. (2006). *The Cambridge handbook of expertise and expert performance.* Cambridge: Cambridge University Press.

Hill, C., & Knox, S. (2013). Training and supervision in psychotherapy. In M. Lambert (Ed.), *The handbook of psychotherapy and behavior change* (6th ed., pp. 775–812). New York: Wiley.

Miller, S., & Bertolino, B. (Eds.) (2012). *ICCE feedback informed treatment training and treatment manuals.* Chicago: ICCE.

Miller, S. D., & Hubble, M. A. (2011). The road to mastery. *The Psychotherapy Networker, 35*(2), 22–31, 60.

Miller, S. D., Hubble, M. A., Chow, D. L., & Seidel, J. (2013). The outcome of psychotherapy: Yesterday, today, and tomorrow. *Psychotherapy, 50*(1), 88–97.

Miller, S. D., Hubble, M. A., & Duncan, B. L. (November/December, 2007). Supershrinks: Learning from the field's most effective practitioners. *The Psychotherapy Networker, 31*(6), 26–35, 56.

PCOMS (2013). Patterns for Change Outcome Management System (PCMOS): International Center for Clinical Excellence (2013). Retrieved January 6, 2016, http://legacy.nreppadmin.net/ViewIntervention.aspx?id=249

Wampold, B., & Imel, Z. (2015). *The great psychotherapy debate* (2nd ed.). New York: Erlbaum.

4

THE PARTNERS FOR CHANGE OUTCOME MANAGEMENT SYSTEM (PCOMS)

Barry Duncan and Jacqueline Sparks

Purpose: To give clients a voice and improve couple therapy outcomes

Introduction

> "However beautiful the strategy, you should occasionally look at the results."
> Sir Winston Churchill

Couple therapy is a good news, bad news scenario. The good news is that research indicates that couples who undertake therapy have a greater chance of improving their relationships than those who don't. The bad news is that, despite this, many couples do not benefit, dropouts are a problem, and therapists vary significantly in success rates, are poor judges of client negative outcomes, and don't have a clue about their effectiveness (Duncan, 2014).

Systematic client feedback offers a solution to these problems. It refers to the continuous monitoring of client perceptions of progress and the therapeutic alliance throughout the course of therapy. It involves a real-time comparison of the client's views of the outcome with an expected treatment response that serves as a yardstick for gauging client progress and signaling when change is not occurring as predicted. With this alert, clinicians and their clients have an opportunity to shift focus, revisit goals, or alter interventions before deterioration or dropout.

Two feedback interventions have demonstrated gains in randomized controlled trials (RCT) and are included in the Substance Abuse and Mental Health Administration's (SAMHSA) National Registry of Evidence-based Programs and Practices (NREPP). Only one, the Partners for Change Outcome Management System (PCOMS; Duncan, 2012), has achieved significant improvement in outcomes with couples. Of the five RCTs conducted by researchers at the Heart and Soul of Change Project that demonstrate a significant benefit of the PCOMS over treatment as usual (TAU), two have specifically addressed couple therapy.

Anker, Duncan, and Sparks (2009), the largest RCT of couple therapy to date, randomized 205 couples to the PCOMS or TAU. *Feedback clients* reached clinically significant change nearly *four times* more than TAU couples, and over doubled the percentage of couples in which both individuals reached reliable and/ or clinically significant change. The PCOMS not only maintained its advantage at the six-month follow-up, it also achieved a 46% lower separation/divorce rate. Reese, Toland, Slone, and Norsworthy (2010) replicated these impressive results.

These studies make a strong case for the use of client feedback with couples. If someone told you that by having your couples answer four brief questions at the beginning and end of each session, you would quadruple their chances of having a successful outcome short-term, and more than double their chances of success long-term, would you say: "Nah, too much trouble?" If that is not your response, this chapter intends to give you enough information about the PCOMS to get you started. More information about the PCOMS, including over 250 free resources (measures, articles, chapters, webinars), can be found at https://heartandsoulofchange.com.

The Purpose of the Partners for Change Outcome Management System

The purpose of the PCOMS boils down to this: partnering with clients to identify those who aren't responding to clinician "business as usual" and addressing the lack of progress in a proactive way that keeps clients engaged while therapists collaboratively seek new directions. The PCOMS is not based on any model-derived assumptions and can be incorporated in any couple approach. Thus, it promotes the values of social justice by privileging the client's voice over manuals and theories, enabling idiosyncratic and culturally responsive practice with diverse clientele. Clients determine the fit and benefit of services as well as intervention preferences.

The PCOMS embraces two known predictors of ultimate treatment outcome. Time and again, studies reveal that the majority of clients experience the majority of change in the first eight visits. Couples who report little or no progress early on will likely show no improvement over the entire course of therapy or will end up on the drop-out list. Monitoring change provides a tangible way to identify those who are not responding so that a new course can be charted. A second robust predictor of change solidly demonstrated by a large body of studies is that taken-for-granted old friend, the therapeutic alliance. Clients who highly rate their partnership with their therapists are more apt to remain in therapy and benefit from it.

As mentioned, the PCOMS is an evidence-based practice, but it is not a specific treatment model for a specific diagnosis. The PCOMS has demonstrated significant improvements for both clients and therapists, regardless of the theoretical orientations of therapists or the diagnoses of the clients. More importantly, the PCOMS is evidence-based at the individual client–therapist level, promoting a partnership that monitors whether *this* approach provided by *this* therapist is benefiting *this* client. In other words, it is *evidence-based practice, one client at a time.*

Description and Implementation of the PCOMS

The PCOMS is a light-touch, checking-in process that usually takes about five minutes but never over 10 for administering, scoring, and integrating into the therapy. The PCOMS works best as a way to gently guide models and techniques toward the client's perspective, with a focus on the outcome. Besides the brevity of its measures, the PCOMS also differs from most systems in that client involvement is routine and expected; client scores on the progress and alliance instruments are openly shared and discussed at each administration. The clients' views of progress serve as a basis for beginning therapeutic conversations, and their assessments of the alliance mark an endpoint to the same. With this transparency, the measures provide a mutually understood reference point for reasons for seeking service, progress, and engagement.

The PCOMS starts with the Outcome Rating Scale (ORS; Miller, Duncan, Brown, Sparks, & Claud, 2003), which is given at the beginning of a session and provides client-reported ratings of progress. Rather than a symptom checklist, the ORS is a visual analog scale consisting of four 10-centimeter lines that correspond to four domains (individual, interpersonal, social, and overall). Clients place a mark on each line to represent their perception of their functioning in each domain. Therapists use a 10-centimeter ruler (or a computerized version that scores automatically) to sum the client's total score, with a maximum score of 40. Lower scores reflect more distress.

The Session Rating Scale (SRS) (Duncan et al., 2003), which is also a four-item visual analog scale, serves to measure client views of the therapeutic alliance and is given toward the end of a therapy session but with enough time to discuss any concerns. Similar to the ORS, each line on the SRS is 10 centimeters and can be scored manually or electronically. Use of the SRS encourages all client feedback, positive and negative, thus creating a safe space for clients to voice their honest opinions about their connection to their therapist and to therapy. Appreciation of any negative feedback is a powerful alliance builder. Both the ORS and SRS can be downloaded for free at https://heartandsoulofchange.com.

Given that at its heart, the PCOMS is a collaborative intervention, it is important that couples are on board and understand two points at the start: 1) the ORS will be used to track the outcome in every session; and 2) the ORS is a way to make sure that the client's voice is not only heard but remains central. In the first meeting, the ORS pinpoints where the client sees him/herself, allowing for an ongoing comparison in later sessions. It helps to put the forms (or laptop or other device) out on an open surface (e.g., coffee table) where everyone can take a look.

The ORS allows everything to be literally on the table right from the beginning—the agreements and disagreements that everyone knows about, except the therapist, until now.

Research on the ORS has identified clinical cutoff scores that differentiate between clinical and non-clinical populations: 25 is the cutoff for adults, meaning that, on average, persons seeking therapy will fall below that, and those not typically seeking counseling will score above it. After the ORS is scored, the clinical cutoff facilitates a shared understanding of the ORS and is often a step toward connecting the scores to the reason for services. For those who score below the cutoff, the therapist can assure them that they made a good decision to come in. For those who score above the cutoff, the therapist can simply validate their score by saying that it looks like things are going pretty well, which leads to the next logical question—what are the reasons for meeting now?

Couples either agree about their views of the level and areas (domains) of distress, or they don't. When folks agree, therapists can comment on it as a strength, highlight the commonality, and use it as a stepping stone to establish mutual goals. Disagreements between clients in their scores on the ORS simply speak to the dynamics frequently present in couple therapy. The instrument just puts those differences front and center in the first minutes of the session. The ORS gives you an instant read on things like who is in the most distress about the relationship, and who perhaps was coerced into therapy. Not surprisingly, the one wanting to work on or save the relationship is often the one demonstrating more distress on the ORS. Also not surprising is that the one who is dragged to therapy or is there to clarify whether the relationship will continue is often over the cutoff. The discussion of distress via ORS scores shines a light on these important issues, allowing their open discussion and subsequent planning for how therapy can meet both individual's needs.

Couples typically will come in with the *interpersonal* domain scoring lower than others, given that is the scale intended to reflect relational distress. Clients often connect that reason to the mark they've made without prompting from the therapist. Other times, the therapist needs to clarify the connection between the client's descriptions of the reasons for services and the client's marks on the ORS. This enables the therapist and the client to be on the "same page" regarding what the marks say about the therapeutic work and whether the client is making any improvement. At the moment that clients connect the marks on the ORS with the situations that prompt their seeking help, the ORS becomes a meaningful measure of progress and a potent clinical tool. And that moment facilitates the next question: "What do you think it will take to move your mark just one centimeter to the right; what needs to happen out there and in here?"

After the first session, the PCOMS simply asks: Are things better or not? The longer that therapy continues without measurable change, the greater the likelihood of dropout and/or a poor outcome. The ORS scores are used to engage the couple in a discussion about progress, and more importantly, what should be done differently if there isn't any. While you may get fairly consistent agreement regarding the two possible change scenarios, it may be that you will encounter different views. For example, as we will see below, a spouse may be seeing things improve because his wife has returned to live in the home, but her view of the situation indicates deterioration. This is, of course, the challenge—to create a therapeutic context where everyone, different views and all, benefits. We believe the best way to judge success is when both persons in a couple benefit.

Regardless of the congruence or discrepancy between client scores, the task of the therapist from session to session is to identify client perceptions of progress and the alliance, and to respond appropriately. When ORS scores increase, a crucial step to empower the change is to help clients see any gains as a consequence of their own efforts. It is interesting to see how a simple jump of even a few points on the ORS can spur conversation about how small changes can be carried forward to address the problems at hand. When change is not forthcoming, or things are worsening, it is time to have a conversation about doing something different. The ORS stimulates such a conversation so that all interested parties may struggle with the implications of continuing a process that is yielding little or no benefit. The intent is to support practices that are working, and challenge those that don't appear to be helpful.

The progression of the conversation with couples who are not benefiting goes from talking about whether something different should be done, to identifying what can be done differently, to doing something different. Doing something different can include, for example, inviting others from the client's support system, using a team, developing a different conceptualization of the problem, trying another therapy approach, or referring to another therapist or venue of service, such as a religious advisor or self-help group—whatever seems to be of value to the client.

More Guidelines From Our Research With Couples

The mass of data collected in the Anker et al., (2009) trial became a gold mine for other analyses about what makes couple therapy tick, resulting in the following guidelines (Sparks, 2015):

1. *Determine each partner's goal for seeking therapy early and use individual outcomes, not only relationship status, to determine success.* We found a relationship between the client's couple therapy goals (strengthen the relationship or clarify if it should continue) at the beginning of therapy and whether they were together at the six-month follow-up. As might be expected, when both members of the couple wanted to improve the relationship, the majority (92%) of them did. In contrast, when both partners sought clarification of the relationship, 56% had split by the follow-up. Early goal identification can assist therapists to work toward client-defined better futures, whether that means couples remaining together or not. Relatedly, we found that all clients, on average,

benefitted from treatment, regardless of their goal at the beginning or their relationship status at termination. In other words, therapy was shown to be helpful even with couples on the verge of divorce. Individual measures of progress can facilitate a more rounded picture of the actual outcome, even in instances of separation or divorce.

2. *There are two clear pathways to become a better couple therapist: building alliance skills and time in the trenches with couples.* We found that therapists' average alliance quality accounted for 50% of the differences among therapists—in short, therapists who form better alliances across couples achieve better outcomes. We also found that therapists' experience with couples differentiated one therapist from another. To ensure that you learn from experience and not merely repeat it, monitor outcomes and use objective evidence from your practice to discern your clinical development without falling prey to wishful thinking.

3. *Become skilled at incorporating task activities, including structuring, directing, and giving input as appropriate.* We found that some couples, while appreciative of therapist relationship skills, wished their therapist had been more active. This may be particularly salient in couple therapy, as therapists may need to interrupt negative or volatile communication interchanges to establish a climate of safety.

Case Example

David was distraught that his wife, Jenn, had moved out, leaving him to care for their two daughters. At the first session, David's ORS score was 14.5 and Jenn's 12.7 (well below the clinical cutoff score of 25), with the *interpersonal* scale coming in the lowest at 3.4 and 2.2, respectively, confirming that these were two highly distressed individuals with a marriage on the brink. When the therapist invited each to tell the story behind the numbers and explain their marks on the *interpersonal* scale, David described his loneliness and said he just wanted his wife to come back home. Jenn pointed to her mark on the ORS and recounted his late nights at work and indifference to her needs. SRS scores reflected a rocky start. When the therapist asked about what was needed to move the SRS in a more positive direction, David said he wanted the therapist to focus more on Jenn moving back home. Jenn said she wanted the therapist to help them talk together so that David would hear her.

At the next session, David's ORS indicated a five-point jump, as he felt more hopeful that Jenn would return given that she attended therapy; by session three, his ORS surpassed the cutoff, because Jenn, perhaps succumbing to David's pleas, moved back. With a note of relief, David described their home life as more or less "back to normal." His SRS scores for sessions two and three increased, indicating a strengthening therapeutic alliance. Meanwhile, despite a similar rise in SRS scores for Jenn, her third session ORS score was a paltry 13. Clearly, something was gravely amiss in her life, and therapy was failing to help.

In session four, Jenn's ORS plummeted to a dismal 7.2 while David's ORS at session four jumped to a 30.2. The therapist printed out a graph of their two change trajectories and placed it on the coffee table in front of them, reflecting in sharp relief the dramatic difference. The two ORS paths provided a compelling rationale to inquire about Jenn's decline corresponding with her return home. With encouragement, Jenn opened up about her dreams to pursue a meaningful career and to have time away from household responsibilities. Though these were not new themes, there was an urgency and clarity absent from previous sessions. The therapist supported Jenn's dreams and encouraged David to respond to his wife in a way that showed that he took her seriously. At the same time, David was asked to talk about his needs to manage the demands of his job, the primary financial support for the household, and his limited ability to share equally in home tasks. This time the conversation was real, significantly different than their usual stalemated communication. Jenn's ORS scores significantly increased over the next three sessions as the couple continued to make necessary adjustments in their relationship.

This therapy may have reached this point without the PCOMS, but the chances of dropout were high, particularly after the first session, without prompt alliance feedback and the fourth session without concrete evidence of their disparate views. Different scores on the ORS in couple work may be interpreted as cause for concern when, in truth, they are cause to rejoice; therapists and their clients are given the opportunity to unambiguously face the reality of their different views and then to gauge and celebrate convergences when they occur. In the case of David and Jenn, session four proved a turning point for strategies to meet their conflictual needs.

Conclusions

Given that the PCOMS is listed in the National Registry of Evidence-based Programs and Practices, it offers a valid choice for clinicians wishing to be evidence-based across their clients while implementing a feasible feedback system that has a proven track record with couples. Lessons from our five couple studies (see Sparks, 2015) provide additional guidance. The PCOMS also provides a ready-made method for couple and family therapy programs to help students accelerate their development (Sparks, Kisler, Adams, & Blumen, 2011). Therapist variables (including a therapist's ability to form strong alliances and experience working with couples) and the alliance (including goal alignment and directive skills) join with the routine incorporation of client feedback to create a practical, research-informed framework for navigating the difficult passages of couple therapy.

Exercises/Points for Reflection:

1. Download the ORS/SRS family of measures from the website https://heartandsoulofchange.com. The measures are free for individual use. Simply click on "Measures" on the home page, indicate your understanding of the

License Agreement, register your email (no marketing materials are sent; the email is only for the registration of your agreement to license), and download the measures in any of 23 different languages.

2. Watch the free webinars and peruse other materials found at the top left of the home page under "PCOMS 101" to facilitate your understanding of how to use PCOMS. "PCOMS Video" is a good place to start and includes the nuts and bolts of using the measures.

3. Reflect whether PCOMS or systematic feedback fits into your value system and can be integrated into your authentic practice of couple therapy. PCOMS (or anything else in therapy) doesn't "work" without your investment of yourself and your genuine desire to partner with clients and appreciate their feedback.

References

Anker, M. G., Duncan, B. L., & Sparks, J. A. (2009). Using client feedback to improve couple therapy outcomes: A randomized clinical trial in a naturalistic setting. *Journal of Consulting and Clinical Psychology, 77*(4), 693–704.

Duncan, B. L. (2012). The Partners for Change Outcome Management System (PCOMS): The Heart and Soul of Change Project. *Canadian Psychology, 53*(2), 93–104.

Duncan, B. L. (2014). *On becoming a better therapist: Evidence based practice one client at a time* (2nd ed.). Washington, DC: American Psychological Association.

Duncan, B. L., Miller, S. D., Reynolds, L. R., Sparks, J. A., Claud, D., Brown, J., & Johnson, L. D. (2003). The session rating scale: Psychometric properties of a "working" alliance scale. *Journal of Brief Therapy, 3*, 3–12.

Miller, S. D., Duncan, B. L., Brown, J., Sparks, J. A., & Claud, D. (2003). The outcome rating scale: A preliminary study of the reliability, validity, and feasibility of a brief visual analog measure. *Journal of Brief Therapy, 2*(2), 91–100.

Reese, R. J., Toland, M. D., Slone, N. C., & Norsworthy, L. A. (2010). Effect of client feedback on couple psychotherapy outcomes. *Psychotherapy: Theory, Research, Practice, Training, 47*, 616–630. doi:10.1037/a0021182

Sparks, J. A. (2015). The Norway couple project: Lessons learned. *Journal of Marital and Family Therapy, 41*(4), 481–494.

Sparks, J. A., Kisler, T. J., Adams, J. F., & Blumen, D. G. (2011). Teaching accountability: Using client feedback to train effective family therapists. *Journal of Marital & Family Therapy, 37*, 452–467.

5

ETHICAL TECHNIQUES TO MAINTAIN CONFIDENTIALITY IN COUPLE THERAPY

Gerald R. Weeks

Purpose: To maintain confidentiality in couple therapy in an ethical way

Introduction

Working with couples requires a different conceptual framework, skill set, and more options regarding confidentiality than working with an individual. The default position in working with individuals is to maintain all information in confidence unless the client gives permission to release information (with the exception of legally mandated reporting). This default position has also been widely used in working with couples. Generally speaking, the issue of confidentially does not arise in individual therapy unless the client asks about it or there is some need to release information. Thus, having an agreed-upon rule of confidentiality from the outset is not always viewed as essential. However, working with couples presents a different dilemma. You are now dealing with the privacy of two partners. One may want to reveal certain information and the other may not wish to disclose information that would be essential for the successful completion of therapy. The commonly accepted default rule does not automatically apply to couples. Therefore, it is essential to discuss various rules of confidentiality in the first session with every couple.

Purpose of Maintaining Confidentiality

The purpose of the techniques described in this chapter is to give the therapist options in choosing from different rules of confidentiality when working with couples. Treating couples creates different ethical challenges because the couple's "relationship" is viewed as the unit of treatment but the relationship consists of two individuals who must be treated ethically. Some couple therapists will refuse to split the couple to have individual sessions for theoretical and/or ethical reasons. These therapists may believe that it is their role only to treat the relationship, and, if individual work is needed, refer that person to another therapist. Perhaps the therapist believes that mixing therapeutic modalities is not appropriate because it might have effects such as blurring boundaries or interfering with the alliance the therapist has formed with the couple. The therapist may believe that seeing one partner without the other will automatically unbalance the therapy by creating an alliance or a perception of an alliance with that partner. Such a coalition or even the perception of it would interfere with the need to maintain both an alliance and neutrality with regard to the couple.

Therapists may also fear that if they are told certain information in an individual session, they must keep it in confidence. One instance where this becomes extremely problematic is when the couple claims they want to work on improving their relationship, but one partner is actively engaged in a secret affair. The presence of an affair in a relationship makes progress in couple therapy impossible. Other couple therapists are comfortable seeing each partner separately from time to time. However, unless the partners are high-functioning, have a good sense of boundaries, and agree to the rule of confidentiality mentioned below, it is not advisable to have individual sessions. Thus, it is essential to establish a rule of confidentially from the onset of couple therapy.

Three Rules of Confidentiality

The couple therapist has a choice of three rules of confidentiality. Each of the three rules has its advantages and disadvantages, and therapists have different comfort levels with the various rules. First, the therapist could suggest that if the couple is seen individually, all information obtained during those sessions or via any other form of communication will be maintained in confidence. The advantage of this rule is that clients may feel more open to disclosing information, as well as the therapist never having to divulge any "secrets" or other reasons the couple therapy is stuck or might fail. The disadvantage is the therapist must act or pretend they do not have this information, and proceed with the couple therapy. The therapist is now in the bind of having to keep the secret, even if the secret has a direct impact on the relationship and treatment. The therapist's only option is to proceed, risking that the therapy will not be successful.

Second, the therapist could suggest what some call the three-way rule. This rule means any information obtained in any context, via any means, is essentially equivalent to it being said in a couple session. The therapist is declaring they will not keep any "secrets" and will freely divulge any information that they believe might interfere with the couple therapy. The advantage of this rule is the therapist is never in a position of keeping "secrets." For some therapists, this appears to be a comfortable position. They do not have to deal with a complex ethical issue. It is a simple rule that everyone can easily understand. The disadvantage of this rule is that the therapist forewarns the clients that anything revealed in an individual session will not be a kept secret. As a result, clients may not be honest with the therapist and not disclose what they wish to keep secret. This can be problematic for the treatment outcome—for example, when clients are actively engaged in an affair, yet want to work on their marriage. They may be secretly thinking that if they can work things out in their marriage, they will stay married; on the other hand, if they cannot, then they already have another relationship they can continue for some period of time. In many cases, the affair partner is viewed as the second-best mate. The newness of the affair relationship makes it very appealing, "pulling" the partner in the direction of the affair partner and draining energy that could otherwise be used to help repair their marriage.

Third, the therapist could suggest a rule of confidentially known as *accountability with discretion* (Karpel, 1980). Karpel suggested the therapist should have the privilege of deciding which information could be kept from the partner without doing damage to the couple therapy, and which information the therapist should be accountable for revealing because it is so detrimental to the relationship and to the process of therapy. However, Karpel never clearly articulated his rule of accountability.

Weeks, Odell, and Methven (2005) and Weeks and Fife (2014) have written extensively about this dilemma and articulated their own rule of accountability with discretion. With this approach, the therapist might suggest the following: "At some point, I might want to see one or both of you individually or you might ask for an individual session. If we have an individual session, it is essential we all agree to a rule of confidentially at the outset of therapy. The rule of confidentiality is I will maintain information in confidence unless I believe it will impede, interfere, or render couple therapy useless. Depending on the information, I might suggest a number of individual sessions with me or another therapist in order for the couple therapy to progress. You will need to be prepared to tell your partner why you are seeking individual therapy. In some cases, it will be clear the information needs to be shared with your partner because it is so destructive to your relationship and the couple therapy. Should this situation occur, I will ask you to reveal this information to your partner, and we will discuss how you might reveal it. If you refuse to reveal the information, I will simply say in the next session (or up to three maximum if the person needs help revealing the information) that I have acquired some information in the individual session (or elsewhere) which I cannot specifically reveal but makes continuing couple therapy impossible at this time." The therapist is essentially waving a red flag, saying there is a secret but not disclosing the secret. The advantage of this technique is the couple therapist is not in the dark about information that is essential to understanding the couple and has not revealed the specific information that was shared. The disadvantage is the level of discomfort in carrying secret information, possibly discontinuing the couple therapy, and basically forcing the spouse to inquire about the nature of this information from the partner.

Many therapists we have trained like this third position because they do not want to participate in therapy that is a sham, but others are so uncomfortable with the idea of carrying a secret and having to confront the situation, they opt for another rule of confidentiality. Whichever rule is chosen, it is always a good idea to put it in writing and have everyone sign it.

Case Example

A couple had been stuck in their therapy for some time. The therapist suggested meeting with each partner individually and explained to them *discretion with accountability* as the guideline for confidentiality. This was the third option regarding rules of confidentiality with couples. Even though this rule was explained in the first session, it is always useful to remind them of the rule whenever an individual session is held. The couple understood and agreed to this rule, affirming the original agreement. The therapist split the couple to determine what might be missing and learned that one partner was having an affair, which was ongoing with no intent to stop. The secret needed to be revealed or therapy discontinued. The partner had suspected an affair for some time. When the couple therapist announced that an issue had arisen in the individual session that would make continuing couple therapy impossible, the suspecting spouse knew that her fear had been confirmed. She pressed her partner for the truth, and within five minutes he disclosed the information. When the affair was revealed, she said it must stop or she would leave immediately. The threat of losing his wife motivated the husband to stop and commit to working on the marriage. To the therapist's amazement, the wife apologized for her husband putting the therapist in such an uncomfortable situation and appreciated that she finally knew the truth.

References

Karpel, M. (1980). Family secrets. *Family Process, 19*, 295–306.

Weeks, G., & Fife, S. (2014). *Couples in treatment* (3rd ed.). New York: Routledge.

Weeks, G., Odell, M., & Methven, S. (2005). *Avoiding common mistakes in couple therapy*. New York: Norton.

SECTION II
Techniques and Interventions

PART A
Enactments

6

ENACTMENT

From the Perspective of the Use of Self

Harry J. Aponte

Purpose: To allow the therapist immediate access to the couple's dysfunctional relationship

Introduction

When couples and families relate to us their perceptions and interpretations of what goes on at home, we seldom find concurrence between any two parties in their depictions of what takes place between them. We then resort to our therapeutic detective work to develop our own hypotheses about their relationships. If our strategy is based on our interpretation of what they say, we act on the hearsay garnered from their narrations.

And, of course, that interpretation of ours is drawn from data strained through the filters of our personal life experiences and world views. The more removed we are from actually witnessing and experiencing the action people are describing, the more influence our own personal filters will have on what we understand. To be able to trust the behavior that we are exploring and weighing, we need to be closer to the action, so we can not only see it directly, but also so that we can feel the heat of it. The question to consider is this: How can we as therapists bring the living drama of people's lives into our space so we can directly see and act on it?

The Purpose of Enactments

The enactment is meant to bring the story of our clients' pathology into our presence for us not only to witness it as it happens, but also to experience it. People cannot convey the fullness of their experience through narration. People cannot fully see themselves, nor can they see others, except through the filters of our own biases. We fill in the blanks with our imagination. We can reason about it, feel it in our emotional receptors, and even track its effect on traces of our personal and professional histories—that is, what we have lived through in our personal lives and seen in our clinical practice. That data still lacks the body that can only be supplied by experiencing clients' live interactions.

Moreover, as therapists we are trying to make a difference in people's lives. This means reaching them at a depth that prompts them to approach their problems in novel and different ways, making possible change that may not have seemed possible. People are accessible to our interventions through different gates, depending on where they are in their relationships with us and what they bring of themselves—emotionally, culturally, and experientially—to the encounter with us. The more of themselves that is present with us, the more gates are accessible to our interventions. However, they cannot open their pain and vulnerability to us through words alone.

Description and Implementation

> The therapist constructs an interpersonal scenario in the session in which dysfunctional transactions among family members are played out. This transaction occurs in the context of the session, in the present, and in relation to the therapist.
>
> (Minuchin & Fishman, 1981, p. 79)

Therapists from various schools have always attempted to make therapy more than just a conversation, and more of an experience. Psychoanalysts did it through the techniques that fostered transference. Structural family therapists, as noted above, did so through what they labeled the *enactment*. Bringing the action into the session can happen in several ways, but what is common to all methods is setting up a situation where clients feel free to or compelled to interact with each other around the focal issue in the session itself. The opportunity may present itself spontaneously when a client triggers another's reaction by a comment or action touching on his or her issue, and the therapist refrains from drawing attention to him/herself. If the enactment is not fully spontaneous, the therapist may help it along by signaling a client to respond directly to the other family member and what was said instead of responding to the therapist, thus prompting them to continue the interaction between them as they would normally do at home. More actively, the therapist may explicitly invite clients to address the issue between them at a given moment, with the therapist involved as an observer. Even more actively, the therapist can read/sense what a family member wants to convey to another and then say it for him or her, looking to instigate an interaction between the family members.

This facilitation of interaction between family members will serve as an opportunity to observe and to understand what goes on between them. It also serves as a chance to intervene for change, a potentially powerful occasion to alter the couple's interaction in a way that is therapeutically helpful to them. When partners are thus engaged with each other, the therapist, by how he or she connects with the couple, can promote a change in their words or behavior with one another. In such a reenactment, clients are emotionally open, and consequently more amenable to changing their patterns of interaction. This kind of engagement is more likely to stick than advice offered when they are less emotionally engaged. When a therapist actively joins family interactions to alter their dynamics, an intervention gains power through the therapist's own emotional presence in what is interchanging among family members. The therapist's live presence in family interactions takes on color, energy, and dimension through the therapist's conscious and purposeful use of "all of self" that may facilitate the process— whether it is through gender, age, race, religious affiliation, or anything else that may make for a more immediate connection with the family.

Contraindications

There is a caution that relates to how directly and intensely partners engage with each other around an issue. Therapists need to be so personally present and connected to the interactions that they can sense and anticipate what could be harmful and even dangerous if not guided by them. Therapists' emotional connection to the process will influence boundaries, patterns, and affective tones among members of the family during the enactment. Therapists also need to be self-aware of how they are influencing what is taking place among family members. Just as they can and should be positive influences in the interactions, they can unwittingly provoke harmful interactions. Therapists must view themselves as personally part of the system that is activated in the enactment.

Case Example

In this case example (see also Aponte, 1994), a Latino family with five children, two boys and three girls, presents an 11-year-old boy, Aldo, who was acting childishly at home and was inattentive in school. The mother was actively engaged with the female therapists in the therapy. The father was peripheral in the family and in the therapy. He hardly spoke in sessions. A consultant to the therapists and the family was also Latino, but as a male, his instinct was to engage the father. He moved chairs and sat right next to the father, taking time to talk with him and get to know him a little until the father relaxed with him. When the therapist felt himself connected to the man, he asked the father to get Aldo to talk with him about what was troubling him. The boy responded with one-word answers, obviously intimidated by his father, who was blunt when addressing Aldo. Finally, the father gave up and turned to the 16-year-old, Esteban, and asked him to help engage the 11-year-old. Esteban could read his brother, and confirmed with him that he was afraid of their father. Esteban himself became emotional and acknowledged to his father that he, too, feared him, and that what he needed from his father was to feel his father's respect. This moved the father, and with encouragement from the consultant, the father said he understood his sons and spoke of how tough it had been for him with his own father. The father ended by owning up to his sons how he failed them and resolving to change.

The peripheral father became central in that therapeutic encounter; he was able to show his personal vulnerability and communicate his caring for his boys, something he was able to do in relationship with the consultant who had connected with him. The consultant had consciously used his Latino background and male identity to join with the father in a way that allowed the man to come out from hiding his fatherly understanding.

References

Aponte, H. J. (1994). *Bread & spirit: Therapy with the new poor.* New York: W. W. Norton.
Minuchin, S., & Fishman, H. C. (1981). *Family therapy techniques.* Cambridge, MA: Harvard University Press.

7

ENACTMENTS IN FIVE DEVELOPMENTAL STAGES

Sean D. Davis

Purpose: To help emotionally reactive couples communicate effectively

Introduction

Broadly speaking, an enactment occurs in couple therapy when both partners are speaking with each other. Couples therapists use enactments as a tool for both assessment and intervention. Enactments are used in assessment when a therapist observes the couple interacting naturally, and usually provides a more accurate picture of communication patterns than if a couple merely describes their communication. Enactments are used as an intervention to shape interaction as it is occurring rather than didactically teaching the couple communication skills and then sending them home to practice without the safety provided by a therapist's structure and guidance. Such an experiential approach is thought to produce better outcomes, as change is more likely to stick if a couple's efforts are coached to success *in-vivo* by a therapist.

Even though enactments are traditionally associated with structural therapy, Butler and colleagues (Butler & Gardner, 2003; Davis & Butler, 2004) claim that enactments can be a logically consistent component of any dyadic approach. Butler and Gardner (2003) provide a framework in which a couple's emotional reactivity determines through which of five developmental stages of an enactment a therapist should guide a couple. Davis and Butler (2004), on the other hand, focus on the specific operational skills that comprise an enactment. In other words, Butler and Gardner (2003) focus on *when* and *to what purpose* to use an enactment, whereas Davis and Butler (2004) focus on *how* to use an enactment. The purpose of this chapter is to outline Butler and Gardner's (2003) five-stage model of enactments.

Purpose of the Five Developmental Stages

The main purpose of an enactment is to gradually foster self-reliant, healthy couple interaction. More specifically, enactments help couples lower their emotional reactivity, learn to be attentive to their partner's needs, and effectively communicate their own needs. Enactments provide a vehicle through which a therapist can foster the skills necessary to achieve these goals.

Description and Implementation

Highly emotionally reactive couples begin in stage 1 and graduate to higher stages as emotional reactivity decreases and self-reliant, healthy interaction increases. Less-reactive couples will start therapy at later stages. Furthermore, some stages may take months, whereas others may take one session. It is also normal for couples to return to earlier stages if the transition happens prematurely. Regardless of the stage, the therapist intervenes through coaching interaction rather than extensive didactic teaching or advice giving (Butler & Gardner, 2003).

In stage 1, *shielded enactments*, the seating is arranged so both partners are facing the therapist. All interaction is channeled through the therapist. The couple is told that each will get half of the session to speak uninterrupted. While one speaks, the other is to listen without interrupting and to try to have empathy for their partner's experience. The therapist explains that while the listener will likely not agree with everything their partner says, it is nevertheless important for the listener to set aside his or her agenda for the moment and try to see the situation through their partner's eyes. They are also instructed to practice monitoring their physiological responses as they listen, and practice self-soothing (i.e., deep breathing) if their anxiety rises to the point that they are not listening. The therapist reassures the listener that they will get the same amount of time to talk; this serves the purpose of helping them relax enough to listen to their partner. This is still difficult for many couples in stage 1, and the therapist will likely have to briefly remind the listener to remain quiet until their turn to speak. The therapist asks the speaking partner to discuss their experience using principles of healthy communication, such as "I-statements," complaining without blaming, and so forth. As the therapist listens to the speaker, the therapist helps the spouse or partner say things in ways that are easier to be heard. This coaching can be either didactic (e.g., "It may be easier for him/her to hear you if you used an I-statement rather than a you-statement there") or through reflecting back what was said in a way that is easier for their partner to hear, such as by focusing on soft, primary emotions rather than harsh, secondary emotions (e.g., "I hear you that you feel angry when she doesn't come home as planned, though I'm wondering if there's some hurt underneath that anger, like you're afraid that she doesn't want to be around you. Is that right?"). Didactic coaching should be brief and kept to a minimum so as to allow time to practice within the enactment. Most instruction in stage 1 occurs indirectly through therapist modeling.

The goals of stage 1 are to help the clients reduce their emotional reactivity by slowing down their process and adopting healthier communication skills. Couples are ready to move to stage 2 when partners can listen without interruption and remain physiologically calm, demonstrate perspective-taking, and frame requests positively when they speak.

In stage 2, *buffered enactments*, seating is arranged as in stage 1 and all of the interaction is still channeled through the therapist, but the speaker will be gently interrupted several times while the therapist checks in with the listening partner to try to elicit a healthy response to whatever was just said. So in stage 1, if the speaker said, "I just feel so hurt when she doesn't come home as planned," the therapist would not interrupt, whereas in stage 2 the therapist may stop and ask the listener, "I know your partner often seems distant to you, but he's saying that during those times he's really feeling hurt. I wonder what it's like for you to hear that?" The listener response is kept brief to maintain a roughly equal distribution of speaking and listening time. If needed, the listener is reminded to use the breathing exercise mentioned earlier.

In addition to the further integration of healthy communication skills, the purpose of the stage 2 buffered enactments is to move the couple closer to self-reliant interaction by helping the listener adopt a deeper, more systemic understanding of the relationship that acknowledges their role in the relationship problems, and allowing the speaker to see their partner softening and taking responsibility. Couples move to stage 3 when the listener focuses on understanding rather than justification or counterattacks, and the speaker uses mostly healthy rather than threatening or blaming communication.

In stage 3, *talk-turn enactments*, couples face each other and all interaction is channeled through the couple, with the therapist actively coaching healthy interaction. Speaking directly with each other often raises emotional reactivity, and thus requires active therapist coaching. Frequent coaching can be frustrating to clients, but it is needed to cement new, healthy communication patterns.

The purpose of the stage 3 talk-turn enactments is to help the couple experience success, further solidify healthy communication, and grow toward self-reliant interaction. A couple is ready to move to stage 4 when the speaking partner avoids provoking the listening partner, the listener focuses on understanding, and the couple exhibits an ability to exit negative cycles on their own.

In stage 4, *episode enactments*, therapist intrusion is greatly reduced, as all interaction is channeled through the couple. Conversations are allowed to run their course, and the therapist processes the experience afterwards, inviting the couple to identify strengths and weaknesses in their communication. Therapy may terminate at this stage, as clients demonstrate self-reliant communication by taking turns respectfully speaking and listening, attending to each other's emotions as well as their own, and resolving long-standing content issues. Stage 5, *relationship enactments*, occurs outside of therapy as the couple maintains healthy communication in their daily life.

Contraindications

As with many couple therapy interventions, enactments are contraindicated if domestic violence is present. Each client must also be willing to take responsibility for their role in the relationship problems. In my experience, failure to do so is often an indication that one or both partners wants to end the marriage or relationship but have not said so yet.

Case Example

During stage 1, Illiana had difficulty listening and Eduardo had difficulty speaking. After about eight sessions in stages 1 and 2, both were able to articulate the primary emotions underlying their stance in the cycle and acknowledge that their partner's behavior made sense in light of their own. Eduardo acknowledged that he unfairly took liberties with time and money, attitudes and behaviors that had gotten worse as Illiana had become increasingly angry. He felt entitled to these liberties as the primary breadwinner raised in a family where such behavior was the norm. Illiana felt disregarded and hurt, and she questioned Eduardo's commitment to her emotional well-being. In stages 2 and 3, Eduardo was able to acknowledge that his behavior was unfair and that Illiana was justified in feeling as she did. Illiana was able to see how her anger made it more difficult for Eduardo to come home. By stage 4, Illiana was articulating her needs nondefensively, and Eduardo was responding to these needs by taking responsibility for his misogynistic behavior. They spent most of stage 4 working out a plan that met all aspects of what previously had been competing desires for separateness and connectedness. They stopped coming to therapy after they successfully navigated several instances where old patterns emerged.

References

Butler, M. H., & Gardner, B. C. (2003). Adapting enactments to couple reactivity: Five developmental stages. *Journal of Marital and Family Therapy, 29,* 311–327.

Davis, S. D., & Butler, M. H. (2004). Enacting relationships in marriage and family therapy: A conceptual and operational definition of an enactment. *Journal of Marital and Family Therapy, 30,* 319–333.

8

EFFECTIVELY STRUCTURING ENACTMENTS

Sean D. Davis and Sandra A. Espinoza

Purpose: To structure healthy couple communication in session

Introduction

An enactment occurs when a couple is speaking with each other in therapy. Enactments provide a vehicle through which couples can learn how to communicate effectively. Effective structuring of an enactment is vital to the mastery of healthy communication skills. With too little structure, enactments often mirror the same dysfunctional communication patterns that brought the couple to therapy to begin with. With too much structure, couples never get the chance to practice communication skills on their own. Much of the theory—the *when* and *to what purpose* to use enactments—is discussed in Chapter 7 in this volume. The purpose of this chapter is to outline the skills necessary for a successful enactment (Butler, Davis, & Seedall, 2008). The techniques discussed in this chapter represent a highly structured enactment. However, not all aspects of the technique will be used in every enactment. Rather, clinicians should use their judgment to gauge how structured the enactment needs to be. Guidance for this decision is offered in Chapter 6 on the developmental stages of enactments.

Purpose of Enactments

An enactment is a therapeutic technique that can be used regardless of theoretical background. The primary goal is to help facilitate increasingly self-reliant interactions by the couple. Enactments can be used as a vehicle for initiating change, facilitating emotional expression, and practicing communication skills in couple therapy.

Description and Implementation

The following description of enactments is meant to provide therapists with a systematic tool to aid in the implementation of the technique (Butler et al., 2008). However, as couples vary in their dynamics and emotional reactivity, therapists are encouraged to be flexible and utilize the intervention as it best fits the couple. The framework of enactments can be outlined in three phases: (a) *initiation phase*; (b) *intervention phase*; and (c) *evaluation phase*. Each phase has a different subset of tasks that aid in the fulfillment of an overall goal of helping the couple sustain positive interaction.

In the *initiation phase*, the therapist helps the couple understand the purpose of the technique by explaining to the clients what he or she would like them to gain out of the enactment (Butler et al., 2008). The therapist explains the roles of each partner (i.e., the speaker and the listener) as well as the therapist's role during the enactment. The speaker is instructed to use first-person language and describe what feelings emerge for them when there is a negative exchange with their partner. Meanwhile, the listener is directed to avoid becoming defensive and instead listen reflectively and try to understand what the speaker is feeling. The therapist also explains that during the enactment, the therapist will intervene occasionally in order to help guide the couple toward their goals. In order to increase the efficacy of the technique, the therapist picks a specific content focus for the couple to talk about (e.g., "Vanessa, please tell Michael what it feels like when he begins to text during an argument . . . and Michael, please tell Vanessa what it feels like when she ignores your calls during the day"). The therapist specifies content to focus on in order for the enactment to unfold smoothly. Selecting a topic helps narrow the focus of the conversation and should be picked carefully by gauging the couple's current emotional state. Throughout the initiation phase, the therapist explains the use of positive communication skills (and models them when clients struggle with implementation). After the couple understands the purpose of the enactment, the therapist arranges the couple by having them face each other in order to foster positive emotional expression. Once the couple is arranged this way, it is important for the therapist to remove him/herself from the couple interaction in order for it to be sustained by the couple. The goal for this phase is to help "set up" the couple for the practice of positive communication and interaction skills.

In the *intervention phase*, the therapist acts as a coach and promotes the implementation of the skills covered in the initiation phase. The therapist facilitates the enactment while it is ongoing, sometimes briefly interrupting the couple by giving a partner a small instruction in order to redirect a negative exchange. Therapists should look for clues that a partner is disengaging, such as losing eye contact, turning away from their partner and toward the therapist, or using third-person pronouns (Davis & Butler, 2004). The therapist focuses on helping the couple sustain their positive interactions by commending them when they are doing well in session. In this phase, the therapist can continue to "coach" the clients by reframing a partner's negative comments and continuing to promote positive expression. In addition to this, the therapist is also trying to promote the expression of attachment-based emotions in order to help the couple connect on a deeper level and acknowledge underlying needs (e.g., "Can you tell Lily a little more about how scared you feel every time she dismisses your feelings?"). The therapist also may help the listener by highlighting the underlying emotion of the partner who is speaking (e.g., "Lily, what is it like to hear how scared Carlos gets when he feels unworthy of your love?"). This attachment-based dialogue can help the couple move toward healing and bonding by becoming aware of one another's emotional experience (Davis & Butler, 2004). The goal for this phase is to help the couple practice their newly learned skills while prompting a new emotional experience that can help them work through attachment needs in order to better resolve their problems.

In the final *evaluation phase*, the therapist reviews the goals of the enactment with the couple. Together, they evaluate the enactment goals, partner roles, and the couple's interaction process. The therapist also incorporates the progress made in the enactment to overall therapy goals for the couple. The therapist focuses on highlighting what each partner did well and invites each partner to commend each other for their successes. The couple is encouraged by the therapist to notice positive changes but also reflect on areas for growth and note where change is needed (e.g., "What about today's interaction made it difficult to achieve your goals?"). This phase also involves the therapist prompting the couple to make commitments to each other in order to help solidify changes in the relationship (e.g., "What will each of you do in order for there to be fewer arguments about Maria's work commitments?"). These commitments can be centered around how the expression of emotions will be made in the future or specific solutions that will be attempted in order to reduce conflict. The purpose for the *evaluation phase* is to help the couple reflect on the enactment process, revisit their goals, and commit to making positive changes moving forward.

Contraindications

Emotionally reactive, volatile couples may not be able to sustain productive dialogue in an enactment as described in Chapter 6. In that chapter, a five-stage model for adapting enactments for use with emotionally reactive couples is described.

Case Example

Married couple Jayden and Kayla presented with "difficulty communicating." Jayden was feeling neglected by Kayla's preoccupation with work and their children. Kayla felt like all Jayden wanted was sex. Attempts to discuss this usually led to fights that would both escalate until one left the house, after which they would be silent for a few days. They had reached the point where they had almost completely stopped talking. We used enactments heavily to help them slow down, clarify what they were feeling, communicate it in a way that could be heard easily, listen to each other, and respond with compassion. This process took about 13 sessions, after which they were able to effectively communicate on their own.

References

Butler, M. H., Davis, S. D., & Seedall, R. (2008). Common pitfalls of beginning therapists utilizing enactments. *Journal of Marital and Family Therapy, 34,* 329–352.

Davis, S. D., & Butler, M. H. (2004). Enacting relationships in marriage and family therapy: A conceptual and operational definition of an enactment. *Journal of Marital and Family Therapy, 30,* 319–333.

PART B

Couple Communication

9

EXPANDING LEVELS OF COMMUNICATION

Gerald R. Weeks and Nancy Gambescia

Purpose: To help couples learn how to communicate with depth and richness

Introduction

One of the most recurrent complaints in couple therapy is the lack of communication between partners; consequently, it is one of the most common issues discussed in treatment (Weeks & Fife, 2014). For some couples, the quantity of verbal communication is insufficient. This problem is addressed through teaching, modeling, and reinforcing clear communication skills in session and through homework assignments that focus on increasing verbal communication at home. In many cases, however, the communication problem is that the partners fail to understand each other because the intent of the communication is not what the other hears (Weeks & Fife, 2014). In other words, one partner is trying to send a message with a particular meaning and the other partner interprets the meaning of the message differently. When intent and effect are very dissimilar, the result is misunderstanding, which can rapidly erupt into conflict. When this problem is detected, the couple is taught reflective listening skills and encouraged to practice them in session and at home, in hopes that the partners will be better able to understand each other.

Another common communication problem is the tendency to focus on negative aspects of the relationship or to underemphasize the positive attributes of each other. In this instance, the couple is helped to recognize the ratio of positive to negative comments and then change the ratio to increase the positive interchanges. For instance, a negative comment could involve blaming or complaining. The couple is aided in understanding that a positive focus will increase the likelihood of getting what is desired. Further, they learn about how destructive negative comments can be to their relationship.

The literature on couple therapy is filled with information and techniques about communication; however, there is inadequate knowledge about the *depth* of communication, ranging from superficial conversation to self-reflective discussions of patterns within a couple's relationship. In order to assess and improve the complexity of interactions between partners, communication is divided into levels based on depth. Additionally, the couple is taught how to measure the deepness of communication and to recognize deficits in order to communicate more effectively.

Purpose of Expanding Levels of Communication

The entire issue of communication is ambiguous and vague. Often couples present for treatment with "communication problems" and therapists repeatedly fail to clarify the difference between quality, quantity, clarity, and positivity of verbal interactions. Another factor that is muddled in ambiguous discussion about communication is the fact that therapists often do not help couples understand that communication occurs at different levels, and that all these levels are important. The level of communication refers to the depth and complexity of the communication. Even if the couple masters the techniques mentioned above and commonly found in the literature, they are still missing a way to self-assess whether their communication is encompassing enough to produce a sense of feeling understood, being able to resolve problems, and learning about the other person. Discussion of the richness and complexity of communication will occur only if the different levels of communication are considered.

The ability to fluidly move among the levels of communication depth and richness will enhance the couple's sense of connection and relationship satisfaction. In many cases, one partner will want to communicate at a "deeper" level and the other will not know what "deeper level" means. Unfortunately, in this type of situation, the partner wanting more authenticity is frequently unable to explain what they mean, or if they can, the partner will become defensive. The therapist should provide a framework through which the partners can assess the level at which they are communicating, determine if they are on the same level, and learn when to move to another level. The key components are agreement on the level of communication and the flexibility to move among the different levels as the situation necessitates.

Description and Implementation

This technique involves educating the couple about different levels of communication. They are then coached to practice these levels in the session and at home, and to self-assess whether they are able to move among the levels in a way that matches that of their partner and deepens the level of understanding when needed. The most important undertaking in couple therapy is to help each partner feel fully understood. Feeling fully understood at each level will help to achieve a number of goals that are critical to durable and lasting couple functioning.

With this simple and straightforward framework, the therapist uses language that is easily understood, and couples are coached to ask questions if they do not comprehend something. The couple is also encouraged to take notes on the different depth levels, review them daily for some time, and report weekly about their ability to talk at these levels. The therapist may need to coach them in the session and give them more specific homework assignments to facilitate discussions at various degrees. It is important that the therapist explain that one level is not better than another. In order to quantify the concept of levels of deepness, the therapist explains that there are five levels and that Levels 1 and 2 are easy, but the other three are more challenging. If a couple is stuck at the first two levels, relational problems will continue.

The therapist begins by describing the five types of communication, asking the couple which one they think they currently use most often, and helping them to recognize that staying in sync with each other is essential—particularly moving to a deeper level when the situation requires it.

- Level 1: *Reporting* or *storytelling.* One partner is simply giving a factual account of an event, talking only about what happened. It is not much different than reading an account in a newspaper. Some partners will talk endlessly about the events of the day and thinking it is communication, but the other partner may be, and probably becomes, quickly bored with it.
- Level 2: *Reacting.* A partner may talk about a number of events and then simply discuss how they reacted to it behaviorally without saying anything about how they felt or what they thought. The communication is about their behavioral reaction to an event. If all communication is about behavioral responses, very little information is being disclosed about feelings; thus, the couple is encouraged toward discussion that is deeper than a reaction to an event. The partners should include how they felt and what they were thinking.
- Level 3: *Openness, self-disclosure, and/or self-reflection.* As communication continues to deepen, the partners will engage in more talk that incorporates *openness, self-disclosure* and/or *self-reflection.* This kind of talk is spontaneous, or it can be a reaction to the other's statements. The partner freely expresses his/her thoughts, feelings, opinions, preferences, wants, needs, dreams, fears, and so on. It involves being open, present, and vulnerable to the other person. This act of self-disclosing communication conveys the essence of the experiences of one person to the other. The therapist must clarify this level using language that makes sense to the couple.
- Level 4: *Relationship talk.* The couple is asked to step back and become observers of their relationship. The therapist might say, "I want you to try to sit in my chair and tell me what you see happening in your relationship." This

description is followed by an explanation of circular repetitions of interaction, looking at underlying patterns in the relationship that may be unconscious, and struggling to dissect the nature of miscommunication and conflict. Furthermore, the couple is warned that the process can be tedious and slowly mastered. It involves self-disclosure, struggling through misunderstandings, and not becoming judgmental, blaming, defensive, or hooked on the idea that they are right.

- Level 5: *Relationship talk plus history.* The final level is an extension of Level 4. When couples begin to reflect on their relational patterns that exist in the here-and-now, it is important to keep the historical context in mind. The present-day interactions or patterns did not just spontaneously happen. They resulted from prior interactions. The couple is asked to reflect on when the pattern started. Did it start in their relationship, a prior relationship, or early in life? Many patterns of communication began early in life. For example, if a partner has trouble expressing their feelings, it may have its origins in early childhood, where children were expected to be "seen and not heard" or when the parent constantly dismissed their feelings. Adding the historical context helps the partners become more compassionate rather than reactive to the other's deficits or problems. Connecting current to past behavior does not come naturally to most couples. The therapist may need to actively intervene in facilitating this process.

Case Example

Harriet and John worked in the same profession. At the end of each day, they would discuss their "cases" and related professional issues. When the therapist asked what else they chat about, they looked blank and said, "What else is there?" They both grew up in emotionally improvised families with parents who had a dismissive attachment style. Learning deeper ways to communicate was a revelation to such a highly educated couple. They required a good deal of in-session work to help them understand the deeper levels of communication and simultaneously discover their own thoughts, feelings, etc. The at-home practice proceeded slowly. The therapy was slow and tedious, but each one fortunately felt something was missing and quickly saw how their families had disabled them. This case was one of the most difficult to teach about communication, particularly Levels 3 through 5. Couples such as Harriet and John will conceptually grasp the idea quickly, but they will need targeted practice on the other levels in and out of session.

Reference

Weeks, G., & Fife, S. (2014). *Couples in treatment.* New York: Routledge.

10

RULE-GOVERNED SPEAKER-LISTENER TECHNIQUE

Rachel M. Diamond and Jay L. Lebow

Purpose: To facilitate "good enough" coordination with minimum communication between divorcing couples

Introduction

In general, communication skills training is a common component of most relational treatments. A primary technique used within this type of training is known as the speaker–listener (SL) technique. When reviewing the literature, Bray and Jouriles (1995) noted that most couple programs promoted the use of active listening and validation of spouses' positions, and by doing this, it was believed that defensiveness during discussions was decreased. A commonly used example of SL can be seen in the Prevention and Relationship Enhancement Program (PREP; Markman, Stanley, & Blumberg, 1994). Within PREP, a clearly defined version of SL is a key component of its curriculum for use with premarital couples. Additionally, most behavioral couple therapy programs use some variation of SL.

The SL technique is a set of skills and procedures that practitioners can teach partners when approaching conflict discussions. In its simplest form, SL involves the act of one person serving in the role of the speaker while another person serves in the role of the listener. The speaker articulates his/her ideas and thoughts while the listener paraphrases back to the speaker what he/she has heard. After the speaker has finished, the two switch roles. The primary goal is for both partners to leave with a sense of feeling heard and respected during the discussion prior to making attempts at solving the point of disagreement. While this technique is typically used with partners who are working on enhancing their relationship in couples therapy (i.e., premarital or marital therapy), we are suggesting that SL can be altered for use with couples who are going through a divorce or separation.

As a growing number of families are divorcing and becoming locked in disputes over issues such as child custody and visitation, some couples find themselves in therapists' offices attempting to communicate around difficult topics. These former couples are unable to resolve issues independently and may be referred to therapy by courts or legal counsel. Often even the simplest communication is difficult. Having a clear structure for organizing communication is of utmost importance when these clients are in session. Emphasizing the transfer of these communication skills outside of sessions is imperative so these couples are able to establish coordination between their households, as necessary.

Purpose of Rule-Governed Speaker-Listener Technique

In high-conflict divorcing and post-divorce families, communication is typically a major issue; it is almost invariably absent or is highly conflictual. Typically, the therapeutic goal for these families, in contrast to other divorcing and post-divorce systems that are better able to work harmoniously in the best interest of children, is for the separate households to function independently with only a minimum level of communication and coordination. For example, when differences between households present difficulties (e.g., differences in rules/structure) or when a child presents with urgent needs (e.g., a new medical diagnosis), the therapist must work with the former couple to create just enough coordination for the children to continue to function successfully. In session, the therapist works to build reliable and agreed-upon methods of communication and coordination between the former couple.

Unlike most instances in which SL is used, the goal of this technique is not to move toward increased communication. The goal of SL with these cases is for the therapist to teach effective communication in order for the dyad to communicate when necessary and allow them to manage conflicts and negotiate child-related issues more successfully. The therapist will encourage the best form of communication that allows for the most flexibility. That is, if and when possible, the therapist will strive to teach the partners to communicate in person using SL. However, if safety becomes an issue with these partners and/or conflict still readily erupts, the therapist can help brainstorm alternative methods of communication. For example, new technologies such as email and text messaging can be valuable as long as clear rules for their use are established (e.g., mutual agreements to keep them from being used as evidence).

Description and Implementation

Too much communication can often be as risky as too little in these families, degenerating into off-topic fights. When this method succeeds, it is expected that most of these former spouses will communicate only when necessary. The goal of this modified version of SL for former couples is to create a known structure for communication so that: 1) communication occurs just enough in order to serve the lives of their children, and 2) when communication occurs, it is highly structured and minimizes the potential for deterioration.

For example, in the context of necessary coordination of care about a child's diabetes, the therapist will instruct the first speaker to focus on one issue related to the coordination of the child's care. The therapist will help the speaker learn to communicate directly about this topic without switching to other topics or prematurely attempting to problem-solve. This is done in crisply delivered small bits so the listener can understand the message being said. The therapist can stop the speaker if something is unclear or if the speaker goes off-task. The listener is similarly helped to listen without interrupting until he or she paraphrases what the speaker says without including personal thoughts or explanations. Once the listener paraphrases what was said, the roles are switched. The listener then becomes the speaker and is given the opportunity to express his/her ideas on the topic while the other person is now in the role of the listener.

Contraindications

In order for it to be worthwhile to have volatile ex-partners come together to establish methods of communication and coordination, at a minimum there has to be some level of established safety in the therapy room. If this cannot be established, in-person SL will not be able to occur. An alternative plan would be for the therapist to help coordinate communication that does not require in-person communication, sometimes involving the monitoring of written communication by a third person (e.g., the therapist or a parent coordinator).

Another instance arises when former spouses do not need SL to communicate. If the former spouses are skillful at speaking and listening to one another and, subsequently, can coordinate the needs of their children successfully, this technique may in fact hinder their co-parenting efforts by interfering with their existing fluid communication and engagement with one another. As Gottman (1999) points out, SL is not a form of communication couples naturally engage in, but a technique for special situations.

Case Example

To discuss how to implement modified SL, we use the case example of Amy and Charles. They have been separated for three months and have two children, ages 10 and 12. The children reside with Amy the majority of the time. Charles picks them up from school on Tuesdays and Thursdays and drops them off after dinner; he also takes them every other weekend. Amy notices the children's homework has not been completed on the nights they are with Charles. They have attempted to better coordinate on their own, but they have struggled. They were referred to therapy by their mediator to address communication issues. One of the first techniques the therapist taught them was SL.

THERAPIST: Amy, I want you to state your concerns without getting into what you think Charles's motives are for the problem. Try to use "I" statements that describe your point of view. To make sure you help Charles understand your message, please keep it brief and avoid accusatory language. Charles, you will listen and restate what you hear. If there is something you miss or didn't understand, Amy can help clarify. It's important to understand this isn't an attempt to trip either of you up, but an attempt for both of you to be heard with the goal of better coordination for your kids. Amy, please start.

AMY: I feel overwhelmed when the kids are dropped off at night and I find their homework isn't complete. Then I have to help them finish their homework, and there is not a lot of time left, and before you know it they're up after their bedtimes. And, I don't get a chance to relax either. You don't get how hard that is for me, you never did! I think . . .

THERAPIST: Amy, why don't we stop here so we don't get off track. As the listener, Charles, it might be hard to not offer your opinion. That is the hardest part of being the listener. I'm going to ask you to be patient until you get the floor as the speaker, because you will want Amy to do the same for you. Instead, I want you to tell Amy in your own words what you heard her say.

CHARLES: You're feeling overwhelmed when the kids don't finish their homework the days they're with me.

AMY: Yes! When the kids didn't have to go back and forth there was more consistency. They knew to come home and do homework. I worry how they are adjusting to every little change.

THERAPIST (*TURNING TO CHARLES*): What do you hear her saying now? Please tell her.

CHARLES: What I hear you saying is that you're also worried about how the kids are handling the changes, and without consistency between our houses this might be adding to these changes.

AMY: Exactly!

THERAPIST: Great job, both of you. Now, I'm going to ask you to switch roles. Charles, please tell Amy what you've been thinking about the children's homework and your time with them.

The conversation will continue as demonstrated above with the partners switching roles. They will continue to practice this skill in sessions and will be encouraged to incorporate the key aspects of the rules into their communication outside of sessions. With continued practice, the hope for Amy and Charles is the ability to learn to use SL as needed. Effective use of this technique will facilitate structured communication to help them improve coordination between their households so they will eventually no longer need the assistance of professionals.

References

Bray, J. H., & Jouriles, E. N. (1995). Treatment of marital conflict and prevention of divorce. *Journal of Marital and Family Therapy, 21,* 461–473.

Gottman, J. M. (1999). *The marriage clinic: A scientifically based marital therapy.* New York: W. W. Norton & Co, Inc.

Markman, H., Stanley, S., & Blumberg, S. L. (1994). *Fighting for your marriage.* San Francisco, CA: Jossey-Bass.

11

PROBLEM-SOLVING STRATEGIES BASED ON PREP (PREVENTION AND RELATIONSHIP EDUCATION PROGRAM)

Aleja M. Parsons, Lane L. Ritchie, and Howard J. Markman

Purpose: To provide structure for couples to resolve problems peacefully

Introduction

All couples encounter problems, and it is important to have tools and skills to resolve these issues without increasing the conflict in the relationship. A structured approach can help couples stay focused on reaching a resolution rather than being sidetracked by common barriers to effective communication. A set structure also establishes an expectation that the couple will work together as a team to resolve the issue.

The most effective approach to help couples learn how to solve problems is to combine communication skills training with training in problem-solving, as is done in the Prevention and Relationship Education Program (PREP; Markman, Stanley, & Blumberg, 2010). PREP is a comprehensive, research-based relationship education curriculum designed to teach couples skills and principles that are the foundations of a healthy relationship. The preponderance of evidence gathered by various research teams shows positive effects of PREP (e.g., Markman et al., 1993), resulting in PREP being listed in the SAMHSA National Registry of Promising Practices. PREP has been widely disseminated across the U.S. and internationally.

In this chapter, we focus on the multi-step PREP approach for effective problem-solving (Stanley, Markman, Jenkins, & Blumberg, 2009). The purpose of the problem-solving skill is to give couples a structured approach to tackle problems in their relationship. It allows partners to express their feelings about the problem and work together to find a mutually agreeable solution.

Description and Implementation of Problem-Solving Strategies

The first step in the problem-solving skill is the Problem Discussion, which allows each partner an opportunity to clarify the topic at hand. An ideal way to structure the Problem Discussion is by using the speaker–listener technique, a PREP skill designed to help couples talk about important problems without fighting (described below). Among other ground rules during this step, couples are instructed *not to solve the problem at this stage*. By discussing the problem before trying to solve it, the Problem Discussion provides a safe space where both partners can feel heard and validated. Thus, it is important not to move on from this step until both partners feel understood. Oftentimes, once couples take the time to have a Problem Discussion, they find that there is no longer a problem to resolve. Two strategies listed at the end of this section may be helpful in facilitating the Problem Discussion. However, sometimes couples still feel like an issue exists after this step. If that is the case, they can move on to the next step of problem solving: Problem Solution. The Problem Solution step is broken down into four distinct stages: 1) Agenda Setting, 2) Brainstorming, 3) Agreement and Compromise, and 4) Follow-Up.

The purpose of the Agenda Setting stage is to specify exactly what issue the couple is trying to resolve. As the Problem Discussion likely covered many different components of the issue, it is important to take the time to focus on one specific aspect of the problem before moving forward. This is a helpful and important stage because it can often make the issue seem much more manageable. Further, couples are much more likely to come to a solution when they focus on a specific problem. It can be reassuring to work through these specific problems one at a time, starting with the easiest piece of the issue first. For example, rather than tackling a conflict over household chores all at once, couples can use the Agenda Setting stage to focus in on developing a schedule for washing the dishes, a more manageable piece of the larger problem. The second stage is Brainstorming. During this stage, the couple should write down a list of ideas generated to resolve the specific problem at hand. The most important guiding principle to keep in mind during this stage is that any and every idea is okay. The couple will have the time to evaluate and pare down ideas in the next stage of problem solving. Giving couples the freedom to include all ideas will hopefully encourage creativity and allow the couple to have some fun with the process. Also, spending time exhausting all options discourages couples from settling on a solution that is not their best idea.

Following Brainstorming is the Agreement and Compromise stage. The goal of this stage is to narrow down the list from the Brainstorming stage to a specific solution that both members of the couple agree to try. The important part of this stage is to be sure that the end solution is as specific as possible, and that both partners are on board with testing it out. The solution can be a combination of suggestions from the Brainstorming stage or can include modifications to one idea necessary for both partners to agree. Partners should be prepared to compromise in this stage. The goal is not necessarily that each partner gets *everything* they want from the solution, but that through teamwork, the couple is able to find a solution that is mutually satisfying.

The final stage of the problem-solving skill is the Follow-Up stage. This stage is important because it builds accountability by requiring the couple to check back in about how things are going with the decided-upon solution. It is also an important stage because it sets up the expectation that things may not go perfectly the first time around. Oftentimes, couples need to slightly alter the solution to work better long-term. The couple should set an agreed-upon time for the Follow-Up stage. The couple should give themselves enough time to implement the solution before checking back in. Sometimes this stage is quite simple and just requires a quick chat to confirm that the solution worked out well for both partners. Other times, it may require a bit more time to work through modifications. If major changes are agreed upon in this stage, the couple should schedule a second Follow-Up to ensure the problem is resolved.

Strategies for Problem Discussion:

- *Speaker–Listener.* When emotions are high, couples may find it helpful to implement the speaker–listener technique. This skill is highly structured and gives each partner the opportunity to be the speaker and the listener in an effort to avoid negative communication patterns. In brief, one person has the floor (literally a piece of tile, carpet, etc.) and talks about their perspective while the other person, the listener, paraphrases what they hear. The conversation continues with the couple passing the floor after a few statements so that each person has a chance in both roles. A full description of this skill can be found in *Fighting for Your Marriage* (Markman et al., 2010).
- *XYZ Statements* ("When you do X in situation Y, I feel Z"). These statements can be helpful during the Problem Discussion because it gives partners specific, usable information rather than vague, non-descript statements that often include a personal attack or overgeneralization. XYZ statements are also useful for avoiding escalation and defensiveness, two common roadblocks for effective communication.

Case Example

Max and Sophia noticed that they often argue about household cleanliness. In order to try the problem-solving skill, they first agree on a time to come together and have the Problem Discussion. They agree to use the speaker–listener technique and to include XYZ statements as much as possible during the Problem Discussion step.

Problem Discussion:

MAX (SPEAKER): I've been really stressed out about how messy the house has been lately. It's difficult for me to feel comfortable when none of the chores are done.

SOPHIA (LISTENER): It's really hard for you when the chores aren't done because you feel stressed out and not at ease at home.

MAX (SPEAKER): YES! WHEN THE HOUSE ISN'T CLEAN, I CAN'T UNWIND AFTER A LONG DAY AT WORK.

SOPHIA (LISTENER): When things are still a mess when you come home from work, it makes it difficult for you to relax.

MAX (SPEAKER): Exactly! That's why it's so important to me that we find a solution for this problem. *(Max gives Sophia the floor)*

SOPHIA (SPEAKER): When you don't put your dishes away after you finish eating, I feel frustrated.

MAX (LISTENER): It's irritating when I don't clean up after myself?

SOPHIA (SPEAKER): Yes—I feel frustrated with the inconsistency in keeping things clean.

MAX (LISTENER): You'd like me to be more consistent in keeping things clean?

SOPHIA (SPEAKER): Not just you, I think we can both be more consistent. I just want to make sure that it's a priority for us both all the time, not just when things are obviously messy.

MAX (LISTENER): It's important for you that we both work on this on an ongoing basis?

SOPHIA (SPEAKER): You got it! How can we make this work?

The couple agrees they both feel heard and understood and move on to the Problem Solution stage.

Agenda Setting:

SOPHIA: This just seems like such a big issue. We have a big house, and there are a lot of chores that need to be done to maintain cleanliness—where can we start?

MAX: Well, it seems like the kitchen is one small piece of the problem that we could address first.

SOPHIA: Great—let's start there.

Brainstorming *(Max writes down the ideas they both suggest)*:

SOPHIA: We could get a dishwasher installed so that it's not so difficult to stay on top of washing the dishes by hand.

MAX: We could try getting a cleaning service to come in and help out.

SOPHIA: What if we just used paper plates and only used the dishes for special occasions?

MAX: We could both wash our dishes immediately after using them so things don't pile up.

SOPHIA: What if we wrote out a schedule of what chore needs to be done on what day. It might help to just have it all written down for us to use as a reference.

MAX: Hmm . . . We could have kids so they can take care of everything! (*Both partners laugh*)

SOPHIA: Okay, I think that's a good list. Are you ready to move on to the next step?

Agreement and Compromise:

MAX: Well, I like the idea of writing everything out. It would help me to just have a sense of what needs to be done throughout the week.

SOPHIA: Okay, that sounds good. What if we also add in one of the ideas that will help us stay on top of cleaning?

MAX: We have a few to choose from. What do you think about getting a cleaning service?

SOPHIA: I'd rather not start with that. Can we try to do it ourselves first and then come back and consider a service if things still aren't working?

MAX: That sounds like a fair compromise. What about trying to wash our dishes right away?

SOPHIA: I'm willing to give it a try. So we're going to write out the list of what needs to be done throughout the week and also keep up on the dishes by washing right after we eat?

MAX: Yup—I'm on board.

(*Couple agrees on a time to come back together for the Follow-Up.*)

Follow-Up:

SOPHIA: So how do you think it's been going?

MAX: Well, the chart has helped me out a lot because it's a visual way to make sure all the chores are checked off each day. What about for you?

SOPHIA: I agree; that part is working great. I don't know about the immediate dishwashing though. I'm usually running out the house right after I eat, so I haven't been the best at this.

MAX: "It's been hard for me to wash things immediately, too. What if we just agreed that we will wash our dishes by the end of the day?"

SOPHIA: "That sounds great."

MAX: "We got somewhere!" (*They hug each other*)

Sophia and Max adapted their solution and found that things were going smoothly at their next Follow-Up meeting. They then moved on to resolve the other pieces of the larger issue that were still problematic. By going through these steps, they were able to resolve their conflict in a constructive way and focus their energies on protecting and enhancing their positive connections.

References

Markman, H. J., Renick, M. J., Floyd, F. J., Stanley, S. M., & Clements, M. (1993). Preventing marital distress through communication and conflict management training: A 4- and 5-year follow-up. *Journal of Consulting and Clinical Psychology, 61*(1), 70–77. doi:10.1037/0022–006X.61.1.70

Markman, H. J., Stanley, S. M., & Blumberg, S. L. (2010). *Fighting for your marriage: A deluxe revised edition of the classic best seller for enhancing marriage and preventing divorce* (3rd ed.). San Francisco, CA: Jossey-Bass.

Stanley, S. M., Markman, H. J., Jenkins, N. H., & Blumberg, S. L. (2009). *PREP 7.0b*. Greenwood Village, CO: PREP Educational Products, Inc.

12

THE DAILY DIALOGUE

Jon Carlson and Sonya Lorelle

Purpose: To increase awareness of what is on the individuals' minds to maintain a more constant connection between partners

Introduction

The Daily Dialogue is an activity that couples can practice in order to build positive and encouraging interactions into their daily life. While this technique can be integrated into various theoretical orientations, Adlerian psychology provides a helpful rationale for incorporating this practice. Adlerian psychology is a holistic systems theory that emphasizes the importance of social relationships and the interactional patterns within those relationships. The Adlerian counselor believes that a couple's problems are not a result of disorders within the individuals, but rather difficulties that result from the relational patterns that they have created. Within Adlerian therapy, the counselor collaborates with the couple in order to assess their current lifestyle or set of beliefs, build clear goals for the couple, identify positive strengths and resources, and incorporate new strategies that can help the couple meet their goals (Carlson, Watts, & Maniacci, 2006). *The Daily Dialogue* is a method of creating regular constructive interactions for the couple. These positive exchanges set the foundation for building a safer and more cooperative relational system.

Purpose of the Daily Dialogue

Couples often come to counseling having tried very hard to make their relationship better; however, they tend to do the things that created and sustain, rather than resolve, the real issues they face as a couple. Most couples are not aware of the skills or actions that can promote healthy and satisfying connection. Their disconnection can lead to partners feeling discouraged, empty, or isolated. Struggling couples describe their interactions as mainly negotiating life tasks or attempting to resolve conflict in emotionally painful, draining, and ineffective ways. *The Daily Dialogue* provides an opportunity for partners to thoughtfully share important and personal aspects about each other in hopes of fostering a genuine connection so that each partner feels encouraged. After drifting apart or getting stuck in a conflictual cycle, couples soon avoid being vulnerable or sharing private thoughts. Feelings of love and caring are difficult to maintain without this type of regular interaction. *The Daily Dialogue* provides the structure for couples to intentionally build this reconnection, prevent continued isolation, and build intimacy (Carlson & Sperry, 2010). *The Daily Dialogue* also has value in fostering the self-awareness of each individual partner. When sharing inner thoughts and feelings, partners are able to gain a deeper understanding of whether they are being authentic and communicating what they truly think and feel (Carlson & Dinkmeyer, 2003).

Description and Implementation

The counselor asks the couple to commit 10 minutes each day to a *Daily Dialogue*. During this time, each partner shares for five minutes while the other person listens. The topic of these discussions should not be facts about the day's events but rather each individual's feelings, including their hopes, fears, insecurities, anger, sadness, or joy. It is important for each person to share insights and reflections about themselves. This is not a time to complain or air gripes about the other partner (Carlson & Dinkmeyer, 2003). Couples often begin by sharing safe or more mundane thoughts and feelings, but with continued dialogue, the depth increases.

The listening partner remains silent and practices listening to their partner's feelings and thoughts with an open and non-judgmental stance. The role of the listener is to seek understanding of what the partner has shared. It may be tempting to argue or contradict what the partner has shared if the partner disagrees. However, the goal is not to agree with what the partner is saying, but to accept their partner's thoughts, feelings, and perspectives as valid, even if they differ from his or her own (Carlson & Dinkmeyer, 2003). It is important to avoid criticism, attacks, or defensiveness during these discussions. It is best if the partner does not respond or ask questions and concentrates on understanding how the thoughts and feelings are true for their partner. If they really do not understand their partner, they can ask for clarification in their counseling session or at a different time.

For couples who have not connected in this way for a while, this process may initially seem awkward and superficial. Learning new skills can take time and practice to become natural. Developing the type of relationship a couple desires takes time and effort. Counselors should encourage couples to continue with the practice as the benefits can deepen with time (Carlson & Dinkmeyer, 2003). It takes time to build the safety and comfort to share the deepest emotions. While couples may come in hoping for big changes, it is important for them to keep in mind that bigger change happens slowly, one step at a time.

Contraindications

Counselors may worry that during these daily conversations, a couple's emotions may trigger another negative conflict. Some couples may be so entrenched in their negative patterns that they revert to their habitual interactions during this activity. While counselors do not want to reinforce negative experiences with couples, this dialogue is a small step toward building some needed positive connection. Therefore, if a couple has difficulty in carrying out this dialogue, the counselor may want to explore barriers that are preventing them from having the 10-minute conversation. For example, if the listeners become defensive during the dialogue, there could be private logic or underlying beliefs that are part of their lifestyle that could foster a more closed position. The counselor may explore their goals or beliefs about their relationship that may be impacting their ability to share their feelings with the partner. The counselor may also ask the couple what would help them detach from taking the feelings or thoughts personally during the discussion.

Caution: Couples need to remember to take turns, with each partner talking for only five uninterrupted minutes and then listening for only five uninterrupted minutes. They should not go any longer, and if they cannot fill five minutes, they should spend the time looking at one another's beautiful faces. Partners should not react to each other's content but concentrate on non-verbal understanding and being present. Understanding does not mean agreement. Partners should not respond to the other's messages, but rather spend the time letting the other person know what they wanted to share with them now that they have their complete and undivided attention or focus.

Case Example

A married couple had a relationship pattern that consisted of intense arguments that would unexpectedly arise from seemingly small, benign differences. Since these arguments were so painful, the husband began withdrawing and distancing himself emotionally from his wife with the hope of avoiding another painful conflict. The counselor introduced *The Daily Dialogue* as a safe way to help the partners to connect in a way that reduced the likelihood of the usual negative intensity of their arguments. Both partners were eager to incorporate the routine, as they both described a strong desire to work through their difficulties. Unfortunately, most couples try to focus more on being heard rather than accurately hearing.

When they returned for the next counseling session, they stated that most of *The Daily Dialogues* had gone well, but they described one that resulted in a conflict. The counselor explored the underlying beliefs as the possible trouble in the conflictual session during this activity. The wife stated that when listening to her husband, she felt he was blaming her for his feelings. The counselor asked what might help her listen in a more open and non-judgmental stance. She stated that since she knew the dialogue was coming and she was aware now of her typical reactions, she could prepare with some different self-talk. She decided she would tell herself that she cared about what her husband had to say, and even if she disagreed with his perspective, it did not invalidate her truth. She understood that they did not have to agree to be connected, only to create mutual understanding and acceptance of one another's views. Taking three deep breaths and preparing with this self-talk prior to *The Daily Dialogue* meeting helped her to be more open to hearing her husband's disappointment and hurt without her needing to feel responsible for them. Once she was able to incorporate these listening strategies, her husband commented that he really appreciated the dialogues because it was now safe, and he was able to share feelings that he was too afraid to share before. The wife shared that she felt relieved to finally be listened to so accurately by her husband. While the couple needed to take many other steps to build their relationship, this deceptively simple shift in the system from distance and conflict to daily safe connection was a necessary and important first step for this couple.

References

Carlson, J., & Dinkmeyer, D. (2003). *Time for a better marriage: Training in marriage enrichment.* Astascadero, CA: Impact.

Carlson, J., & Sperry, L. (2010). *Recovering intimacy in love relationships: A clinician's guide.* New York: Routledge.

Carlson, J., Watts, R. E., & Maniacci, M. (2006). *Adlerian therapy: Theory and practice.* Washington, DC: American Psychological Association.

13

USING SHARED JOURNALING TO PRACTICE COMMUNICATION SKILLS WITH COUPLES

Toni Schindler Zimmerman and Shelley A. Haddock

Purpose: To help couples struggling to use communication skills at home that they learned in therapy

Introduction

In couples therapy, therapists commonly introduce clients to new ways of communicating and resolving conflict as a means of relationship improvement. Therapists typically encourage couples to practice these new skills in therapy in hopes of strengthening the couples' ability to use the skills at home. Some couples struggle to use the skills at home—without the direct input from the therapist—and report, week after week, failed attempts at more effective communication and conflict resolution. Commonly, in attempting to describe these failed attempts to the therapist, the couple has difficulty remembering the interaction or they do not agree on what went wrong. In these situations, we have had success using a Shared Journaling technique. With this technique, the couple uses a journal to communicate and resolve conflict throughout the week instead of talking directly (verbally) to one another. In this way, the process of communication is slowed down and becomes more intentional, thereby increasing the likelihood that the couple will use new skills in their communication. Additionally, the couple can bring the journal into therapy so that the therapist has direct access to the communications, allowing for more direct feedback on both excellent attempts and problem areas.

Purpose of Shared Journaling

The purpose of the Shared Journaling technique is to provide couples with a structured and intentional means of successfully practicing new communication and conflict resolution skills at home.

Description and Implementation

To use this technique, the therapist should first decide the communication and conflict resolution model they will use with the couple. For instance, the therapist may select Gottman's approach (Gottman & Sliver, 1999), in which they will introduce the couple to techniques such as using soft start-ups, repair attempts, complaints versus criticism, and so on. The therapist should introduce these skills to the couple in therapy and/or request that they read Gottman & Silver's (1999) *Seven Principles for Making Marriage Work*. In therapy, the therapist should ensure that each partner understands the skills, and then encourage the couple to use the skills in session. If each partner understands the skills and can practice them successfully in session, yet continues to have difficulties using the skills at home, the therapist then assigns the Shared Journaling assignment.

If the couple agrees to this homework, the therapist gives the couple a journal. On the first few pages, the therapist or couple lists the skills to be used in each journal entry. This summary of skills allows the couple to review these skills prior to any communication. To use the journal, each partner writes his/her thoughts for the other partner. Then, they assess their own entry prior to their partner reading it. Each time they use a skill, they circle it and write the name of the skill in the margin (i.e., soft start-up). Asking the couple to circle and name skills used accomplishes two tasks. First, the writer essentially assesses him/herself as to how effectively the agreed-upon communication skills are being used with his/her partner. As a result of this self-assessment, the writer can rewrite or edit his/her journal entry, if deemed necessary. Second, the partner reading the entry can see where the partner made efforts to use the skills and to be thoughtful about his/her communication. When the partner writes a response, she/he also will circle and name the skills used. In this way, both partners are accountable for using the agreed-upon skills in their communication. When the couple brings the journal to therapy, the therapist can unpack the journal entries with the clients, reviewing what went well and what could have been improved. The couple can continue to use this technique until the skills become more readily accessible to them for use in verbal communications.

Contraindications

Some couples may have difficulty with this technique due to difficulties with or a dislike of writing or reading.

Case Example

Barbara and Jessica are a couple who, despite their best intentions, have difficulty using communication skills learned in therapy at home. The couple reports that they understand the skills and believe the skills would improve their communication and relationship. They also have successfully used the skills in therapy sessions with their therapist acting as a coach as they worked to resolve issues. Yet, time and time again, when they attempt to resolve an issue at home, the conversation does not go well. When the couple is next in session, they become frustrated trying to describe what went wrong to the therapist, and very little progress is made in translating the skills to communications outside of the therapy session. The therapist introduces the idea of and rationale for the Shared Journaling technique to the couple, and the couple agrees to try the technique for one week. The therapist instructs the couple to avoid trying to problem-solve even the smallest issue verbally, but instead to use the journal. The therapist gives the couple a journal, and together they write the communication skills they hope to use in their communications. In this case, the communication skills are based on Gottman and Silver's *Seven Principles for Making Marriage Work* (1999). The therapist then instructs the couple to write their thoughts to their partner in the journal and attempt to use the skills listed. After completing the entry, the writer is to circle each time they used a skill and to write the name of the skill used in the margin. For instance, if the writer uses a "soft start-up" in the entry, she will circle the "soft" words or sentences and write in the margins "soft start-up." In her response, the writer's partner uses this same process. The next week in therapy, the couple brings in their journal for the therapist to read and comment on. The couple reported that the process of writing helped slow down communication and created more thoughtful exchanges. They pointed out areas that went well and areas that didn't. The therapist added circles where she saw excellent repair attempts. The couple continued this process and gradually worked toward being about to talk openly without the journal to one another at home.

Reference

Gottman, J., & Silver, N. (1999). *Seven principles for making marriage work*. New York: Crown Publishers.

14

SOFT/HARD/SOFT COMMUNICATION

Patricia L. Papernow

Purpose: To provide a structure for couples to speak truth kindly and to say hard things in a way that they can be heard

Introduction

Soft/Hard/Soft is a communication technique that is useful in all relationships. It is a simple structure for speaking truth kindly and saying hard things in a way that they can be heard. This technique can be particularly useful in stepfamilies because of the differences between the biological parent and the stepparent, especially before a deep attachment is forged. Stepparents usually want more limits and boundaries with stepchildren. Parents want more love and understanding. For one adult, a "comfortable" living room may be one that is completely cleared of clutter and confusion. For the other, it may be strewn with books, toys, and other familiar items (Papernow, 2013). Successful stepcouples face the same typical challenges as struggling ones. However, thriving stepcouples communicate constructively about their differences. Less-successful stepcouples avoid conversation or get stuck in corrosive conflict.

Soft/Hard/Soft communication (Papernow, 2013) provides a structure for engaging over differences in ways that build connection and collaboration rather than disconnection and divisiveness. Most clients cannot easily master the empathic mirroring involved in "joining." However, almost all of them can easily grasp Soft/Hard/Soft, and most can use it on their own at home.

Description and Implementation of Soft/Hard/Soft Communication

I say to stepcouples, "*The flood of differences between being a biological parent and a stepparent is stunning, isn't it? You do need to talk to each other about these things. But I want to help you express yourselves in a way that creates connection, not disconnection."* Then I tell them I have something called Soft/Hard/Soft that goes like this:

- When you have something "hard" to say, *start* by looking for something "soft." Try not to open your mouth until you can start with something soft! (See the list below.)
- Next, say the hard thing, but with that same soft energy.
- You can then add another "soft" statement.

I sometimes describe this as a "reverse Oreo cookie." Couples therapist and researcher, John Gottman, stresses the importance of a "soft start-up" (Gottman, 2011). Soft/Hard/Soft operationalizes this principle. "Soft" can be:

- *Find your caring:* "I love you."
- *Express confidence:* "I believe we can work this out together."
- *Look for positive feedback and express appreciation:* "I noticed that your daughter did say hello to me yesterday. I appreciate that."
- *Own your own contribution:* "I know I got kind of sharp."
- *Look for positive intentions:* "I assume this just slipped your mind."
- *Find your empathy:* "I know it isn't easy for you when my kids leave a mess!"

Just the act of looking for "soft" statements often opens the speaker's heart enough to significantly shift the way in which a "hard" thing is expressed. Sometimes it is also necessary to teach some very concrete guidelines for effectively expressing "hard" things:

- *Stick to descriptions, not labels.* A description is, "There are a lot of dishes in the sink!" A label is, "Your daughter is a slob."
- *Make a request, not a criticism.* A request is: "Can we work together on getting your daughter to clean up her own dishes?" A criticism is: "You never taught your children anything about cleaning up."
- *Reach for "I" messages, not "you" messages.* An "I" message is, "I'm having a hard time with the mess in the kitchen." A "you" message is, "You clearly don't care that your children are slobs."

Case Example

Tony and Delia are arguing, yet again, over the level of mess in their home. Like many stepparents, Delia feels Tony should be much firmer with his daughters. She wants him to insist that they clean up after themselves. Like many parents in a stepcouple, Tony feels Delia has unrealistic expectations of his children and that she is unreasonably harsh when those expectations are not met. The first round of the conversation goes like this:

DELIA: *"You let them get away with murder. They don't lift a finger around here and you don't say a thing about it! Then when I'm upset, you race around like an idiot and do it for them!"*

TONY: *"What is the big deal? Can't you just back off?"*

DELIA: *"If you would just listen to me, maybe I would!"*

TONY: *"I do listen to you. But it's never enough!"*

Tony and Delia are spiraling yet again into what I call a "polarization polka." The stepfamily structure pulls Delia, the stepparent, toward more and more harshness, and Tony, the parent, toward more and more permissiveness (Papernow, 2013). I begin the conversation by sharing the research with them: What children need most is "authoritative" (both loving and firm) parenting. Parents must remain the disciplinarians. Stepparents often need to help parents be firmer, and parents need to help stepparents be more understanding. Due to this difference, both parents need help communicating with each other. I put my hands up in a time-out sign and say, *"This is another of those parenting polarities, right?"* Tony grimaces, *"Yup, we're right in it again!"* I let a little silence go by while we all take a breath. *"It's such a pull, isn't it, to find yourselves at further and further extremes? Let's try this conversation again. I want to teach you something that may make it easier for you. It's called Soft/Hard/Soft."*

Tony greets my explanation with, *"Why can't we just express ourselves honestly?"* My response to this common objection is, *"It is important to be honest with each other. And I know you are longing for Delia to hear you, right? What if the choice isn't to either stuff it or dump it?"* I let that idea sink in for a moment. *"It turns out, if you use labels and criticism, most people, barring saints, will respond defensively. There is a way to say hard things kindly. It takes some muscle and there's no guarantee. But, the chances you will be heard do go way up. Want to try?"*

Delia agrees to go first. I say, *"So, Delia, see if you can find a 'soft' way to start the conversation."* With some help, Delia considers several possible "softs." Round 2 begins very differently:

Delia: "Actually, I did notice that you asked the girls to clean up their stuff yesterday. Thanks. I appreciate it." I say to Delia, "Notice how your body feels as you find that 'soft.'" She sits back. "Maybe just a little more open?" She looks surprised and smiles a tiny sheepish smile.

I continue, "Now, can you say the hard thing, but say it with that same soft energy?" Delia is silent for a moment. Then she says, with some tenderness in her voice, "But I am getting really frustrated with the mess in the living room." Now I ask her to find another "soft." She looks at me like I have just asked her to do a double backflip. But, with what I sense is actually some relief, she looks at Tony and says, "I do love you, you know. Let's work this out."

"You go!" I say, giving her a thumbs-up sign. I turn to Tony: "Now it's your turn. Can you respond to Delia with your own Soft/Hard/Soft?" We look together at the list of possible "softs," and Tony also begins his second round very differently. "Thanks for the appreciation! It really helps. I do get that our mess is hard for you."

"Now," I say, "add a 'hard.' But see if you can use that same soft energy." Tony says, "Honey, I really do want to help. But when you tell me how I'm doing it wrong, I'm afraid I get really defensive." I say softly, "And now, another 'soft.'" Tony ends with, "I know it has to get really frustrating!"

It is important to anchor and integrate new experience. I turn to Delia. "What's that like, Delia, to hear Tony respond this way?" She smiles broadly, "So much better!" I say to Tony: "What's this like for you?" Tony looks at Delia: "I'm sorry I get so defensive. I really do want to make things better for you. It really helps when you approach me this way." I say to both of them, but especially to Tony, "It works, doesn't it?" A silly grin spreads across Tony's face. "Yup!"

I say, "I'll bet you two can work this out now." As they both calm down, Tony and Delia become less polarized. A very different conversation unfolds. Tony offers, "I know we're all slobs in comparison to you. I do want you to know I'm working on it with the kids." Delia responds, "I know. It's just so hard for me when there's stuff everywhere." He twinkles at her: "We've improved a lot! Remember what it used to be like?" Delia giggles. "It's true! But, Honey, when I get home from work, I am so longing for peace. To me, peace is clear, uncluttered horizontal surfaces. You have to admit, we are really far from that." Tony says sheepishly, "True!"

Now, rather than fighting with each other, Tony and Delia can tackle the issue as a more collaborative team. We agree that Delia notices "mess" way before Tony does. I observe, "That's probably not going to change right away." They make a deal that Delia will approach Tony and let him know, kindly, when she needs him to ask his children to pick up. If either gets sharp, they commit to try asking each other to "Try it again, Soft/Hard/Soft," and to take a break until they can, rather than getting defensive. They also begin carving out one area in the house that can be a "Delia Zone," a clutter-free retreat space that provides the peaceful sanctuary Delia so craves.

References

Gottman, J. M. (2011). *The science of trust*. New York: Norton.

Papernow, P. L. (2013). *Surviving and thriving in stepfamily relationships: What works and what doesn't*. New York: Routledge.

15

MULTIDIRECTIONAL PARTIALITY

Janie K. Long and Daniel Kort

Purpose: To validate the differing perspectives of each partner while modeling the capacity to understand and empathize with many types of experience, even those seemingly in conflict with one another

Introduction

Contextual therapy was developed to deal with family-related problems. However, it can also be applied to couples. Overriding goals in contextual therapy are to: foster a more equitable give-and-take between partners; encourage dialogue and help uncover relational resources; and emancipate partners from total control of loyalties, legacies, and destructive entitlement by encouraging *separation-individuation* (Boszormenyi-Nagy & Krasner, 1986). The key intervention is *multidirectional partiality* (Boszormenyi-Nagy & Krasner, 1986; Krasner & Joyce, 1995). When using this intervention, the therapist validates the differing perspectives of each partner and models the capacity to understand and empathize with many types of experience, even those seemingly in conflict with one another. No partner is considered to have the one and only truth, but all are validated as living a truth that deserves its due. Exploring any individual's truth may also involve discussing injustices suffered in the past that may be impacting the actions and expectations in the present. The therapist leaves it up to the couple to work toward finding solutions, using previously untapped *relational resources* uncovered through dialogue (Boszormenyi-Nagy & Krasner, 1986).

Purpose of Multidirectional Partiality

When all persons in the therapy room feel validated in their experiences and encouraged to share them, dialogue can open up, allowing them to support one another in ways that they may not have previously been willing or capable of doing. The therapist's aim is to "loosen the chains of invisible loyalty and legacy, so each partner can give up symptomatic behaviors and explore new options" (Boszormenyi-Nagy & Ulrich, 1981, p. 174). Thus, the relational needs of both partners have the potential of being met as well as evoking more understanding of the actions of past generations.

Description and Implementation

One of the primary interventions in contextual therapy is *multidirectional partiality* (Boszormenyi-Nagy & Krasner, 1986; Krasner & Joyce, 1995). With multidirectional partiality, the therapist models the process of understanding and empathizing with others' experiences by validating the various perspectives of each partner, even when they may seem to be in conflict with one another. No person in the therapy session is considered to have the one and only truth; all perspectives are validated, and each person is regarded as living a truth that deserves consideration. Exploring partners' experiences may also involve discussing wrongs from the past that may influence present-day expectations and behaviors. The therapist leaves the responsibility for finding solutions to their problems up to the couple, helping them identify and draw upon unused or dormant relational resources the couple and therapist discover through dialogue (Boszormenyi-Nagy & Krasner, 1986). The key element in the use of this technique is the therapist's own inner freedom to take turns in siding with each partner.

Contraindications

The ability of the therapist to have empathic understanding with each member of the couple is key to the utilization and success of this technique. This level of empathy may challenge inexperienced therapists or therapists who have experienced trauma related to the particular presenting issue of the couple. Should the therapist have a similar unresolved trauma, they will not be able to effectively help the couple. The therapist must be courageous enough to enter into areas such as murder, exploitation, incest, child abuse, and rape, and balance feelings of sympathy and wanting to help alleviate suffering with the desire to also have couples acknowledge responsibility for their actions.

Case Example

The use of the multidirectional partiality approach may be exemplified by the case example of Linda and Swathy, two women in their thirties who have been in an exclusive relationship for two years. Linda, who has been open about her sexual orientation since her teenage years, frequently invites Swathy to join her as a date to family and company functions, where her identity is embraced. Swathy, who has two children and divorced the father of her children three years ago, frequently declines Linda's invitations or makes last-minute excuses to avoid these occasions. Linda communicates to the therapist her frustration and disappointment with Swathy's unwillingness to appear together in public. Swathy claims that Linda is not sensitive to her situation and circumstances, given that she had only recently become aware of her attraction to women and is still very much closeted to many relatives and friends.

In addition to paying careful attention to personal biases, the therapist in this scenario must also be mindful of the differences in culture and background between the two women.

The contextual approach and multidirectional partiality, in this case, may assist the therapist in simultaneously validating the two women's perspectives, which appear to be at odds with one another. By allowing for multiple truths, the therapist may facilitate candidness and empathy between Linda and Swathy, which may uncover the roots of each woman's attitudes toward outness, openness, and public displays of romance.

In this instance, Swathy's family of origin and current relationship with Linda may unveil contradictory perspectives of heteronormativity and same-sex attraction. Simultaneously, Linda may feel torn between her feelings toward Swathy and her personal value of outness. These conflicting loyalties, Swathy to her children and Linda to her identity, may exacerbate pre-existing relational conflicts.

By validating both Linda's and Swathy's viewpoints and familial ties, the therapist can assist the women in better understanding one another's values and experiences. Ultimately, this greater mutual understanding may lead the partners to reconsider and address the pressures they place on each other in social situations.

References

Boszormenyi-Nagy, I., & Krasner, B. R. (1986). *Between give and take: A clinical guide to contextual therapy.* New York: Brunner Mazel.

Boszormenyi-Nagy, I., & Ulrich, D. N. (1981). Contextual family therapy. In A. S. Gurman & D. P. Kniskern (Eds.), *Handbook of family therapy* (pp. 159–186). New York: Brunner/Mazel.

Krasner, B. R., & Joyce, A. J. (1995). *Truth, trust, and relationships: Healing interventions in contextual therapy.* New York: Brunner Mazel.

PART C
Reframing

16

SYSTEMIC REFRAMING

George M. Simon

Purpose: To frame a couple's presenting problem in a systemic context

Introduction

When couples enter therapy, they usually have a fairly well-defined problem on which they would like the therapy to focus. Sometimes, the problem is a symptom: "He's depressed." Sometimes, the problem is relational: "We fight all the time." Either way, couples almost invariably have an individualistic, linear understanding as to why their problem is occurring. If the problem is a symptom, they tend to see it as residing inside the symptom-bearer, rooted in his or her biochemistry and/or psychological development. If the problem is relational, each partner usually sees the other as the cause of the problem.

Structural couple therapy (SCT)—along with numerous other models of couple therapy—is founded upon a very different understanding of the problems couples bring into therapy. Its systemic world view leads it to see problems as residing not in individual couple members, but in the structure of the relationship that binds them together into a single, psychosocial organism (Minuchin, 1974). Both members of the couple are seen by SCT as playing a crucial role in maintaining that structure. Moreover, these roles "fit" together in a complementary way, with each role functioning simultaneously as both the cause and the effect of the other.

The practical upshot of all this is that SCT therapists and their clients almost always begin therapy on very different pages. Everything SCT therapists do in therapy is going to be based on their systemic understanding of clients' presenting problem. Meanwhile, the clients are going to continue to operate out of their individualistic framing of their presenting problem. Unless this mismatch is remedied, the chances of forging a therapeutic alliance are next to none, with the result being that therapy is likely to fail.

Purpose of Systemic Reframing

Thus, by the end of the first session of therapy, the SCT therapist almost always engages in the technique of systemic reframing, the purpose of which is to expose the clients to the therapist's systemic view of their problem.

A word must be said here immediately about what the SCT therapist hopes to accomplish when she/he engages in systemic reframing, and what she/he in no way expects this intervention to accomplish. As it is conceptualized and implemented in SCT, systemic reframing is simply an exercise in "informed consent," intended to manifest to clients the systemic framing of their presenting problem that will guide their treatment if they choose to remain with their SCT therapist. Of course, the therapist hopes that the clients will "buy" the reframe sufficiently in order to continue treatment and to engage thoroughly in the therapeutic process. However, the SCT therapist does not expect a systemic reframing, even one "bought" by the clients, to change the dysfunctional relational structure that is described in the reframing. The pull that each couple member exerts on the other—which, in the view of SCT, is the fundamental mechanism that maintains the structure—is much too powerful to be undermined by a cognitive intervention like reframing. Later in therapy, the SCT therapist will use more powerful, experiential techniques to undermine the couple's relational structure and elicit a new, more functional structure. In delivering a systemic reframe during the first session, the therapist is looking to do nothing more than to get her/himself and the clients on the same, systemic page (Simon, 2008).

Description and Implementation

If a therapist is to "sell" a framing of a couple's presenting problem that is so divergent from the couple's own individualistic framing, the therapist needs some evidence to support her/his alternative framing. Specifically, therapists need to label and to punctuate how the couple members pull from each other in a circular fashion—behaviors that elicit and maintain their presenting problem. Thus, early and then repeatedly in a first session, the SCT therapist will elicit what in SCT parlance are called *enactments*, i.e., extended periods in which the couple members interact with each other directly. Later in therapy, the therapist will intervene into enactments to challenge and modify the structure of the couple system. But during the early part of the first session, the therapist will allow the enactments to develop in a naturalistic fashion so that the relational structure of the couple is brought into the therapy room as it exists outside of it.

As soon as the therapist derives from the enactments a sense of the complementarity between the couple members that maintains their relational structure, she/he begins to express "curiosity" about the behavior of one or the other couple member: "I noticed right now that after she began to cry, you moved away from her on the couch. What did she do to you just there?" "When his voice just now began to rise in anger, you chose to stop talking with him and you began to talk with me. What did he do to you just there?" With questions and observations such as these, the therapist begins to inculcate the idea that, whether they are aware of it or not, the couple members are constantly acting upon each other in ways that elicit particular responses from the other.

After establishing that the couple members are constantly eliciting behaviors from each other, the therapist "closes the loop" by labeling how the behaviors fit together in a circular, complementary fashion. "So, when you, Susan, feel cut off from Sam, you try to engage him by playing a game of '20 Questions.' That feels to you, Sam, like nagging, and you bury your head in the computer. That just turns the '20 Questions' into '40 Questions,' and the beat goes on."

Finally, as the *piece de resistance* of the reframing process, the therapist asserts how the couple's presenting problem is embedded in and maintained by the complementary structure that she/he has punctuated. "And that, Sam, is when your Internet browsing invariably winds up on some Internet porn site."

Contraindications

The only clinical situation in which the technique of systemic reframing is contraindicated is when the therapist encounters a certain kind of couple violence. Some couples are able to talk openly about the occurrence of violent episodes between them, and the perpetrator(s) of the violence admits readily that it is unconditionally inappropriate. Other couples, however, in which violence occurs never reveal that fact in conjoint sessions; the therapist only discovers the violence when she/he meets with the partners in (unusual for SCT) separate, individual sessions (Simon, 2008).

Violence that cannot be talked about in conjoint sessions—which almost invariably is violence not owned by the perpetrator(s) as wrong—renders systemic reframing a contraindicated intervention. In fact, violence of this kind serves, in my opinion, as a contraindication for conjoint couple therapy itself.

Case Example

Pam and Dan enter therapy with not one, but two, presenting problems: Dan's extramarital affair and Pam's excessive drinking. Each asserts with certainty early during the first session that the other's behavior is *the* problem that is undermining their marriage.

In early-session enactments, the therapist observes each spouse trying to gain the upper hand over the other's problem behavior. She sees Pam angrily interrogating Dan about the details of his affair, with the obvious intention of trying to make him feel guilty. Then the therapist sees Dan angrily interrogating Pam about how much she drank the previous night, with the same obvious intention. While under interrogation by the other spouse, both Pam and Dan withdraw into sullen, defensive silence, which has no other effect than to increase the intensity of the interrogation to which they are being subjected.

After observing several go-rounds of this oscillating, interrogate-withdraw complementarity, the therapist interrupts Dan's interrogation of Pam and says to her, "Do you think he notices how thoroughly he has silenced you? Tell him how he managed to do that." A few minutes later, after Pam herself lapses into interrogating Dan, the therapist interrupts again. "Dan, she seems to have the same ability you do to render a spouse mute. How did she just silence you?" After pointing out several more times the silencing effect each spouse was having on the other, the therapist says, "So, I see that the two of you take turns playing 'cat-and-mouse' with each other. Neither of you is a very smart cat, since the way you hunt always allows the mouse to disappear. Here in this room, the mouse always disappeared into silence. In your lives at home, you, Dan, disappeared from her hunting into your clandestine affair, and you, Pam, disappear from his hunting by secretly drinking. We will have to work here on helping both of you replace your *hunting* of each other with some *inviting* of each other."

References

Minuchin, S. (1974). *Families and family therapy*. Cambridge, MA: Harvard University Press.

Simon, G. M. (2008). Structural couple therapy. In A. S. Gurman (Ed.), *Clinical handbook of couple therapy* (4th ed., pp. 323–349). New York: Guilford.

17

TAKING OWNERSHIP

Jon Carlson and Sonya Lorelle

Purpose: To refocus a couple's attention on how they each are responsible for change rather than having a focus on blame

Introduction

According to Adlerian therapy, the meaning that each person brings into couple counseling impacts how they understand their experiences (Englar-Carlson & Carlson, 2011). Adler discussed how individuals have *private logic* and patterns of perceiving and responding to the world, which are part of their *lifestyle*. As part of this private logic, individuals may have hidden expectations of their partners, such as expectations that their partner is responsible for making changes to improve the relationship. With this *Taking Ownership* technique, the counselor will encourage a shift in this thinking in order to focus more on the personal role each person has in the relationship dynamics.

Purpose of Taking Ownership

Behavior has a purpose and is attempting to achieve a goal, even if the couple is not aware of that goal consciously (Carlson & Dinkmeyer, 2003). *Taking Ownership* is a technique that encourages individuals to accept the responsibility for their behavior, which may include becoming aware of the underlying purposes of the choices they make in the relationship. With this focus, counselors want to move the couple away from blaming their partners to accepting responsibility for the choices they are making and understanding they have power to choose differently.

Description and Implementation

There are several ways that counselors can encourage couples to *Take Ownership*. The counselor should provide psychoeducation about the change process. They introduce the idea that each of the individuals will need to look at themselves during this process instead of attempting to change their partners. It is impossible to change anyone else. Metaphors that use the idea of teamwork, such as pairs volleyball, skating, or dancing, help to illustrate the concept that it takes effort from both partners to be successful. Carlson and Dinkmeyer (2003) described how accepting responsibility for personal behavior and acknowledging this power to make different choices is a first step in improving marriage satisfaction. Assigning a homework reading, such as the first chapter in *Time for a Better Marriage* (Carlson & Dinkmeyer, 2003), reinforce these concepts.

When clarifying goals, it is important to help each of the individuals focus on what they can each do to work toward that goal. Questions encourage the couple to reflect on their own role in the dysfunctional patterns: "What choices are you making to nurture or hurt the relationship?" "What are the changes you could make that would be most beneficial for the relationship?" "How likely are you to change?" Other questions might ask the individuals to describe their role in a conflict: "If I were to watch you at home, what would I see you doing?" "What were you hoping to accomplish with that action?" "How might you have responded differently in order to achieve that desired goal?" The question, "What would it take for you to do that differently?" not only asks the couple to think of what might impact their motivation for change, but it also implies that there is a choice they are making currently to *not* do it differently.

The counselor may ask questions that encourage self-reflection about hidden underlying blame. Carlson and Dinkmeyer (2003) introduced four questions that invite self-reflection:

- What excuses have you used that keep you from changing your behavior?
- Have you blamed your partner for problems in your marriage?
- Have you blamed yourself?
- Are there other circumstances in your marriage that you have felt are to blame for the shortcomings in your relationship?

Counselors also use reframes and challenges to redirect a couple stuck in a blame cycle. A reframe identifies the unknown positive intentions underneath an ineffective action and reveal the purpose or goal of the behavior. Counselors may also playfully challenge the individuals' commitment or motivation when reasons are given for why change is impossible or unlikely. For example, a husband might state his daily demands prevented him from spending time with his wife. The counselor asks the client, "Could you find time to put effort into your relationship if you were paid $5?" If the answer is no, the counselor then raises it to $100. If this is an unacceptable offer, then the client quickly sees that it is a matter of choice and that he could do it if he really wanted to (Carlson & Dinkmeyer, 2003). Once the client understands that he could make the changes for a certain price, then their power to make different choices is clear. The counselor then focuses on what the couple would need to increase their commitment or motivation to take advantage of that power.

Contraindications

There are several aspects to keep in mind when incorporating this technique with couples. Counselors should remain aware of their biases that could impact how the technique comes across. Does the counselor subtly agree with one partner over the other? For example, Englar-Carlson and Carlson (2011) stated that men may often feel resentment when coming to therapy as they may have been pressured by a spouse to be there. The authors also stated the male partner may be worried that the counselor will align with the female partner because counseling endorses actions that are more often associated with feminine ways of interacting. In a case like this, it would be especially important for the counselor to listen to both perspectives equally rather than side with just one of the partners, or to only encourage one of the partners to accept responsibility. This equal attention to both partners being responsible for change will help to put each partner at ease if they had a concern that one of them would be blamed and was going to be the only one required to change (Englar-Carlson & Carlson, 2011).

Counselors may also be cautious when using this technique in the case of working with couples who have a history of or are experiencing domestic violence. While many counselors recommend working with these couples on an individual basis, researchers have been exploring the dynamics of couples experiencing domestic violence in order to understand ways in which counselors can work with them conjointly that encourages responsibility but does not put the victim at risk of additional violence or blame the victim (Bischoff, 2006). By encouraging each person to take responsibility, it is important not to imply the victim of domestic violence is somehow to blame for the abuse.

Case Example

Carl and Helen were stuck in a cycle of blaming when they first presented to counseling. During the assessment phase, the description of the problem revealed a pattern of finger-pointing and defending their individual positions. Carl stated the problem was that Helen was not available enough since she worked long hours, and she was always too tired for sex. Helen stated that she did not desire to be intimate because she felt the need to 'walk on eggshells' as she never knew when his temper would flare up. When discussing a specific conflict, Helen described how her husband left the room angry and slammed the door. She complained that he needed to work on his temper. Carl defended his actions by stating that she pushed him away when he kissed her neck and asked her a question. Helen stated she had a deadline and was under pressure to get the assignment complete by that night. She thought he over-reacted and should know the pressure she is under.

The counselor recognized that they were caught up in the blame cycle again and interjected. The counselor reframed the angry slam of the door for Carl and then invited him to take responsibility for making different choices: "Carl, it sounds like you really wanted to connect with Helen and to get her attention with the door slam." Carl agreed that he was hoping for affection and stated that he was hurt by her dismissiveness. After discussing how a different message came through for Helen, the counselor asked him if there was another way he could express the hurt he felt in a way that may be more effective. Carl was then able to identify an alternate method. They reversed the roles, and the counselor asked Helen to think about what she was trying to accomplish and how she could do that in a way that did not hurt Carl as much. As the sessions progressed, they became more comfortable with looking at the conflicts from these perspectives, and the blaming language decreased.

References

Bischoff, R. J. (2006). The implications for couple therapy of recent research on domestic violence. *Journal of Couple & Relationship Therapy*, 5(2), 70–76.

Carlson, J., & Dinkmeyer, D. (2003). *Time for a better marriage: Training in marriage enrichment*. Astascadero, CA: Impact.

Englar-Carlson, M., & Carlson, J. D. (2011). Adlerian couples therapy: The case of the boxer's daughter and the momma's boy. In D. S. Shepard & M. Harway (Eds.), *Engaging men in couples counseling* (pp. 81–104). New York: Routledge.

18

REATTRIBUTION

Norman B. Epstein

Purpose: To help partners consider alternative explanations for causes of each other's distressing actions

Introduction

When members of a couple observe each other behaving in distressing ways, it is natural for them to ask themselves why the other person is acting in such a manner, and to make attributions or inferences about such causes. The process of making attributions about events that one observes is a natural aspect of human information processing. However, those inferences are susceptible to distortion. There is substantial research evidence that individuals who are unhappy in their couple relationships are more likely than those who are satisfied to make negative attributions regarding a partner's unpleasant actions (Epstein & Baucom, 2002). They commonly conclude that the partner's actions were due to negative intentions (e.g., to exert control or punish the individual) or negative personality traits (e.g., selfishness). Although a negative attribution about a partner may be accurate, people generally assume the validity of their attributions without considering whether there may be alternative, more accurate explanations. Consistent with the concept of "automatic thoughts" described by cognitive therapists (e.g., Beck, 2011), an individual observes a partner's current behavior or has a memory of a past behavior and spontaneously makes an inference about factors that caused the behavior. The attribution seems plausible to the individual, and therefore in that moment it becomes his or her experience of the partner. The individual who makes the attribution experiences emotions and behavioral responses that are consistent with his or her thoughts about the partner. For example, an individual who attributes a partner's late arrival for a planned event as being due to the partner considering him or her a low priority may feel angry and refuse to talk to the partner. Even if the partner's late arrival actually was due to being stuck in traffic, the individual's immediate angry response may trigger an argument.

Therapists commonly encounter couples whose conflict is worsened by partners making negative attributions about each other and failing to examine evidence that supports or refutes the distressing inferences. On the one hand, if evidence tends to support a negative attribution (e.g., if the partner indeed was late because he or she decided to attend to personal matters while knowing that the other person was waiting), the couple may need to discuss where their relationship fits into each person's priorities. On the other hand, if the evidence indicates that the negative attribution was inaccurate, the person who made the inference may need to practice self-monitoring of his or her cognitions and evaluating the negative inferences.

Purpose of Reattribution

Reattribution is a therapeutic intervention that is intended to increase partners' identification and evaluation of the validity of their attributions, especially those that lead to emotional upset and negative couple interactions. It is most commonly associated with cognitive-behavioral couple therapy (Epstein & Baucom, 2002), but therapists with varied theoretical orientations use it. It is conceptually related to the technique of reframing, in which a therapist provides a more benign meaning for a behavior that a member of a couple has interpreted negatively. Whereas the new inference in reframing typically is provided by the therapist, in reattribution the therapist coaches clients in thinking of alternative meanings for the other person's behavior. Because a variety of couple therapy models are designed to change the ways that partners view each other as well as how they behave toward each other, it is not surprising that research has shown that negative attributions are reduced not only in cognitive-behavioral couple therapy, but also in other theoretical approaches (Hrapczynski, Epstein, Werlinich, & LaTaillade, 2011).

It is not assumed that all negative attributions are distorted; therefore, therapists must approach assessment and modification of attributions cautiously. The purpose of the technique is to assist members of couples to be aware of attributions they make and to consider their degree of accuracy carefully. Thus, reattribution involves self-monitoring and systematic evaluation of evidence bearing on the validity of an inference about one's partner. In addition, individuals make attributions about the causes of their own responses (e.g., "I did not miss my partner while he or she was out of town, so I probably do not love him or her any more"). The same procedures that are used for reattribution regarding another person's behavior are used in considering causes for one's own responses.

Description and Implementation

In general, a cognitive-behavioral approach to couple therapy requires that the therapist avoid making assumptions about partners' inner experiences, but rather use open-ended questions to elicit each person's subjective thoughts and emotions. Sometimes an individual spontaneously expresses an attribution about a partner (e.g., "Here you go again, being the selfish person you are and ignoring the fact that I was waiting for you!"). In other instances, the therapist notices from verbal or nonverbal cues that the individual has had a negative response to the partner, and the therapist inquires about his or her thoughts (e.g., "You seem upset that your partner was late and didn't call you. What were you thinking was going on with him/her?"). Sometimes the initial thought that the person reports is not the negative attribution, so the therapist may need to use the "downward arrow" technique of follow-up questions to identify the underlying upsetting inference about the partner (Epstein & Baucom, 2002). For example, the upset individual may first say, "I'm angry because this isn't the first time he/she disregarded plans we had." The therapist then may ask, "What does it mean to you that he/she has done that more than once?" The client may respond, "It means that my getting upset about it before had no effect on him/her." The therapist then asks, "If your getting upset before seemed to have no effect on him/her, what does that mean to you?" The individual then may respond, "It means that his/her own plans mean a lot more to him/her than I do." This sequence of inquiries and responses zeros in on the upsetting negative attribution that the individual has made about the partner.

Once a negative attribution has been identified, the therapist explores with the client its link to negative emotions. Although the client may be aware of one emotional response (e.g., anger that the partner seems to be self-focused), it is important to explore whether there are other emotions as well (e.g., sadness that the partner does not seem to care about him or her). The therapist also inquires about the tendency for the attribution to trigger negative behavior toward the partner (e.g., verbal attacks, withdrawal), which may exacerbate tension in the relationship. Once the negative emotional and behavioral consequences of the attribution have been identified, the therapist can point out that it is crucial to evaluate the accuracy of one's attributions that have such negative effects.

The therapist then coaches the individual in examining evidence regarding the validity of the attribution. One approach to doing so involves logical analysis of possible alternative explanations for the partner's upsetting behavior ("What are some other possible reasons why he/she was late meeting you?"). The therapist also can encourage the individual to think of other times when the partner behaved in ways that seemed to reflect caring. Furthermore, in couple therapy the partner typically is present in the session, and the therapist can coach the upset person to ask the partner in a constructive way (not in a sarcastic, attacking manner) to explain why he or she behaved that way. Even though feedback from the partner initially may be viewed as making excuses, often the information helps the upset person to consider alternatives to the negative attribution.

Contraindications

Reattribution is not intended to absolve individuals of responsibility for negative actions toward their partners, such as aggressive behavior, infidelity, and other breaches of trust and safety. Its goal is to increase the accuracy of the inferences that partners make about each other. If an individual behaved violently toward a partner, the therapist does not pursue reattribution to identify benign motives for the abusive actions. In fact, an exploration of causes of the person's aggression may help identify motives (e.g., an attempt to retaliate for partner behavior that hurt the person's feelings) that need to be addressed in individual and/or couple therapy. Thus, although reattribution may identify more positive causes of upsetting behavior, it is not used to re-interpret negative actions as justified and acceptable.

Case Example

Throughout this chapter, an example has been used of a couple in which an individual made negative attributions about the characteristics of a partner who was late for a planned meeting, a process that occurs in many couples who seek therapy. The procedures for assessing the content of the upset person's attributions and linking the cognitions to emotional and behavioral responses have been outlined. The therapist introduces reattribution through a brief psychoeducational explanation of what attributions are, their tendency to occur automatically, the fact that people commonly accept their inferences without examining evidence for their accuracy, and the negative consequences of responding to one's partner based on unexamined negative attributions. The therapist inquires about negative attributions that each member of the couple tends to make, and how those inferences contribute to relationship conflict and distress. The therapist then explores the content of each person's negative attributions and coaches the individual in considering alternative explanations. Each member of the couple can be used as a source of disconfirming information. The burden for change is not placed solely on an individual who has responded automatically to a negative attribution, as the person's partner is helped to see how causes of his or her behavior were ambiguous. If the partner wants to reduce the likelihood that his or her actions will be misinterpreted, clearer communication about one's intentions will help. Consequently, communication skills training is often used in conjunction with reattribution for couples such as this case example.

References

Beck, J. S. (2011). *Cognitive behavior therapy: Basics and beyond* (2nd ed.). New York: Guilford Press.

Epstein, N. B., & Baucom, D. H. (2002). *Enhanced cognitive-behavioral therapy for couples: A contextual approach.* Washington, DC: American Psychological Association.

Hrapczynski, K. M., Epstein, N. B., Werlinich, C. A., & LaTaillade, J. J. (2011). Changes in negative attributions during couple therapy for abusive behavior: Relations to changes in satisfaction and behavior. *Journal of Marital and Family Therapy, 38,* 117–132.

19

CLARIFYING THE NEGATIVE CYCLE IN EMOTIONALLY FOCUSED COUPLE THERAPY (EFT)

Sue Johnson and Lorrie Brubacher

Purpose: To clarify a couple's negative cycle in order to shift partners from blaming each other to framing the cycle as a common enemy that blocks connection

Introduction

The technique of clarifying a distressed couple's negative emotional-behavioral cycle is rooted in the systemic and attachment orientations of emotionally focused couple therapy (EFT). The systemic view is that self-reinforcing repetitive patterns of demand-pursue/withdraw-defend characterize distressed couple relationships (Gottman, 1994). Attachment theory (Bowlby, 1969; Johnson, 2013) views these patterns as partners' unsuccessful attempts at regulating attachment anxieties and seeking secure connection from their partners that paradoxically heighten insecurity. Clarifying that it is the repetitive negative cycle that is responsible for the couple's distress creates a safe space in which to explore the hidden and unexpressed attachment fears and needs that are driving the cycle, which is usually one of criticism and withdrawal (Johnson, 2004). It is not conflict that leads to relationship dissolution so much as it is the failure to repair and reconnect following relationship ruptures. Hence, clarifying the negative cycle that consistently blocks reconnection is the first step to reshaping a relationship in distress.

Purpose of Clarifying the Negative Cycle

The purpose of clarifying the negative cycle is to create a meta-perspective that shifts the problem away from being the fault of one of the partners, and to frame this cycle as the common enemy that blocks satisfying connection. Framing the negative cycle as the relationship problem is consistent with the de-pathologizing and collaborative nature of EFT. Each partner is outlined as unwittingly triggering responses in the other that maintain the stuck dysfunctional dance and undermine safe connection. EFT therapists collaborate with a couple to recognize and begin to shift the default behaviors and underlying fears that are blocking secure connection. The first step is to identify which position of critical pursuit or defensive withdrawal each partner automatically takes when their attachment fears are triggered. These fears of abandonment or rejection are phrased, for example, as, "You don't care about me" or "I can't do anything right with you—so I just stand still." After each partner recognizes the default behaviors that automatically take over when attachment safety is threatened, they begin to accept a non-pathologizing reframe for their relationship problem. The pursuing partner is able to recognize, for example, "The more I try to get a response from you, the more you hear criticism and the message that you are disappointing me, and so the more you fire back in defense and then disappear from me." And the more withdrawn partner is able to recognize, "The more I defend myself from hearing that you are unhappy with me, and then withdraw in frustration, the more lonely and unimportant you feel, and then the louder you shout." This non-blaming picture, in which each partner sees the real relationship problem as a two-step interactive dance, lays the foundation for creating new, clearer, and more nurturing ways of interacting.

Description and Implementation

From the first moments of meeting a couple, the EFT therapist listens to partners' stories of negative events and attends to *how* the partners interact in session. The therapist listens beyond the content of the stories for the dominant negative cycle into which partners unwittingly pull one another, and also observes interactions in session (Johnson, 2004; Johnson et al., 2005). Most couples present with short cross-complaining attack-attack cycles we term "Find the bad guy" and more substantive pursue-withdraw or even withdraw-withdraw cycles. Gottman (1994) identifies cycles of criticize-blame-demand in tandem with defend-withdraw-stonewall to be the most common. As couples tell their stories of negative events, the EFT therapist attunes to and explicitly outlines their typical positions and ways of regulating emotion under threat. The pursuer typically pursues for contact and tends to take a critical stance when in separation distress, fearing disconnection and abandonment. They say things like, *"He is never there for me when I need him"* or *"I can never trust she really ever wants to be close to me."* The withdrawer tends to shut down and revert to flight or freeze responses, fearing rejection and sensing the partner is disappointed in him or her: *"Nothing I do is fast enough or polite enough for her"* or *"I wish we could just get along without the big heavy talks he wants to have."*

Clarifying the negative cycle includes the following aspects:

1. Identifying the steps in the dance of distress: Outlining the steps in a couple's negative cycle from the story they tell and from observing and capturing the

cycle as it happens in session; and linking these responses together into a self-perpetuating loop.

2. Helping partners "own" their steps in the dance ("I do shut down"; "I do lash out") and validating how normal and natural these steps are.

3. Helping partners see how they impact one another by:

   • Evoking and reflecting attachment meanings triggered in or triggering the cycle. ("What did it say to you, Sam, that she was late?"; "What does his loud outburst followed by his silence say to you, Sara?");

   • Attuning to and validating the secondary emotions of each partner. (Sara is frustrated and angered by Sam's distance; Sam is briefly frustrated, followed by numbness.)

4. Catching bullets where necessary (reframing aggression as unspoken difficulty, pain, etc.: "When you don't know how to tell her how unwanted you feel, it's so easy to slip into irritation and trying to change her").

5. Evoking and making sense of the underlying emotional music that drives the dance and fuels distress: Loneliness, attachment fears of rejection and abandonment, and negative views of self ("I'm unlovable") and other ("She is unpredictable and unreliable").

6. Summarizing the negative cycle, the fears that trigger it, and the attachment consequences of this cycle for both partners: "Sara, the more you complain about Sam's distance and try to pull him close, the more Sam hears he's letting you down and the more angrily he shuts you out. When Sam shuts down, you become frantic and aggressive. Underneath, Sara, you are lonely and afraid you'll lose him at any moment. And Sam, you're afraid she doesn't really love and accept you. When this cycle takes over, you are both so alone."

7. Framing the dance of distress as the joint enemy and helping couples to step out of it in session. It then becomes something they can contain and move beyond.

This approach then de-escalates the cycle and creates a secure base for the next stage of therapy—restructuring positive contact and responsiveness. The lay version of this process is outlined in *Hold Me Tight: Seven Conversations for a Lifetime of Love* (Johnson, 2008). More detail can also be found at www.iceeft.com.

Contraindications

When it becomes clear to the therapist that there is violence or abuse in the relationship and that exploring the couple's interactive pattern would put one partner at greater risk of violence or abuse, it is contraindicated to clarify the negative cycle as the primary problem of distress. Situations where one partner has already detached from the relationship or is heavily invested in proving their partner is mentally ill contraindicate clarifying the negative cycle. One or both partners engaged in an active affair or addictive process that he or she is not interested in giving up are also contraindications for engaging a couple in clarifying their negative interactive cycle.

Case Example

Sam and Sara arrive 10 minutes late for their second session. Sam mumbles a complaint about how Sara can never be ready on time. A plethora of criticisms tumble forth from Sara, while Sam's eyes turn down and his arms fold across his chest. He disappears into stony silence.

THERAPIST: This is a very difficult moment—both of you feeling the other one upset with you! (*reflection and validation*) Right now, Sara, you looked at Sam fold his arms and go silent, and you became very agitated. Your voice sped up as you recounted many struggles of the past few days. You sound so very frustrated!" (*tracking the present-moment process and reflecting her secondary emotion of frustration*) What happened for you, Sara, as you heard Sam's complaints about your being late?" (*evocative question*)

SARA: I heard, "Here we go again!"—I've tried for years to tell him he is good enough, that I am so proud of him, that I just want him to open up to me, but he is always on guard, ready to defend himself and put the blame on me—then he won't talk to me for days.

THERAPIST: So you hear Sam's complaint and you hear that you are being shut out, that he is pulling away from you, and you become desperately frustrated, trying to tell him he has no reason to shut you out—yes? (*tracking process, empathic reflection of Sara's attachment distress*)

SARA: Exactly!

THERAPIST: And Sam, just before Sara exploded with her frustration at you, you were saying how angry you are that she was late to come to this appointment (Sam nods definitively). Can you tell me what it means to you when she is late? (*evocative question to access the attachment meaning for Sam of Sara's lateness*)

SAM: That I'm not important enough for her to care about getting ready on time!

THERAPIST: Ah, so is this how many of your unhappy times play out? Sam, what you hear is that Sara is dissatisfied with you. You are on guard for little signs that she cares, and when she forgets something or is late, your massive concern that you are not measuring up in her eyes rips through your heart, and before you know it, you fire back in defense and step far, far away from the trigger of your pain. And Sara, you live on the edge of fear that he is going to turn away from you, looking for ways to pull him close and grasping for messages that you are precious to him, getting annoyed each time you sense even a hint that he is stepping back or going silent—is that it? (*tracking the cycle with underlying attachment fears*)

The cycle continues to get triggered in the session, and each time, the therapist tracks what is happening, validates their reactions and reflects any hints of their underlying fears and attachment distress. By the end of this part of therapy, known as de-escalating the negative cycle, Sam and Sara will have clarified their dominant negative cycle and begun to understand how they trigger this cycle in each other. Sara is beginning to grasp, "You shut me out because you think I don't care. You are looking for signs that I care about you." Sam is absorbing a new sense of Sara: "You get angry with me because you are afraid I'll turn away from you and shut you out."

References

Bowlby, J. (1969). *Attachment and loss: Vol. 1. Attachment*. New York: Basic Books.

Gottman, J. (1994). *What predicts divorce?* Hillsdale, NJ: Erlbaum.

Johnson, S. M. (2004). *Creating connection: The practice of emotionally focused couple therapy* (2nd ed.). New York: Brunner/Routledge.

Johnson, S. M. (2008). *Hold me tight: Seven conversations for a lifetime of love.* New York: Little, Brown.

Johnson, S. M. (2013). *Love Sense: The revolutionary new science of romantic relationships*. New York: Little, Brown.

Johnson, S. M., Bradley, B., Furrow, J., Lee, A., Palmer, G., Tilley, D., & Woolley, S. (2005). *Becoming an emotionally focused therapist: The workbook*. New York: Brunner/Routledge.

20

EXTERNALIZING CONVERSATIONS

Gene Combs and Jill Freedman

Purpose: To counter cultural practices and assumptions that see people as problematic

Introduction

Externalizing conversations are one of the central features of narrative therapy. These conversations are based in the assertion that ". . . it is not the person who is the problem. Rather, it is the problem that is the problem" (White, 1989, p. 6). Michael White originally developed externalization as a way to deal with extreme instances of childhood problems such as encopresis and temper tantrums, but it has since proved useful in practically any situation where people are being perceived as problematic. In developing an externalizing conversation, therapists use language that describes problems as objects or entities located outside of people and operating on those people. For example, if a partner in a couple says that their partner is "mad all the time," the therapist might begin to inquire about what it's like to have anger as a constant third wheel in their relationship. In order to conduct meaningful externalizing conversations, therapists must step into a world view where they genuinely perceive problems as separate from people, and develop skill at asking questions that are based in that perception.

The theoretical basis for externalizing practices comes from the work of the philosopher and historian of ideas Michel Foucault (1995), who described how, over the course of the Age of Reason, people were increasingly classified into categories (medical diagnoses, psychological personality types, races, criminal classes, etc.), measured according to norms (of height, weight, intelligence, athletic ability, beauty, etc.), and assigned individual rights and responsibilities according to those categories and norms. In the field of psychotherapy, these trends have led to practices of assessment that focus on pathology and locate that pathology in individual bodies. Externalizing conversations offer possibilities for working in ways that do not pathologize individuals and that are relationally and systemically, rather than individually, focused.

Purpose of Externalizing Conversations

In his original article on the externalization of the problem, White (1989) lists six purposes of externalizing (paraphrased below):

1. To decrease unproductive conflict between people, including disputes over who is responsible for the problem;
2. To undermine the sense of failure that can develop in response to the continuing existence of the problem in spite of attempts to resolve it;
3. To pave the way for people to unite with each other in escaping the influence of the problem over their lives and relationships;
4. To open new possibilities for action outside the influence and effects of the problem;
5. To free people to take a lighter, less stressed approach to "deadly serious" problems; and
6. To present options for dialogue, rather than monologue, about the problem.

Description and Implementation

Externalizing conversations do not focus on expert assessment and diagnosis. The focus is on developing a clear and detailed description of whatever it is that is of greatest concern to the person or persons seeking therapy. According to White (2007, pp. 26–27):

> The form of inquiry that is employed during externalizing conversations can be likened to investigative reporting. The primary goal of investigative reporting is to develop an exposé on the corruption associated with abuses of power and privilege. Although investigative reporters are not politically neutral, the activities of their inquiry do not take them into the domains of problem-solving, of enacting reform, or of engaging in direct power struggles with those who might be perpetuating abuses of power and privilege. Investigative reporters are not usually 'hotly' engaged with the subjects of their investigations. Rather, their actions usually reflect a relatively 'cool' engagement.

As a definition and description of the problem emerges in the language used by the couple, the focus shifts to developing an understanding of the effects of that problem in their lives and relationships. The therapist inquires about how the problem affects each partner's life and their relationships with other family members, school, work, and social settings; their hopes, dreams, and sense of what's possible; and each partner's commitments and projects in the present.

As the problem's effects are identified, the therapist shifts to asking for an evaluation of those effects: What does each partner think of them? Is that what the person wants for their relationship? What is good and what is bad about the effects? Then the person is asked to explain or justify their evaluation: Why do they want that? What values are they drawing on to have this preference? This careful, patient inquiry invites people to stand outside of their problems and examine them in a "cool" way. It lets them look at their relationship with a problem, which is easier than struggling to cope with internal, relatively fixed, aspects of each other's identity.

Contraindications

Perhaps the only significant contraindication to pursuing an externalizing conversation is the absence of a highly problematic internalized problem definition. If a couple comes to therapy with a clearly defined intention or purpose, and there are no ossified obstacles, it might be superfluous to pursue an externalizing conversation.

Case Example

At their first therapy session, Jennifer and Joe were not talking as they entered the room. It felt like one spark would make the air between them explode. I (GC) asked if they could each tell me a little about themselves outside of the problems that had brought them. Jennifer told me that they had met when she was a bartender at the club where Joe's old band used to play. She was still working as a waitress, but only part-time now that they had a three-year-old son, Burke. She had dreams of going back to school and studying nursing. Joe was working as much shift work as he could get on the loading dock at a shipping company, and he was playing keyboards in a new band.

Joe said that what made them schedule the appointment was that he and Jennifer had gotten into a huge fight in front of Burke. He said, "Once we start to argue, Jennifer goes crazy. You can't reason with her, Burke started crying because we were fighting and she nearly hit him."

Jennifer cut in, saying, "I scream because I can't get Joe to hear me. He's selfish. We need him at home and all he cares about is his music."

I said it seemed to me that there were some things that they each cared a lot about and that they had reached a point where it was very difficult to even bring them up without "intense feelings" (my initial try at an externalized description) taking over. They both nodded. I said that they both seemed worried that the intense feelings were spilling over onto Burke. They continued to nod. I said that I understood that the intense feelings often made Jennifer scream, and I asked Joe what the intense feelings did to him.

He said, "They really get to me. I get mad and scared, and I can't talk; I can't even think straight."

I asked questions about the effects of the anger and fear (the words Joe had used instead of "intense feelings"). We learned that the anger and fear had him questioning his fitness as a parent. They had him taking a dim view of the future for their family. They had him avoiding coming home, often staying on after a club date to drink with his bandmates rather than struggle with the fears of failing as Burke's dad. I asked how this was affecting his relationship with Burke.

He said, "We're becoming more distant; it's like sometimes he thinks I'm a stranger."

I asked if that was what he wanted, and he said, "Of course not, I want to be a good father. I want to be close with him and have him know he can count on my love." At that point, I turned to Jennifer, and we were able to have several minutes of calm conversation in which she remembered and recounted moments of closeness and tenderness between Joe and Burke. She said that she was really missing those kinds of moments with Joe, and that's what made her want to scream sometimes. I was then able to initiate an externalizing conversation with her about "the sense of abandonment" (her words) and its effects on her, on Burke, and on the relationship.

The externalizing conversations about anger, fear, and the sense of abandonment allowed Joe and Jennifer to describe their difficulties in ways that didn't pathologize either of them. It allowed each to get a glimpse of the other's desires and preferences for where their relationship might go. We still had work to do, but we were off to a good start.

References

Foucault, M. (1995). *Discipline and punish: The birth of the prison*. New York: Vintage.
White, M. (1989). *Selected papers*. Adelaide, Australia: Dulwich Centre Publications.
White, M. (2007). *Maps of narrative practice*. New York: Norton.

21

RE-STORYING THE PROBLEM

Janie K. Long and Daniel Kort

Purpose: To develop alternative stories, offering couples different relationships to the problem so that they may feel empowered and successful

Introduction

Narrative therapy is a postmodern social constructionist approach pioneered by Michael White and David Epston that focuses on "re-storying." Given the social nature of client dilemmas, this approach entails the understanding that there are multiple interpretations and understandings of social phenomena (Gergen, 1985). Clients' ideas, memories, and social concepts are communicated via language or narratives (Hoffman, 1992).

Re-storying is accomplished by "externalizing" a problem so that it becomes a separate entity and something with which the couple grapples (White & Epston, 1990). Problems are viewed as the result of stories we develop to describe our lives and ourselves. Often these descriptions are "problem-saturated," perpetuating feelings of powerlessness and failure. Therefore, the goal of therapy is to develop alternative stories, offering couples different relationships to the problem so that they may feel empowered and successful (White, 1991).

Therapists engage with their clients' concerns from individual and local (micro) levels to large-scale social and legal (macro) levels. At the micro-level, the therapist identifies with the oppression of clients when their voice may not be heard or is dismissed altogether. At a macro-level, the therapist identifies with the couple against those ways in which Western culture oppresses them via the media and general social milieu around issues such as body image, marriage, having children, and gender roles. Exploring those oppressive forces, both overt and covert, helps the couple to examine their own internalized beliefs and allows their beliefs to be acknowledged and validated (White & Epston, 1990).

Purpose of Re-Storying the Problem

Re-storying the problem is a technique that grows from the belief that problems are stories we agree to tell ourselves that are embedded within social and cultural contexts. These social and cultural contexts and their dominant stories wield a lot of power over individuals, couples, and families to constrain, disempower, and objectify them. Through utilizing this technique, clients are empowered to externalize the problem from their own self-identity narrative, de-objectify themselves, and re-author new stories. Through re-storying the problem, couples often bring back into focus vital and neglected aspects of their lived experience that have been constrained or pushed out of focus, and thus underutilized. The couple is then able to envision new solutions or new ways of viewing solutions and becomes unstuck.

Description and Implementation

The clinician is an active participant in re-storying the problem, helping the couple redefine and deconstruct the problem as something external to them and pinpointing their influence on it (White & Epston, 1990). Once the problem is externalized, questions are posed to clarify each partner's relationship to it. In addition, times in the past when they were able to have control over the problem (called *unique outcomes*) are discussed because problem-saturated stories often obscure success (White, 1991). These questions often lead to new stories and new definitions of themselves and their relationships. The clinician plays an active role in this process, maintaining a position of openness and curiosity while sharing personal beliefs and biases (White & Epston, 1990). The result is a co-created narrative that allows for new possibilities for the couple.

Contraindications

When working with same-sex couples, it is important that sexual orientation not be externalized as the "enemy." Rather than rallying against an important part of their identity, members of the couple system can map the problem to external factors other than their sexual orientation.

Challenging assumptions and "truths" regarding sexual orientation may help in the re-storying process. This approach asserts that the label itself (the term *homosexual,* for example) and the pathologizing conversations around that label are the real problem. Therefore, deconstructing these labels may help the couple and their family realign themselves and lessen the load that the oppressive beliefs may have had (White & Epston, 1990). For example, parents who believe that same-sex attraction automatically leads to acquiring HIV, or that a lesbian daughter may never become a mother, may be asked questions regarding their assumptions about same-sex orientation. Deconstructing those beliefs can be very difficult, as sexuality itself is still a taboo subject in our society. The following is a brief description of the challenges encountered when using a narrative therapy framework with a couple trying to deal with the meaning of monogamy in their relationship.

Case Example

To demonstrate the use of the re-storying narrative approach, we point to the case example of Aaron and Connor, who have been in a committed, sexually monogamous relationship for more than a year. Aaron has expressed to Connor that he is "bored" sexually and misses the time when he frequently slept with several different men he had met on an online gay mobile application. He suggests that he and Connor create online profiles to find other sexual partners to join them individually or as a group. Connor fervently refuses Aaron's suggestion out of concern that violating the monogamous nature of their relationship will make them "impure" and "socially unacceptable." This dispute has resulted in a lack of intimacy between the two men, and Aaron has even threatened to move out.

In this scenario, the re-storying approach could be used effectively with the therapist bringing attention to the social forces at play in engendering Aaron and Connor's attitudes toward monogamy. In doing so, the therapist helps Aaron and Connor "externalize" the concept of monogamy and unpack the reasons behind their perspectives toward it. On a micro-level, the therapist would highlight each partner's concerns with the couple's sexual dynamic, understanding the manifestations of Aaron's "boredom" and Connor's commitment to "purity." On a macro-level, the therapist could shed light on the broader social factors at play, including social norms related to heterosexual versus gay male cultures' perceptions of monogamy, purity, and sexuality.

The therapist might then probe Aaron to discuss times when he had control over his sexual boredom. Also, the therapist may prompt Connor about times when purity has been in his control, drawing from the aforementioned cultural factors. Once these narratives have been externalized, the therapist can help Aaron and Connor clarify their relationship to the problem. Finally, the therapist and the couple can come up with a few options to help them navigate possible resolutions to their dilemma that hold to the values and principles that each partner has externalized, on both micro- and macro-levels.

Finally, we want to note that in this particular scenario, it is important that therapists make an effort to check their personal biases about sexual orientation and monogamy. Furthermore, therapists must keep an open mind to cultural differences between their own backgrounds and those of their clients.

References

Gergen, K. J. (1985). The social constructionist movement in modern psychology. *American Psychologist, 40,* 266–275.

Hoffman, L. (1992). A reflexive stance for family therapy. In S. McNamee & K. J. Gergen (Eds.), *Therapy as social construction* (pp. 7–24). London: Sage.

White, M. (1991). Deconstruction and therapy. *Dulwich Centre Newsletter, 3,* 21–40.

White, M., & Epston, D. (1990). *Narrative means to therapeutic ends.* New York: W. W. Norton.

22

REATTRIBUTION AND NARRATIVE CHANGE

Rachel M. Diamond and Jay L. Lebow

Purpose: To create new narratives that are less blaming and destructive for divorcing couples

Introduction

Problems often exist in the constructed perspectives, stories, and narratives people create. Many events occur every day, but only some are given meaning and are incorporated into our narrative (Freedman & Combs, 2008). What we give significance to becomes our constructed reality. From a narrative perspective, the re-authoring of one's story to include neglected, but important, aspects of the dominant narrative can create a starting point for creating change. In a related but more directive frame, reattribution involves changing the meaning given to events and behaviors so other ways of viewing an experience can be better considered. Broadly speaking, reattribution work includes techniques to modify the attributions people make for behaviors or events in their life (Metalsky, Laird, Heck, & Joiner, 1995). People are essentially taught to engage in new methods of self-talk regarding how they assign meanings to situations so they can interpret and deal with life's problems in new, more constructive ways.

As a growing number of marriages end in divorce, former partners often find themselves locked in disputes over issues such as child custody and visitation. Many of these former couples are being referred to therapy by the courts or legal counsel because they are unable to resolve issues independently. Family members stuck in this conflict often present with powerful stories of blame and victimhood. Research conducted on married couples in distress has found that these partners make attributions for negative events that accentuate their impact. They tend to see behaviors as stable or unchanging, see the problem as global, and find fault in the other person (Fincham & Bradbury, 1992). High-conflict divorcing and post-divorce couples show an even greater frequency and intensity of such attribution patterns. At times, these even extend into kin-wars of extended family.

Purpose of Reattribution and Narrative Change

Negative attributions are influential forces in many post-divorce interactions. Each partner views the actions of the other through a negative filter. Among such former partners, any action that creates problems or tension by the other person is invariably viewed as mounting evidence of character flaws and/or hostile action. Alternatively, behaviors that are cooperative or constructive are seen as disingenuous and/or temporary. All in all, the attitudes and beliefs of both parties sum up to the view that their former partner is to be blamed for any current (as well as past and future) problems. Such beliefs, in turn, impact actions toward one another, which can create a vicious cycle of negative exchanges. For example, one former partner attributed her ex-partner's abstinence from alcohol and regular attendance at Alcoholics Anonymous to be a manipulative plan to win their court case rather than actions for the betterment of himself and their family. She convinced herself that he would convert back to drinking immediately following the court proceedings. Alternatively, he perceived his wife's attitude toward his behavior as proof of her vendetta against him. Each attribution that leads to negative behavioral outcomes deepens the entrenchment of the negative interactions and beliefs toward one another.

A process goal of treatment when utilizing reattribution and narrative change is for the therapist to help former partners modify narratives that describe events. This is done so they do not include blame or cause further damage to the family. In the example above, the goal would be to challenge each partner's interpretations of the sequence of events. Their existing narratives are not based so much in actual events, but in each person's interpretations. By challenging their viewpoints, the therapist is able to help the former partners reframe a new narrative that includes alternative attributions for behaviors and considers factors that may have been previously overlooked or avoided. Generating an alternative narrative creates the possibility of a greater range of constructive attributions to facilitate positive interactions in the future.

Description and Implementation

When former partners present in therapy, it is helpful to first assist them in identifying when they fall into patterns of negative attribution in order to replace the maladaptive attributions with more adaptive ones. The process begins by listening to the client(s) and helping to create a sense of being understood. This provides a foundation of alliance in which the client's (or clients') behavior can be challenged while their positive intention is underlined. The therapist helps each partner break down cognitions that underlie the attributions invoked to explain the problems. In order to facilitate reattribution and the development of a new narrative, it is useful to follow this sequence: First, the therapist and client(s) identify an issue in which one former partner finds fault with the other or there is mutual fault-finding. Second, reasons for why the other person is thought to be at fault are explored. Third, other potential meanings are considered and explored, challenging each person to consider more benign meanings. Finally, potential tangible benefits of changing attributions are examined as well as the cost in a cost-benefit analysis. Bringing a more objective frame to the worst-case beliefs often active in these couples can promote change. Throughout this process, the way in which the perceptions are formed should be examined and challenged in order to help the partners determine whether all available information is being used to create their narrative, as well as if the information is valid. The therapist will work with the former partners to generate a more adaptive narrative that includes information that may have been previously excluded and/or alternative reasons for a given problem. For example, a therapist can help partners consider attributions that relate to situational forces (e.g., normative reactions to divorce) rather than those that blame the personal dispositions of the former partner.

Contraindications

Even though former spouses who come to therapy during or following a divorce are often engaged in a substantial level of conflict, the use of reattribution and narrative change can typically be used to prompt change in session. However, this technique would not be therapeutic if a parent/ex-spouse presents danger to the family and is in fact unsafe. Instead, the focus must first be on helping that parent become less dangerous and also on helping the other parent and children differentiate between which behaviors present as threatening and which do not.

Case Example

The most frequently encountered events that a parent negatively attributes to the behavior of the other parent relate to difficulties children manifest in divorce or transitions between homes. For example, the parents may not want their children to experience the difficulty of moving back and forth between homes or feel sad. That is, if there are any signs of behavioral changes in children, parents are quick to attribute problems displayed by children to the former partner's contribution. To discuss how to utilize reattribution and narrative change in a case like this, we use the example of Eric and Stacey. Since their separation two months earlier, the couple's five-year-old daughter had resided in Eric's new residence one day a week and every other weekend (Stacey remained in the family home). They entered therapy at the suggestion of their mediator because the daughter began wetting the bed at nights and throwing tantrums almost daily when taken to school. Both parents reported that these changes began since the separation. Stacey reported to the therapist that Eric had not made sufficient efforts to make his "bachelor pad" cozy so their daughter could feel at home. Eric, on the other hand, reported that Stacey had not made efforts to adjust her work schedule. Their daughter spent more time with other caregivers than she was accustomed to. Both parents directly attributed the daughter's changes to the other's "bad parenting."

The therapist worked with the ex-spouses to modify their narratives away from viewing one another as bad parents who were not making sufficient effort. The therapist empathized with the parents' difficult situation and helped them understand how, given their differences, it was easy to fall into the process of attributing their daughter's behavioral changes to character flaws in one another. Some simple psychoeducation about children and divorce helped place their daughter's problems in a different context in which no one needed to be blamed. The therapist suggested additional possible sources for the daughter's distress other than "bad parenting," such as powerful feelings she might have about the separation and/or the natural difficulties in learning to live in two households that many children experience in their own way (i.e., situational forces versus personal dispositions). In a related vein, each parent was also encouraged to consider behaviors of the other that were inconsistent with their views. For example, Stacey had not considered how Eric purchased a bed set for their daughter's room that matched the one in the other home, as well as several similar toys. Eric, alternatively, had not taken into account that Stacey could not afford to change her work schedule, having gone from a dual-earner home to a single-earner home. Stacey had her mother babysit for the few hours that their daughter was home from school before Stacey returned from work because this is the relative with whom their daughter was closest. The conversation then segued into ways of working better together in the best interest of their daughter as well as holding onto more positive views (or at least not such extreme negative views) of one another.

References

Fincham, F. D., & Bradbury, T. N. (1992). Assessing attributions in marriage: The relationship attribution. *Journal of Personality and Social Psychology, 62*, 457–468.

Freedman, J., & Combs, G. (2008). Narrative couple therapy. In A. Gurman (Ed.), *Clinical handbook of couple therapy* (4th ed., pp. 229–258). New York: Guilford Press.

Metalsky, G. I., Laird, R. S., Heck, P. M., & Joiner, T. E. (1995). Attribution theory: Clinical applications. In W. T. O'Donohue & L. Krasner (Eds.), *Theories of behavior therapy: Exploring behavior change.* (pp. 385–413) Washington, DC: American Psychological Association.

PART D

Anger and Conflict

23

ANGER MANAGEMENT SELF-TALK

Norman B. Epstein

Purpose: To reduce unregulated anger and aggressive behavior in couple relationships

Introduction

Acts of physical and psychological aggression occur at high rates in couple relationships, especially among couples who seek therapy for a variety of relationship problems (Epstein, Werlinich, & LaTaillade, 2015). The severity of physical aggression ranges from relatively mild actions such as pushing, slapping, and grabbing, to intense and life-threatening behavior such as choking and the use of weapons. Whereas physical actions tend to be more readily identified as aggression and inappropriate, forms of psychological aggression (which include denigrating remarks about one's partner, intimidating actions such as smashing objects, hostile withdrawal from the partner, and restriction of the partner's access to resources such as money) often are viewed by lay individuals as normal aspects of couple conflict. Nevertheless, research has demonstrated that physical and psychological forms of aggression have similar negative effects on the psychological well-being of victims, such as anxiety, depression, and low self-esteem. Both types of partner aggression also undermine partners' perceptions of safety, trust, and intimacy in their relationship, and decrease their relationship satisfaction (Jose & O'Leary, 2009).

Partner aggression also has been classified as either *intimate terrorism* or *battering*, which tends to be severe, unilateral, and perpetrated more by males than females, or *common couple violence*, which involves psychological and mild to moderate physical aggression, and tends to be perpetrated by both members of a couple (in the context of poor conflict resolution skills). Whereas perpetrators of battering tend to use aggression to subjugate their partners, those who engage in common couple violence tend to use it to express upset with their partner and to punish him or her. Given the high level of danger associated with battering, therapists avoid treating such couples with conjoint therapy, typically referring perpetrators to anger management groups and victims to shelters. However, couple therapies have been developed to treat common couple violence, and research has indicated that couples can be treated safely and effectively with careful monitoring and active structured interventions, in particular using cognitive-behavioral and solution-focused approaches (Epstein et al., 2015).

One of the key treatments for partner aggression is anger management training. It includes interventions that address the cognitive, affective, and behavioral components of aggression. Affective interventions include coaching partners in being aware of cues that they are beginning to become angry (e.g., bodily sensations) and engaging in self-soothing behaviors (such as muscle relaxation or taking a warm shower). Behavioral interventions include the development of constructive communication and problem-solving skills as a couple, as well as the use of "time-outs," in which partners agree to disengage from each other for a specified amount of time in order to calm themselves and prepare to talk constructively. Cognitive interventions focus on decreasing thoughts that contribute to anger and individuals' choices to behave aggressively toward their partners, as well as increasing thoughts that guide constructive couple interactions.

Purpose of Anger Management Self-Talk

Individuals who are aggressive toward their partners commonly think in ways that elicit their anger and contribute to their choices to behave aggressively. "Hot" cognitions that elicit anger commonly include themes of injustice ("You have no right to treat me that way!") and attributions of negative characteristics to the partner (e.g., "You just want to control me!" or "You are a jerk!"). Furthermore, some individuals hold beliefs that the use of aggression is justified and that it serves a positive function (e.g., "A person who treats you badly deserves to be punished," or "If I hit her she'll get the message to be more respectful of me"). Consequently, therapists need to modify such cognitions that elicit anger and aggressive behavior. Because these ways of thinking commonly are ingrained, therapists need to be tactful in challenging them and helping aggressive partners to see the advantages of developing more constructive cognitions and behavior.

Description and Implementation

The core of this technique is engaging the individual in conscious, systematic self-talk focused on reducing anger and aggressive behavior (Epstein & Baucom, 2002; Epstein et al., 2015). The first step involves psychoeducation about the association between one's thoughts and one's emotional and behavioral responses to a partner. The therapist uses examples from the couple's recent interactions to demonstrate these principles (e.g., noting how a particular "hot" thought angered an individual and led her to verbally attack her partner). The psychoeducation includes describing how people commonly "talk to themselves," giving themselves instructions to accomplish tasks.

When members of a couple hold beliefs that aggression is justified and useful, the therapist must intervene to challenge and modify those beliefs before coaching the partners in non-aggressive self-talk. Major approaches include more psychoeducation about the negative consequences that aggression has for the individuals and their relationship, and collaborating with the clients in listing and weighing the advantages and disadvantages of venting anger through aggressive behavior (Epstein & Baucom, 2002).

The therapist then models two types of self-instruction: (a) coaching oneself to engage in self-soothing actions (e.g., slow, deep breathing and muscle relaxation) to reduce anger, and (b) guiding oneself in constructive alternatives to aggression, such as avoiding escalation with the partner (e.g., "Don't take the bait. Just because he is being aggressive doesn't mean I need to do it too"), using good communication, or requesting a time-out.

Because such self-talk represents a new pattern for many individuals, it is important to discuss with clients that it takes repeated practice to develop new habits. The therapist can set up role-play practice exercises during couple therapy sessions, coaching the partners as they rehearse constructive self-talk and non-aggressive behavior. It also is important to identify self-statements that feel natural and believable to each partner. The therapist can guide each person in devising the wording and having a copy of one's self-instructions written on a card or as a message on one's cell phone, for easy reference. As the members of the couple become adept at using self-talk during therapy sessions to manage anger and aggression, the therapist can assign them "homework" of practicing the new skills in daily life situations that have tended to elicit conflict and aggression.

Contraindications

Members of some couples experience such high levels of unregulated negative emotions that coaching in self-talk in couple therapy may be ineffective, as their strong emotional responses are triggered very easily by the mere presence of their partner. Others may have deeply ingrained beliefs in retribution or traditional gender roles that involve male domination of female partners, which require more intensive intervention than is feasible in couple therapy. In such cases, it may be necessary to forego couple therapy, at least temporarily, and refer aggressive partners for individual therapy.

Case Example

Marie and John sought couple therapy for chronic conflict that had escalated to the point where an argument led to pushing and slapping each other, which was very distressing to both partners. In discussing their therapy goals with their thera-pist, they expressed a strong desire to communicate better and resolve conflicts without aggression. Given that they did not hold beliefs that justify aggression, the therapist began with a psychoeducational discussion of anger management strate-gies, including self-talk to reduce anger and encourage constructive communica-tion. The couple agreed that in conjunction with work on their communication skills for expressing themselves and listening empathically, they would focus on constructive self-talk. Consequently, the therapist divided the time in each ses-sion between developing the couple's communication and problem-solving skills (Epstein & Baucom, 2002), and coaching the partners in identifying and practic-ing self-instructions for self-soothing, using time-outs to de-escalate conflict, and applying the communication skills they were learning.

By interviewing each partner to uncover the thoughts that typically elicited his or her anger during their arguments (Epstein & Baucom, 2002), the therapist identified that John tended to become angry when he perceived Marie as failing to listen to him, whereas Marie was angered by John's persistence in pressuring her to adopt his views. Both partners responded to their anger by engaging in aggressive criticism of each other, which further increased each other's anger. The therapist reviewed this pattern with Marie and John, who agreed with the therapist's proposed goal of substituting good communication and negotiation for the negative exchanges. The therapist then guided each partner in devising self-instructions to facilitate positive communication (e.g., "If she doesn't seem to be listening to me, I can take slow, deep breaths to relax and then tell her calmly that I would like her to reflect back what I am saying to her, using the listening skills that we have practiced"). Through repeated practice in sessions of positive self-talk combined with communication and problem-solving skills, supplemented with additional practice through homework assignments, the couple improved their anger management and ability to understand each other's position during conflict, and subsequently improved their ability to negotiate solutions.

References

Epstein, N. B., & Baucom, D. H. (2002). *Enhanced cognitive-behavioral therapy for couples: A contextual approach.* Washington, DC: American Psychological Association.

Epstein, N. B., Werlinich, C. A., & LaTaillade, J. J. (2015). Couple therapy for partner aggres-sion. In A. S. Gurman, J. L. Lebow, & D. K. Snyder (Eds.), *Clinical handbook of couple therapy* (5th ed., pp. 389–411). New York: Guilford Press.

Jose, A., & O'Leary, K. D. (2009). Prevalance of partner aggression in representative and clinic samples. In K. D. O'Leary & E. M. Woodin (Eds.), *Psychological and physical aggres-sion in couples: Causes and interventions* (pp. 15–35). Washington, DC: American Psycho-logical Association.

24

UNBALANCING

George M. Simon

Purpose: To elicit an in-session enactment of productive conflict in conflict-avoidant couples

Introduction

Couple therapists are supposed to help their clients resolve conflict, right? Well, not necessarily. Structural couple therapy (SCT) views the avoidance of conflict, or its premature termination, to be as potentially deleterious to a couple as is engagement in chronic, unresolved conflict. Both avoided conflict and chronic conflict bespeak a relational structure that deprives the couple system of resources it would otherwise have if its structure permitted both the airing of differing perspectives by the partners and the "marrying" of those aired perspectives into novel solutions (Minuchin, 1974). Couples beset by chronic, unresolved conflict have a relational structure that is inhibiting the "marrying" of differences; couples that avoid conflict altogether or that prematurely terminate it have a structure that is inhibiting the airing of differences. Skill in addressing both kinds of dysfunctional relational structure is crucial to the successful practice of SCT.

Purpose of Unbalancing

Unbalancing is the technique that SCT therapists use to challenge the structure of couple systems that avoid conflict (Minuchin & Fishman, 1981; Simon, 2008). With couples that never initiate conflict, the technique is used to elicit conflict in the first place. With couples that do initiate conflict on their own but then prematurely flee it, unbalancing is used to extend an episode of conflict beyond the cutoff point prescribed by the couple system's norms.

Whether it is used to instigate or to prolong an episode of conflict, unbalancing is designed to produce that conflict *in the therapy room*. This is in keeping with SCT's overall preference for experiential interventions that elicit in-session enactments of novel relational arrangements for couples. Before we examine what such a conflict-producing intervention looks like, a few words about the name of the intervention are in order.

Why is the intervention called *unbalancing*? SCT's systemic world view leads the practitioner of this model to see both couple members as playing equal, though usually complementary, roles in maintaining the couple's relational structure. Thus, an SCT therapist never sees a "hero" and a "villain" when the therapist observes couple members interact in a dysfunctional manner. The therapist's theoretical perspective inhibits him/her from attributing the dysfunctionality of the interaction to one member of the couple. Yet, as we are about to see, when engaging in unbalancing, the SCT therapist strategically *acts as if* one couple member is, in fact, "wrong," and the other one is "right." In doing so, the therapist enters into a (temporary) alliance with the member who is "right." This coalition with one couple member against the other *unbalances* the otherwise balanced, circular interactional process that maintains the relational status quo in the couple system. By throwing his/her weight behind one couple member and against the other, the therapist destabilizes the conflict-avoiding structure of the couple system.

Description and Implementation

Like so much else in SCT, unbalancing works hand-in-glove with the model's signature intervention, *enactment*, which refers to periods when, at the therapist's behest, couple members interact directly with each other. When the therapist intends to unbalance, he/she begins by eliciting an enactment focused on content material that the therapist knows, based on his/her experience of the couple, the members have differences about. True to form, a conflict-avoidant couple will, in the ensuing enactment, either avoid altogether a discussion of those differences, or discuss them only briefly before either detouring toward another, uncontroversial topic or simply ending the enactment altogether.

Before that can happen, the therapist interrupts the enactment with a comment that clearly indicates the therapist is on one member's "side." Moreover, the therapist incites his/her "ally" to advocate for his or her perspective with the other member: "Just now, Nikia, he was talking to you as if you don't know anything about this topic, when, in fact, I think your point of view is more on the ball than his. Don't surrender so easily. I think you need to make him see the error of his ways." The therapist then backs off and elicits another enactment.

It might take a couple of repetitions of such "inflammatory" remarks, but eventually this behavior on the part of the therapist usually succeeds in lending the therapist's "ally" a sufficient sense of righteous indignation to prompt the "ally" to push his or her perspective longer and with greater intensity than is usually allowed by the couple system's norms. What the therapist does next depends upon how the ensuing enactment plays out.

It might happen that the therapist's "ally" abandons his or her newfound assertiveness in the face of resistance from the other couple member. If that occurs, the therapist is likely to repeat his/her "incitement" of his/her "ally," and then once again elicit an enactment.

Alternatively, the newfound assertiveness of the "ally" might elicit a dramatic display of submission by her or his partner. This development will not be deemed as a positive outcome by the therapist, since what the therapist was trying to achieve via his/her unbalancing was not the prevailing of the therapist's "ally's" viewpoint on the content matter being discussed, but rather a restructuring of the couple system in a manner that promotes adaptive conflict. Therefore, if the other couple member merely gives in, the therapist will likely abandon his/her former "ally" and switch "sides" in an effort to elicit the conflict that is still being avoided: "Stan, you have given in way too easily. While Nikia is mostly right about this, she is not entirely right. Stand up for your point of view." Whether the therapist remains anchored on one "side" during the intervention or works both "sides" against the middle, the therapist will continue his/her unbalancing until it achieves an airing of the conflict that the couple has been avoiding.

Contraindications

Since the purpose of unbalancing is to elicit or prolong conflict in a conflict-avoidant couple, its use is not appropriate with a couple already beset by chronic, escalating conflict. Even when used appropriately with a conflict-avoidant couple, unbalancing runs the risk of rupturing the therapist's joining with one couple member (or perhaps with both, if the therapist engages in the kind of serial side-taking just described). This risk is mitigated by the systemic reframing that the SCT therapist offers during the first session of therapy, which emphatically states the therapist's view is that *both* couple members play a crucial role in maintaining the couple system's relational structure (see Chapter 16 on systemic reframing). Therefore, the therapist should never engage in unbalancing until he/she has delivered and "sold" a systemic reframing to the client couple.

Case Example

Kyra and Philip enter couple therapy to discuss some shared concerns they have about their 14-year-old son. Over the course of the first two sessions, the therapist detects some simmering conflict between the spouses on issues unrelated to their son. However, every attempt he makes to nudge the couple toward an airing of their differences is greeted by a redoubled determination on their part to discuss nothing but their son. Assessing that the son's reported difficulties are very likely related to his parents' use of him as a detour around the spousal conflict that they are assiduously avoiding, the therapist decides to unbalance during the third session.

Early in the session, the therapist sees during an enactment a piece of interpersonal process that has occurred almost every time he has gotten the spouses to speak with each other: Philip interrupts and speaks over Kyra, who despite being obviously annoyed, fails to protest and allows her husband to claim the floor. The therapist sees his opportunity to begin his unbalancing:

THERAPIST: Kyra, why do you let him do that?
KYRA: He does it all the time. I really don't mind.
THERAPIST: Sure you do. It's written all over your face. The thing is, you were making a very cogent point when he silenced you.
PHILIP: Hey, I don't silence her.
THERAPIST (IGNORING PHILIP): You really should get him to stop doing that. Talk with him about it and see if you can get him to stop.

In the ensuing enactment, Kyra slowly but steadily builds in intensity as she complains to Philip about his "incessant"—her word—interrupting of her. Philip vigorously defends himself, but Kyra refuses to withdraw her complaint. Judging that his unbalancing has begun to attenuate the couple's conflict-avoidance, the therapist simply tracks the enactment in silence.

References

Minuchin, S. (1974). *Families and family therapy*. Cambridge, MA: Harvard University Press.
Minuchin, S., & Fishman, H. C. (1981). *Family therapy techniques*. Cambridge, MA: Harvard University Press.
Simon, G. M. (2008). Structural couple therapy. In A. S. Gurman (Ed.), *Clinical handbook of couple therapy* (4th ed., pp. 323–349). New York: Guilford.

25

CONFRONTING SPLITTING

Judith P. Siegel

Purpose: To help partners regain emotional and cognitive balance when they are reacting to each other in polarized ways

Introduction

There are times when therapists find themselves working with highly volatile, emotionally reactive couples. Partners who react to each other in a polarized or extreme way can be very challenging for even the most experienced couple therapist. Such extreme volatility and frequent conflict may be a sign of "splitting." Once you have seen one couple and recognized that they are using splitting, it will become much easier to detect it in the subsequent cases. Helping partners learn to restore a balanced perspective is an important skill for therapists to master.

Although splitting is an analytically based concept that involves an unconscious defense mechanism, it is played out in the couple in a systemic way. Object relation theorists suggest that, as part of normal development, young children need to separate, or split apart, the "all good" aspects of self and others from the "all bad" qualities. For most people, splitting is eventually replaced by more mature defenses, but we are all capable of reverting to it under certain conditions.

I conceptualize splitting as a two-drawer filing cabinet that holds all the memories and references we draw upon in assigning meaning. While one drawer holds the best experiences, expectations, and beliefs associated with positive encounters, the other drawer contains everything we wish had never happened. The emotions that were felt during these positive and negative experiences can be revived or re-experienced when memories are triggered. Just like a two-drawer file cabinet, when one drawer is open, the other remains shut, so that memories of positive experiences are not accessible when splitting has opened the bad drawer.

When splitting is activated, an individual interprets his/her partner through a distorted lens. A relatively minor frustration or disappointment can easily cause a downward spiral, as rekindled memories add fuel to the fire. Under the influence of splitting and the influx of "all bad" memories and emotions, partners may experience pessimism, despair, and/or rage, resulting in a distorted view of the other partner or the relationship as "all bad." This one-sided perspective may lead to threats to end the relationship or to drop out of therapy. There are also harmful consequences of one partner being in the "all good" drawer, as potentially negative aspects of the situation are minimized or denied in order to maintain an idealized view of the other partner and the relationship.

The research on splitting in couples shows that partners experience their relationships as being unstable, as they never know when things can quickly spiral downward (Siegel, 2006). These couples also have compromised problem-solving skills, as areas of potential conflict are avoided when the couple is in an "all good" phase. When problems do surface, the couple has difficulty maintaining a focus on the situation at hand and keeping things in perspective so that problems can be discussed and resolved constructively. Instead, former problems add to the issue at hand, making problems appear insurmountable.

Purpose of Confronting Splitting

Partners who frequently engage in splitting can learn to become aware of "extreme" postures and develop ways to regain a more balanced stance. It is helpful for both partners to address the ways that engaging in splitting harms relationship security and well-being, rather than locating the tendency to split in only one of the partners. It is also useful for the therapist to identify the pattern early in the therapy process so the therapist can help couples catch things before they deteriorate beyond the couple's and therapist's ability to manage.

Description and Implementation

It is wise for therapists to raise the subject of splitting as soon as there is any indication that it is part of the couple's problem. If partners describe relationship cycles of "ups and downs," or describe their partner or the relationship as being "all bad," I focus immediately on splitting and ask them about episodes of idealizing/devaluing in earlier and other aspects of their lives. If there is reason to believe that splitting has added to the couple's difficulties, I provide psychoeducation about the power of past memories, beliefs, and emotions to color the present. Neurobiology research has provided explanations of the power of memory networks to influence cognition and emotion and can be understood by most individuals. I describe neural networks as a vine with many leaves that spring into action whenever we need to interpret an event. I also explain the file cabinet analogy and how memories that are kept in the "all good" or "all bad" drawer influence our perception, interpretation, and conclusions, leading to one-sided, restricted viewpoints and responses that are often regretted (Siegel, 2008).

I work with the couple to help them identify the emotional responses, thoughts, and patterns that occur when either of them is reacting to an event in an extreme or polarized way that suggests splitting. A number of techniques can help partners learn to deescalate, but the most difficult challenge is helping partners develop enough self-awareness to recognize when splitting has taken over. Some indicators might be polarized or "all-or-nothing" thinking; extreme anger, defensiveness, or aggression; or deep despair or withdrawal. Once couples understand what splitting is and recognize when it occurs, I advise partners to work together in challenging a splitting cycle. The therapist can help each partner to identify strategies that help them deescalate and restore calm, as well as what their partner can do (or stop doing) to help them do this more efficiently. Many individuals find that asking for a small "time-out" to step back and do deep breathing is particularly helpful. However, while some individuals need space in order to return to a more neutral posture, others prefer that their partner stays connected, or even help lighten the situation through humor.

The therapist who has taken the time to explain the potential damage of splitting and ways to move past it is better prepared to help the couple when splitting takes over a therapy session. A partner who becomes disgusted or disparaging toward his/her partner or the therapist can be prevented from storming out of the session or ending therapy altogether. It is important for the therapist to remain calm, acknowledge that there is something important that needs to be looked at more fully, and ask the individual whether they think they are in the "all bad" drawer. Because the therapist has previously helped partners understand how strong the world view and emotions are in an episode of splitting, and has helped the couple develop a collaborative relationship to help fight splitting, it is easier to restore a calmer and more thoughtful exchange. This intervention prevents damage and helps partners build trust and confidence in their ability to work together in better ways.

Contraindications

While the technique is helpful for most populations, it is essential that splitting itself not be seen as an indication of pathology. A partner who becomes condescending or belittling in telling his/her partner that he/she is splitting every time the partner has a strong emotion or is unhappy is using feedback about splitting in an inappropriate way to retaliate or gain power. It is therefore important for the therapist to recognize power imbalances in the couple's relationship, particularly in couples who use blaming or pathologizing to create a one-up/one-down position. In such cases, the therapist should work with the couple to identify power imbalances and the potential for weakness to be used against each other, and to focus on this dynamic until it is resolved.

Case Example

I worked with a young couple who were on the verge of divorce. In our first session, the husband defined his wife as being senseless, lazy, and incompetent. When I asked him what led to these conclusions, he told me that another check had bounced because she "forgot" to keep track of the checks she had written. Worse yet, another of his prize orchids had died because she overwatered it. When I asked about expectations and disappointments with other people, my concerns about splitting were confirmed. Both partners could see how the cycles of seeing something as being perfect crash into something worthless had ended friendships and professional relationships for both of them. Both were able to see how triggers like disappointment could open the "all bad" drawer and make problems seem overwhelming. Acknowledging the bad drawer and learning to step back, breathe, and challenge a one-sided perspective was helpful in managing differences at home and in the therapy setting.

References

Siegel, J. P. (2006). Dyadic splitting in partner relational disorders. *Journal of Family Psychology, 20*(3), 418–422.

Siegel, J. P. (2008). Splitting as a focus of couples treatment. *Journal of Contemporary Psychotherapy, 38*(3), 161–167.

26

IDENTIFYING AND WORKING THROUGH PROJECTIVE IDENTIFICATIONS

Judith P. Siegel

Purpose: To help partners recognize when they are reenacting unfinished business from the past by projecting disowned parts of their self onto the other

Introduction

Projective identification is most simply understood as a reenactment sequence in which unresolved themes from the past are played out between partners. One partner stimulates or entices the other to react in a way that allows the projective identification process to unfold. It is as if one partner offers the other a script that allows an emotionally troubling theme from the past to be replayed in the present. For example, if a client wishes to disown some aspect of their personality they find unacceptable, the client may relocate that aspect of their self and see it as belonging to their partner.

The concept of unconscious reenactment is fundamental to analytic and object relations theories. According to these approaches, identity is heavily influenced by early interpersonal experiences. For example, children who are made to feel valued and secure by parents, caretakers, and other family members form a level of self-confidence and trust in others that will carry over into adulthood. Children who are overvalued or rejected will have a different self-view and expectations of how others will treat them. While a sense of competency is an important aspect of well-being, it is only one of several themes that can linger from childhood and resurface in intimate relationships. Vulnerable areas may lie dormant for years before a partner revives them. This may be partially due to the fact that intimacy creates a dependency on a partner, who then has an influence over security and self-esteem (Siegel, 1992).

In intimate relationships, partners can unconsciously trigger each other to respond in ways that allow aspects of earlier relational experiences to be revisited.

The unconscious reenactment allows a theme to be repeated, but with the advantage of more control or opportunity for a different outcome. As the projective identification sequence unfolds, there is a blurring of past and present as beliefs, expectations, and emotions from earlier experiences infiltrate the here-and-now. Partners tend to come to rapid conclusions about their partner's intent and respond to each other in ways that allow for a repetition of former interpersonal sequences. For example, an adult who was repeatedly criticized or demeaned by parents may become extremely sensitive to perceived or potential criticism. He/she may resolve this by either becoming a person with high expectations who is quick to criticize others, or by becoming self-doubting and easily crushed by a negative evaluation. Projective identification distorts the person's perception of their self and others, so that experiences from the past are replayed. Regardless of which role partners take, both share a theme where expectations that are not met lead to failure, blame, and rejection. Any situation that has the potential to lead to criticism or failure can rapidly lead to much stronger emotions and responses than would ordinarily be called for.

Purpose of Identifying and Working Through Projective Identification

Projective identification episodes often lie at the heart of the most painful relationship patterns (Siegel, 1992). Because partners are re-experiencing the worst aspects of their childhood, their sense of trust and security can be challenged or eroded. A painful emotional and behavioral reenactment does not necessarily lead to insight, and without therapy, it does not generate new ways of handling the situation. In fact, in many cases the process of projective identification continues indefinitely and polarizes the relationship. Helping couples step out of the sequence and approach the theme in a different way allows partners to support each other and work collaboratively to construct a happier ending to an unhappy theme.

Description and Implementation

Therapists can usually detect an unfolding projective identification sequence by how quickly partners escalate, often responding to each other in a manner that is confusing to an observer. Reactions may seem excessive and/or uncalled for, and the therapist may feel caught up in an emotional minefield. The different perspectives and responses can feel "crazy-making" to the therapist. When I find myself confused and fighting impulses to do something outside of my normal therapeutic style, I interrupt the interaction. I say that I am a little confused about the energy and emotions in the room, and want to backtrack so that I can make sense of what's going on and how we got here. When each partner sees the world or events in radically different ways, it is hard to make any sense of what is being conveyed. I work with the couple to identify the conversation just before things started to shift, and explore what was said, done, or not said or done that I may not have noticed. As the couple works with me to recreate the sequence, it is usually easy to pinpoint the beginning of the projective identification. The therapist's role at that point is to probe for the meaning and emotions from the partner's subjective perspective and to set a frame where both partners can be curious about the way things unfold between them. It is important to establish that this is not about right or wrong, or the "truth," but the opportunity to learn a new way of understanding and relating to each other.

I put considerable effort into making sure that I fully understand the emotion and the theme that has surfaced for each partner. Once I have correctly labeled the theme, I suggest that this is an important theme that not only causes stress in the here-and-now, but likely had meaning in their childhood family as well. Some individuals are comfortable allowing old recollections to surface for discussion, while others are uncomfortable acknowledging "old" memories that have been repressed for years. When I first meet a couple, I ask about early family relationship patterns, and this information can often help guide the conversation and generate thought-provoking questions. The conversation can also be stimulated by asking about the ways this theme was managed in their parents' marriage or in relationships the client has had in the past. If partners have trust in the process and can feel the therapist's genuine concern and nonjudgmental stance, it is typically not difficult to locate the theme from the past that has resurfaced for this couple.

While the themes or projections (usually what each wants to disown in their self or accept from the other) for each partner may not be identical, they usually overlap or are complementary. The therapist needs to balance the conversation so that there is sufficient time to explore the meaning and emotional experience of both partners. Many times, partners hear stories about the past that are new to them and are able to feel empathic for the childhood pain their partner endured. The ability to help partners acknowledge each other in this accepting and supportive way is an important aspect of healing (Siegel, 2010). I then bring the couple's attention back to the sequence that got out of control between them and help them look at the ways that the partners inadvertently rekindled old memories and associations. Again, the therapist works to keep blame outside of this experience, and focus instead on the theme that has meaning to both of them. The final aspect of working with projective identifications involves exploring ways to approach the problem or complaint in a way that feels more open and supportive.

Contraindications

This intervention assumes that there is goodwill and genuine motivation to improve the relationship. Sharing painful memories from the past makes partners vulnerable in terms of sensitive information that has been exposed. This material should never be used against a partner in an argument or as a power tactic. Partners who lack impulse control or who are vengeful should not be trusted with sensitive information that can be misused.

Case Example

Sheila and Ryan called me when pressure about purchasing a home led to unbearable tension and crippling arguments. Ryan wanted to use all of the couple's savings for a down payment in order to qualify for a reduced mortgage rate. Sheila felt uncomfortable with this plan, even though Ryan assured her that he would be getting a commission in a few months' time based on sales he was closing now. As the couple engaged in the argument in my office, I could see Ryan's expressions of contempt for his wife. He snarled at her that she was an imbecile about financing and had no reason not to trust his judgment. I stopped the argument and backtracked to see how the sequence had started. Sheila had become flooded with anxiety when Ryan told her that he was confident that money would come in to replenish some savings. Ryan became furious because he interpreted Sheila's refusal to go along with his plan as a statement of no confidence in him. When I asked Sheila to tell me more about feeling anxious about promises regarding money, she immediately told me about growing up with an alcoholic father who liked to gamble. She recalled her mother collapsing in tears when there was no money to pay the rent or buy school supplies after her husband had lost his entire paycheck on a "sure bet." Sheila had been warned repeatedly to always keep money in reserve just in case. Ryan knew that his now deceased father-in-law liked to play the horses, but he had never before heard this story. Sheila's reluctance could now be seen from an entirely different perspective.

Ryan's aggression had been stimulated by a belief that Sheila didn't trust that his plan was well thought out. When we explored times he had experienced similar feelings growing up, he recalled how his parents had preferred his elder sister, who always stood top in her class. The parents had joked that she had gotten all the best brain genes, and they discounted Ryan's potential. The way Sheila had not supported his plan made him feel that he was once again discounted. When Sheila understood this, she was able to correct his conclusion and talk about the way her anxiety prevented her from taking any risks. We also explored how the couple had taken polarized positions, with Sheila holding all the worry and Ryan holding all the risk-taking. In that way, Ryan could allow Sheila to express trepidation for both of them and experience strength in relation to her weakness. This conversation allowed them to find other ways of providing reassurance, developing a plan that kept just a little in reserve for Sheila, and allowing both to express the part that was excited and confidant, as well as the parts that were a little nervous about the biggest purchase of their lives.

References

Siegel, J. P. (1992). *Repairing intimacy: An object relations approach to couples therapy.* Northvale, NJ: Jason Aronson.

Siegel, J. P. (2010). A good enough therapy: An object relations approach to couples treatment. In A. S. Gurman (Ed.), *Clinical casebook of couple therapy* (pp. 134–152) New York: Guilford.

27

HELPING PARTNERS BREAK FREE OF ADVERSARIAL RELATIONSHIPS

Transitioning From I-It to I-Thou

Stephen T. Fife

Purpose: To help partners move from an adversarial stance toward each other to an affirming, collaborative stance by drawing upon Martin Buber's ideas regarding *way of being* and relationships

Introduction

Couples often come to therapy entrenched in patterns of mutual criticism and blame. Each partner holds the other at fault for the problems in their relationship. When asking couples why they have come to therapy, clinicians often hear partners essentially pointing their finger toward the other: "I am here because of *him/her*"; "She does this and this and this"; "He spends all of his time . . ."; "He never . . ."; "She always . . .". The partners' description of the relationship and reasons for coming to therapy blame each other for their problems and imply that the other person is the one who needs to change: "If he would only stop _____, we wouldn't have these problems"; "If she would just change _____, we would be happy." When both partners see the situation this way, neither is focused on their own participation in the relationship troubles, nor are they thinking about what they can do to help bring about positive changes. Not surprisingly, couples who are entrenched in this kind of adversarial blaming and waiting for the other to change do not experience many benefits from therapy. If they cannot shift from this stance, they are likely to drop out of treatment.

Martin Buber's ideas regarding human *being* and relationships help illuminate the source of this kind of intractable problem in couple relationships, and they suggest a way for couples to break free. Buber's ideas are grounded in a perspective of human beings as fundamentally relational. He held that we are not isolated, self-contained individuals; rather, we are constituted by our relationships and the way in which we relate to others. In other words, who we are is who we are with others. In his seminal book *I and Thou*, Buber (1958) describes two fundamental ways of being: *I-Thou* and *I-It*. *Way of being* is a concept that reflects a person's in-the-moment stance or attitude toward another (Fife, Whiting, Davis, & Bradford, 2014). With the I-Thou way of being, others are regarded as people whose feelings, needs, hopes, and fears are as legitimate as one's own (Fife, in press). This way of being is other-affirming, as one acknowledges and responds to the humanity of another. With the I-It way of being, others are regarded as objects: They are seen as either obstacles to one's happiness or as vehicles or something to be used to satisfy one's needs/desires (Fife, in press). This way of being is other-negating (i.e., others are merely objects whose needs or experiences are not as real or important to a person as his or her own). Buber's philosophy suggests that the root of conflict and adversarial relationships between partners is an I-It way of being. Relationships that are characterized by I-It relating may become inundated with conflict, and partners may have difficulty developing or maintaining closeness.

Purpose of Transitioning From I-It to I-Thou

The purpose of this technique is to invite relationship partners to move from an other-negating, adversarial stance toward each other to an other-affirming, collaborative relationship. This shift also invites each partner to take responsibility for their part in bringing about desired changes.

Description and Implementation

The intervention begins with psychoeducation and a discussion about the two ways of being.

1. Teach couples about the two ways of being: I-It and I-Thou. Therapists can include stories to illustrate the concepts—stories of people who were criticized, blamed, used, abused, or otherwise regarded as objects, and stories in which people were regarded with empathy, kindness, compassion, and respect. Additionally, having clients read a short article (e.g., Boyce, 1995) or book (e.g., Arbinger, 2015) may enhance their understanding of the two ways of being.
2. Help couples understand these concepts by reflecting on their own experience. Clients' personal experiences can help increase their understanding of the two ways of being because they usually know what it is like to be treated as an object and as a person. Likewise, most can remember times when they have been I-It or I-Thou toward others.
3. Discuss the relationship implications of the two ways of being by considering the following questions. How does the way of being affect closeness in relationships? Does being treated or treating one's partner as an object bring people together or push them apart? What about partners whose way of being is I-Thou? Is this more likely to draw partners closer or create distance in their relationship? Most clients clearly recognize that the I-It way of being

leads to emotional (and perhaps physical) distance between partners. It also tends to inhibit listening, empathy, and understanding. On the other hand, the I-Thou way of being tends to draw people and their hearts together. It may be helpful to discuss other relationship implications, such as dealing with conflict. Who is more likely to be able to resolve a difference or solve a problem: Two people who see each other as objects, or partners who see each other as people, with needs and desires as real to each of them as their own?

4.   Discuss the systemic implications of the different ways of being. In some respects, a partner's way of being is contagious. Like tends to beget like. Behaviors arising from an objectified view of one's partner are likely to invite one's partner to reciprocate with an I-It way of being. On the other hand, I-Thou tends to invite I-Thou. Although seeing another as a person does not guarantee that he or she will respond the same, it is more inviting because the other is less likely to feel objectified, attacked, or criticized. Remind couples that in every moment, they have the option of regarding their partner as a person or an object.

After discussing the two ways of being and the relationship implications, the focus shifts to application and inviting clients to move from an I-It relationship stance toward their partner to an I-Thou way of being. In session, therapists may utilize enactments to help facilitate I-Thou relating (see Chapter 8 on Enactments by Davis and Espinoza). Encouraging clients to adopt an attitude of sincere, empathic listening may help them connect with the humanity of their partner and see them as a person (rather than as an obstacle, threat, or thing to be used). Likewise, experiencing a partner listening with I-Thou acceptance, understanding, and compassion may invite mutual softening, empathic listening, and understanding. The application of the concepts can also be facilitated through homework. In order to increase clients' awareness of their way of being with each other, therapists may ask clients to pay attention in between sessions to how they are feeling toward their partner and how they are regarding them: as a person or an object (I-Thou or I-It). Additional exercises may help partners regain a view of the other's humanity and regard each other more consistently as people rather than objects. For example, therapists may encourage clients to carefully reflect on the following questions (particularly when there is a disagreement or conflict): "What is my partner feeling?" and "What does my partner need?" Sincere consideration of these questions typically invites clients to see their partners as people. Usually if clients take these first two questions seriously, they readily discover an answer to a third humanizing question: "What can I do for my partner?"

Contraindications

An I-Thou way of being cannot be faked. It is either genuine, or it is not. Way of being is not a description of behavior, but of one's attitude toward another.

Warner (2001) argues that people sense how others feel about them, and it is that to which they respond (see also Arbinger Institute, 2015). So adopting an I-Thou way of being is not something that occurs at a behavioral level, but it represents something more fundamental and comprehensive—it is how one regards others, how one feels about them, and how one sees them. Behavior arises from one's way of being.

Case Example

Collin and Jessica were a married couple that contacted me for therapy to help them overcome their constant arguing and improve their communication. They described their marriage as emotionally depleted and lacking in warmth and kindness. They reported that most of their interactions turned into arguments, often followed by hours or even days of grim silence (they called these periods the "ice age"). They wanted to stay married, but they seriously doubted whether they could turn their marriage around. As part of treatment, I introduced them to Buber's ideas concerning the two ways of being. We discussed the meaning of the concepts and experiences in their lives that were reflective of the two ways of being. We also discussed the relationship implications of the two ways of regarding each other.

After discussing these concepts, I asked Collin and Jessica to pay attention during the coming week to how they were seeing and feeling about their partner: as an object or as a person. The following session, Jessica reported, "I realized that I am often I-It with Collin. I see him as an object—primarily as an obstacle or irritation. I've noticed that sometimes I'm already irritated or defensive before I even see him. I realized this one day when he came home from work. As I heard his car pull into my driveway, my mood shifted and I began feeling frustrated and angry with him—before we even talked to each other!" Collin said he had a harder time recognizing whether he was seeing Jessica as an object or person. However, in the session he realized that he is often defensive before she speaks to him, and this might lead him to take her words as an attack or criticism when neither is intended. He concluded that he was likely seeing Jessica as an object in these moments.

We discussed what could help them shift from being I-It to I-Thou toward each other. They suggested that they needed to be more sensitive to each other's desires. As they began acknowledging each other's feelings and needs, they begin to express more empathy and understanding. The following session the couple described their efforts during the week to maintain an I-Thou way of being with each other. Jessica described that she had tried to see him as a person and think about his feelings, needs, hopes, fears, strengths, and shortcomings. She said that as she did this, her mood softened, and she was able to speak with him in a manner that invited conversation and connection rather than conflict and coldness.

References

Arbinger Institute (2015). *The anatomy of peace: Resolving the heart of conflict* (2nd ed.). San Francisco, CA: Berrett-Koehler.

Boyce, W. (1995). The ecology of the soul. *National Forum, The Phi Kappa Phi Journal, 75*(1), 29–32.

Buber, M. (1958). *I and Thou* (R. G. Smith, Trans.). New York: Charles Scribner's Sons.

Fife, S. T. (2015). Martin Buber's philosophy of dialogue and implications for qualitative family research. *Journal of Family Theory and Review, 7*(3), 208–224.

Fife, S. T., Whiting, J. B., Davis, S., & Bradford, K. (2014). The Therapeutic Pyramid: A common factors synthesis of techniques, alliance, and way of being. *Journal of Marital and Family Therapy, 40*(1), 20–33.

Warner, C. T. (2001). *Bonds that make us free: Healing our relationships, coming to ourselves.* Salt Lake City, UT: Shadow Mountain.

28

TRACKING PROTECTIVE SEQUENCES IN INTERNAL FAMILY SYSTEMS THERAPY

Toni Herbine-Blank

Purpose: To help couples understand the ways in which their vulnerable and protective parts contribute to patterns of conflict in their relationship

Introduction

Internal family systems (IFS) therapy developed by Richard Schwartz (1995) views multiplicity of mind as a normal human phenomenon and makes use of systems thinking in the realm of the mind. IFS therapy holds that each partner has an internal system of sub-personalities or "parts," as well as an unwounded Self. The IFS model sees couple conflict as various parts of the partners reacting to each other. IFS couples therapy has a protocol for helping couples resolve their conflicts that moves from internal exploration to interpersonal connection.

According to Schwartz (1995), all human beings are born with a resilient Self capable of regulating their internal system of parts with wisdom and compassion. When therapists are able to help client couples access this intrinsic internal resource with qualities such as clarity, compassion, and confidence, they are more capable of restoring balance to their inner systems. What Schwartz (2008) found as he experimented with this concept in couples therapy is that when people accessed this state of Self, they experienced themselves and each other differently and their interactions began to change.

Purpose of Tracking Protective Sequences

Tracking protective sequences is one of an IFS therapist's first inquiries with a couple. A protective sequence is defined as a predictable and repeating pattern of behavior between internal parts in a couple. Partners fight in similar ways regardless of content, and the seemingly constant loop of reaction/counter-reaction can feel inescapable and hopeless. The purpose of tracking protective sequences is to help couples understand the vulnerable feelings and needs that fuel the fire of their repetitive fights. This supports them in breaking old patterns of relating (Herbine-Blank, 2013).

Description and Implementation

IFS holds that partners who are caught in patterns of conflict usually have vulnerable parts and protective parts that contribute to these patterns. With the tracking of protective sequences, we invite couples to imagine what life might be like with less reactivity toward one another. In order to do this, however, we ask them to make a radical *U-turn*, a term coined by Schwartz (2008), and begin to focus away from the other person as wounder or redeemer.

Because a sequence has no simple beginning and can only end when partners put down their weapons, no one is to blame. In IFS couples therapy, we make this invitation: "What if there was a way to help you both so that when he or she did that, you didn't react like this?" In other words, our invitation is for each partner to take responsibility for internal parts of them that engage in conflict, understand what drives their reactivity, and shift the dynamics from the inside out (Herbine-Blank, 2013).

There are four basic steps to tracking protective sequences:

1. Describe what occurs inside when a partner engages in a certain way and what they do or say in response.
2. Ask protective parts what would happen if they disengaged.
3. Illuminate the vulnerable feelings beneath the defensive reaction.
4. Make an invitation to help them lessen their reactivity and respond differently.

Case Example

Alan and Sue were a married couple who came to therapy seeking to address the persistent patterns of conflict in their relationship. Their case illustrates the process of tracking protective sequences.

> "We fight all the time," Alan complained to me one morning during a session. **"Can you describe your fight to me?"** I asked him.
> "I'll just say something and Sue will over-react."
> "Over-react?" Sue exclaimed. "Any reaction is an over-reaction in your mind!"
> "Come on, Sue," Alan said, "give it a rest."
> "Is this a tiny example of what you're talking about?" I addressed them both. Yes, they both nodded.

"Let's use this as an example. I'm curious about what happened just now. Sue," I said, turning toward her, **"when Alan said** *you over-react,* **what did you notice came up inside you?"**

"I got angry."

"And when that part of you gets angry with Alan, what do you hear yourself saying to yourself?"

"Here we go, he's judging again."

"And what's your very first impulse?"

"To snap at him and get him to stop talking."

"Thanks," I said, and turning to Alan, I asked, "Do you know this part of Sue that snaps at you?"

"I sure do."

"And what comes up in you when the part of Sue snaps?" I asked.

He paused. "I guess I do what I just did."

"Which is?" I asked.

"Try to calm her down."

I looked at Sue, who was nodding. "And Sue," I said, **"what happens when Alan's part tries to calm you down?"**

"I get madder."

And then to Alan, **"And what happens to you and what do you do?"**

"I leave."

"And when you leave?" I asked him and waited.

"I get it, she gets madder."

"Is this a familiar dynamic?" I asked.

"Yes, and one that doesn't get us anywhere," Sue said.

"I'd like to ask you both something," I said. "Starting with you this time, Alan. The part of you that wants to calm Sue down, **would you focus on it?"**

Alan paused. "As you focus inward, ask that part, '**What's the concern about not trying to calm her down?'"**

"Things will escalate."

"And then what?" I asked gently.

"We'll be fighting longer."

"And then what?"

"I don't know, a lot of bad feelings," Alan responded.

"Oh, I said, this part of you is trying to prevent bad feelings."

"I guess it is," he said.

We tracked back and forth this way, fleshing out the protective parts of each person. In this model, we believe all parts, even the ones that might appear negative, have an inherent positive intention for the relationship. If you stay with the process long enough, this becomes apparent. In Alan's case, his protector part was attempting to limit the interaction with his wife in order to prevent bad feelings.

With more exploration, we learned that bad feelings equaled feeling disconnected from Sue. This was a great surprise to her.

On the other hand, Sue's attempt to stop Alan had a similar intention. She felt belittled and judged by his language. Snapping, said her protective part, was an attempt to get him to be less critical and more accepting. In other words, both protective parts (which manifested as anger) were protecting more vulnerable ones. In this model, we understand that vulnerability of this kind is generated in childhood and becomes projected into the relationship. With further exploration, we discovered their childhood histories, which impacted their present-day relationship.

Finally, I made another invitation. Addressing them both, I said, **"If there was something we could do here in this office so that when the other person was angry or tried to shut you down, your vulnerable parts were not so intensely impacted and you had more choice in how to respond to the other person, would you be interested in exploring that?"**

"Yes," they both agreed, "we want to change how we react and respond."

The invitation we make is not to try to change one person, nor is it to offer solutions. Our goal is to invite both people to do the work required to change their relationship. Our invitation then is to heal wounds of the past so childhood pain and protective adaptation is not fueling present-day interactions.

References

Herbine-Blank, T. (2013). Self in relationship: An introduction to IFS couple therapy. In M. Sweezy & E. Ziskind (Eds.), *Internal family systems therapy: New dimensions* (pp. 55–71). New York: Routledge.

Schwartz, R. C. (1995). *Internal family systems therapy*. New York: Guilford Press.

Schwartz, R. C. (2008). *You are the one you've been waiting for: Bringing courageous love to intimate relationships*. Oak Park, IL: Trailhead Publications.

29

EMPATHIC JOINING

Patricia L. Papernow

Purpose: To calm high-conflict interaction and help open pathways to understanding

Introduction

Empathy is a key regulating, soothing, and binding force for couples. However, in a stepfamily, parent-child bonds pre-date the stepcouple relationship. As a result, every time a child enters the room or a conversation, the stepfamily structure places the biological parent and the stepparent on seemingly opposite sides of an emotional divide. Stepparents are consistently left out of established parent-child connections. The stepchildren often need to distance their stepparents, which can make the stepparent(s) feel rejected. As a result, stepparents are "stuck outsiders," often feeling invisible and lonely. Parents are "stuck insiders," torn between the people they love (Papernow, 2013). These differences create recurring, disappointing misconnections that can easily spark painful arguments, and are often interspersed with a collapse or withdrawal in the relationship.

In a stepcouple, connection does not usually come from both individuals feeling the same way. It must come from skillfully expressing their feelings and needs, and slowing down enough to fully take in and empathize with the other's very different experience. Ultimately, we want conflicted couples to master skills for engaging more constructively. However, when arousal is very high or very low, or when despair has set in, changing the pattern of interaction is often very difficult. The therapist must take the reins and forge an experience of soothing connection. Empathic joining is a kind of heart-led mirroring that interrupts chronic "but, but, but" responses and begins to rekindle the hope and caring that stronger bonds can be made among all parties.

Description and Implementation of Empathic Joining

On the surface, helping couples join through empathic listening is quite simple. However, using it well requires staying firmly and confidently in charge, while remaining deeply compassionate and acutely attentive to nonverbal cues. One member of the couple volunteers to begin. I invite him or her to say, in just a sentence or two, "the nub of what you most want your partner to hear." The other partner is instructed, "Before you answer, take a breath. Find what you DO understand. Not what you agree with, or what you think. Just what you DO understand." We stay with this until the speaker feels that the listener really "gets" what was just said. The listener is then invited to add a sentence of his or her own, "What you most want your partner to get is . . .," and the process repeats. We go very slowly, sentence by sentence, letting each round of understanding soak in before moving to the next. Although the process may begin with somewhat rote restatements of words, we want to move toward a felt sense of understanding (Siegel & Hartzell, 2003)

Case Example

Delia, a stepparent, is the stuck outsider in her family. Tony, the parent, is the stuck insider. Their attempts to communicate about this are leaving them both ever more raw and alone. Delia launches, *"Your daughter completely ignores me. She is a rude brat. You get so defensive I can't talk to you!"* Tony shoots back, *"You're just too sensitive. She's just being a kid."*

I want my office to be safe. I know where this conversation is going, and it is not a good place. I step in and put up a time-out sign and say, *"I'm betting this is a conversation you've had before. Am I right?"* They both nod. I continue, *"I am guessing that each of you is so longing to be understood. But I am sensing that you are both feeling really unheard and alone. Am I right?"* They both nod again. Tony looks interested. Delia looks guarded. *"I'd like to try something that I think will help,"* I say. *"It's called 'joining.' Who wants to go first?* Delia volunteers.

PP to Delia: "Delia, I know you have a lot to say. I'm going to ask you to say just a sentence or two. Just the very nub of what you most want Tony to get."

Delia: "I want you to get that your daughter is a rude brat." Although Delia is aching for Tony's support, the "rude brat" label is almost guaranteed to trigger him. Ultimately, I want Delia to learn how to make a heartfelt request, rather than a damning criticism. However, in this moment, she is much too upset to learn a new skill. I reach for the vulnerable longing underneath her anger.

PP: "And that must hurt. I'm guessing you are longing for Tony to see and to know that it hurts. Am I getting that right? That you are longing for him to see the hurt? OK, can you tell him that?"

Delia: "I want you to see that she's rude. She hurts me!" Half of the label is still there, but Delia has moved toward her own vulnerability. Not surprisingly,

Tony looks poised to shoot back. He starts with, "But . . ." Ultimately, it will be in Tony's best interest to learn how to take a breath, let his defensiveness pass, and turn "toward" Delia, rather than against her (Gottman, 2011): "I can see you're upset. I want to help. How about we start again without the labels?" However, Tony is just as lonely and desperate as Delia is, and way too raw to learn anything new.

PP to Tony: "Here's what I'd like you to do, Tony. It sounds kind of simple. But it's actually hard. I'll help. Before you respond, I'd like you to take a breath. Find your heart. I know that you love Delia. Take a moment to look in your heart for what you DO understand about what Delia just said." Tony pauses. He looks a bit bewildered. I repeat myself, staying "low and slow" (Johnson, 2004): "Just look into your heart for what you DO understand about what Delia just said. Not what you agree with. In fact, I am betting that you feel very differently. But see if you can find what you DO understand."

Tony looks directly at Delia for the first time. "She hurts you." Delia's shoulders drop just slightly. PP: "Yes," I say, looking over at Delia and letting them both feel emotionally held by me. "So, Tony, now it is your turn to say just a sentence to Delia, just the nub of what you most want her to get." Tony: "I feel so torn. It's so hard. She's my daughter, and you say such awful things about her."

Delia starts with, "But. . . ." I again put my hands up in a time-out sign and step in. "Delia, it's so easy to shoot right back, isn't it? This sounds simple, but it's hard! Take a breath. Take a moment, Delia, to go inside. See if you can find what you DO understand about what Tony just said. It's not easy, but it's actually your best bet for getting him to open to you."

Delia: "You're feeling torn. When I say I'm hurt, you feel torn." PP: "Great!" To Tony: "Did she get it?" Tony replies, "Almost. She says such awful things about Jenny. She over-reacts." Now I want to help Tony speak for the vulnerability underneath his critical defensiveness. "You want Delia to know that it hurts inside. It hurts to hear those things about your daughter. Is that right?" He nods. I ask him to tell Delia directly.

PP to Delia: "Can you find the place inside where you do understand what Tony has just said?" Delia: "It hurts you when I say bad things about Jenny." She has said this somewhat woodenly, but she is considerably calmer. We are headed in the right direction. "Did she get it, Tony?" He nods. Back to Delia: "Well done. And now can you add a sentence, just a sentence about what you'd like Tony to understand?"

Delia launches into a paragraph explanation. I can see Tony getting flooded. Ultimately, he will need to be able to ask her to stick to a sentence or two. I stop her again, tenderly but firmly. "I know you have lots to say. But, it turns out that listening is a bit like eating. Your partner can take in just so much at a time! So, it turns out, if you want to be heard, it's best to stick to one or two sentences. It's hard, isn't it? I'll help. Take a breath. Find just the nub of what you most want Tony to get."

Delia looks flustered, but she tries again: "I think you don't see it. Or maybe you don't want to see it. But Jenny makes awful faces at me. It's so painful." Delia has calmed enough so that she is slightly less blaming and more descriptive. Back to Tony: "Your turn again, Tony. Just go inside and see what you do understand. Stay with it until you get that little nod."

Tony: "You're right, I don't see it. You're saying Jenny makes faces at you." Delia nods. PP to Tony: "Good job. You got it. Now add a sentence of your own." Tony: "You're right. I don't see it. That must hurt!" Tony has calmed enough to access his empathy. Delia nods. There is a tear at the corner of her eye. They are looking fully, softly, at each other now.

Now Tony and Delia are engaged in a very different conversation. We continue from there. As they open to each other, I begin to loosen the reins. When they miss each other, we return to the structure of joining, going sentence by sentence: "Oops, looks like there was a miss there. Let's slow down again."

As the sense of intimacy and closeness strengthens, it is critical to help Delia and Tony to anchor this new experience in their bodies and in their thinking minds. I say to Delia, "What's this like, Delia, to feel Tony getting this, getting your hurt?" She replies, "It makes such a difference." I ask her to tell Tony, "Just the feeling that you're with me! I don't feel so alone!" I turn to Tony: "What's that like to hear, Tony? That you've reached Delia and comforted her?" Tony's cheeks flush: "Such a relief. I do love you, Honey."

Finally, I say, "You might notice, you are so fully connected with each other. You both feel seen, heard, and cared about. Right? But, did you notice, it didn't come from agreeing. It came from slowing down and really hearing each other." I often add, "You may not be able to do this at home yet. Over time, we'll work together so that you can find it on your own. Meanwhile, I want you to go home with the confidence that this connection is here for you."

Other Uses for Empathic Joining

Decreasing interparental conflict is key to children's well-being. I also use empathic joining to structure meetings with hostile ex-spouses. However, in these cases, I do not elicit vulnerable feelings. Until they are calm enough to learn better skills, I translate each criticism (*"She never answers my texts!"*) into a request (*"You would like to know what would help her to respond more quickly"*). We go one sentence at a time, using joining to help each partner hear the other's concerns so that, on behalf of their children, they can begin to collaborate.

Empathic joining is also very useful in shaping parent-child attunement. Here, however, joining goes in only one direction, *from* the parent *to* the child. When the child feels fully heard, I allow parents to express a sentence or two. With adolescents and young adults, joining remains one-sided until the child feels fully "gotten." Once the child feels fully heard and understood, we can then turn to helping an older child provide this key experience of empathic attunement.

References

Gottman, J. M. (2011). *The science of trust: Emotional attunement for couples.* New York: Norton.

Johnson, S. M. (2004). *The practice of emotionally focused couple therapy.* New York: Routledge.

Papernow, P. (2013). *Surviving and thriving in stepfamily relationships: What works and what doesn't.* New York: Routledge.

Siegel, D. J., & Hartzell, M. (2003). *Parenting from the inside out.* New York: Penguin.

Intimacy, Growth, and Change

30

ASPECTS OF INTIMACY

Stephen T. Fife

Purpose: To help couples create connection and maintain intimacy in their relationship

Introduction

Couples often come to therapy primarily focused on what is going wrong in their relationship. Their explanations for why they are seeking therapy tend to emphasize their problems, and their goals center on eliminating these problems. However, many couples also seek out therapy with an interest in restoring the love and closeness they once had in their relationship. Couples may have neglected their relationship and feel that it is depleted and lacking in intimacy (Fife & Weeks, 2010). Intimacy may also have been damaged or lost through destructive behaviors, such as chronic conflict, abuse, or infidelity (Weeks & Fife, 2009). Whether it is a primary or secondary reason for seeking professional help, couple therapy often includes relationship enhancement and intimacy building.

Some couples find it difficult to build intimacy because they define it too narrowly or rely on only one type of connection to sustain their relationship (e.g., sexual intimacy). However, with this intervention, intimacy is defined more broadly as closeness, connection, and sharing between partners. Intimacy is considered a multidimensional phenomenon, meaning that there are a number of different ways a couple can experience closeness, connection, and sharing (Schaefer & Olson, 1981; Weeks & Fife, 2014). For example, couples can experience emotional, physical, spiritual, intellectual, or recreational intimacy in their relationship. Experiencing intimacy through multiple avenues can be very liberating for couples, as it provides a variety of options for sharing closeness and connection between partners. Additionally, the personal, exclusive connections that partners share with each other help define the relationship as unique and establish protective boundaries around the couple unit.

Purpose of the Aspects of Intimacy

The purpose of the Aspects of Intimacy technique is to facilitate the creation and rebuilding of intimate connection between partners in a committed relationship.

Description and Implementation

As discussed above, multidimensional intimacy allows couples to connect with each other in a variety of ways. The Aspects of Intimacy intervention provides a useful framework for helping partners assess the current state of their closeness and connection with each other and create goals for increasing the intimacy in their relationship. The intervention is facilitated through the use of the Aspects of Intimacy handout (see Appendix A). The handout can be used for multiple purposes: to educate couples about the multidimensional nature of intimacy, to help couples broaden their definition of intimacy, to examine and increase understanding of partners' expectations or desires regarding intimacy, and to facilitate conversation and collaboration about how they can increase intimate connection in their relationship.

Therapists may introduce the intervention by explaining that the purpose is to help couples create or rebuild closeness and connection in their relationship. The therapist may point out that each person likely has his/her own definition or understanding of intimacy, and that this exercise is designed to help partners find a variety of ways to connect with each other. Each partner should be given a copy of the handout, and the therapist asks them to individually mark two to five aspects of intimacy that they believe are strengths in their relationship. They are also instructed to mark two or three areas in which they would like to see growth or improvement. The therapist then facilitates a discussion between partners in which they share their reflections on the areas they identified as strengths and those in which they desire increased closeness and connection. Prior to letting couples discuss their respective ideas, it is important to encourage them to discuss their reflections in non-accusatory and non-defensive ways.

Although there may be some overlap in partners' answers, it is likely that they will find that some of their responses differ. Individual partners come into the relationship with different ideas and expectations about intimacy and ways they would like to connect with an intimate partner. Areas that are identified as strengths by both partners should be celebrated! When there are differences, the therapist should help clients seek understanding of how their partner feels about the different aspects of intimacy. For the areas in which one or both partners desire improvement, the therapist can help partners talk about why that particular aspect is important to them, what changes he or she desires, and what the couple can do to bring about greater intimacy in these areas. Additionally, it is important to let couples know that successful relationships do not require that couples connect in every aspect of intimacy. Most successful couples have a small core collection of ways they are intimate that help keep the relationship healthy and strong.

When partners identify aspects of intimacy that they would like to improve, it is critical that couples move beyond merely understanding to identifying specific behaviors that will strengthen intimacy in these particular areas. It may help to have couples first reflect on behaviors and activities that brought closeness in the past. They may realize that they already know a variety of ways to connect with each other. They can then brainstorm additional ways to build greater intimacy in specific areas. Some activities may target multiple aspects of intimacy simultaneously.

Rebuilding intimacy takes time, and clients should not try to focus on all desired aspects of intimacy at once, nor should they expect things to change dramatically right away. The therapist should ask clients to identify one or two aspects of intimacy they want to work on during the coming week and help the couple plan what and when they will do their intimacy-building activities. In the next session, the therapist should follow up with clients on their homework by asking them to describe what they did and the outcome of their efforts. If they did not follow through on their commitment, the therapist should help the couple examine what prevented this and what they need to do in order to complete the homework in the future.

Contraindications

Some clients may have a deep-rooted fear of emotional and/or physical intimacy (Weeks & Fife, 2014). Such fears may preclude healthy intimate connection, as they may lead to a fight-or-flight response when an interaction or relationship becomes too intimate. For example, a partner may verbally express a desire for increased closeness in their relationship, but continually push his or her partner away or sabotage the relationship. In cases when one or both partners exhibit a persistent fear of intimacy, it may be helpful to address this prior to intimacy enhancement work.

Case Example

Paul and Anya sought therapy because they were struggling in their communication and were experiencing frequent and occasionally intense verbal conflicts. Anya said that nearly all of their interactions ended in arguments, she felt emotionally distant from Paul, and she was losing hope that their marriage was going to last. Paul said he was sick of the fighting and Anya's persistent criticism. He, too, was questioning the viability of their marriage. As part of treatment, I suggested that in addition to addressing the communication problems and conflict they described, they might benefit from a concerted effort to enhance their relationship by building greater closeness and connection between them. They enthusiastically agreed. Anya said she missed the fun and connection they used to have. Paul was also excited: "I thought that all we'd do in here would be talk about problems—which is what we already do at home."

I explained that some couples fail to nurture intimacy in their relationship, or they define intimacy too narrowly. I suggested that intimacy could be defined broadly as "closeness, connection, and sharing between partners," and I explained that couples benefit from having "multidimensional" intimacy in their relationship. I gave each of them a copy of the Aspects of Intimacy handout, and asked them to take a few minutes to identify two or three areas that they felt were strengths in their relationship and two or three that they would like to improve. I then facilitated a conversation between them about the aspects of intimacy they felt were strengths in their marriage. I had them explain why and provide examples of times when they felt connected in these ways. This allowed them to talk about their successes as a couple. We then moved to the areas they would like to improve. This discussion was framed as each person desiring to create more connection with their partner rather than emphasizing deficits in the relationship or criticisms. Paul and Anya then discussed what they could do in the next week to improve their closeness and connection by focusing on one or two of the aspects of intimacy they identified. This process continued over the course of therapy while we concurrently worked on their communication and efforts to resolve conflicts. Their work on building intimacy brought increased closeness in their relationships and greater hope for their future together.

References

Fife, S. T., & Weeks, G. R. (2010). Barriers to recovering intimacy. In J. Carlson & L. Sperry (Eds.), *Recovering intimacy in love relationships: A clinician's guide* (pp. 157–179). New York: Routledge.

Schaefer, M., & Olson, D. (1981). Assessment of intimacy: The PAIR inventory. *Journal of Marital and Family Therapy, 7*, 47–60.

Weeks, G. R., & Fife, S. T. (2009). Rebuilding intimacy following infidelity. *Psychotherapy in Australia, 15*(3), 28–39.

Weeks, G. R., & Fife, S. T. (2014). *Couples in treatment: Techniques and approaches for effective practice.* New York: Routledge.

APPENDIX A

Aspects of Intimacy

Review the list and identify the top two to five aspects of intimacy that are strengths for you as a couple. Also, note two or three areas in which you would like improvement or growth. Share your reflections with each other in an open, non-defensive way. In the areas where you both desire improvement, discuss specific steps which can be taken to increase closeness in your relationship. You will likely find that some of your answers differ. In those areas in which your partner wants improvement, seek to understand why that particular aspect of intimacy is important to them, what changes they desire, and what you can do to help intimacy grow. In areas where you are both satisfied, congratulate each other. Most successful relationships have a few (but certainly not all) core areas of intimacy that help keep the relationship strong. (Note: some items adapted from Schaefer, M., & Olson, D. (1981). Assessment of intimacy: The PAIR inventory. *Journal of Marital & Family Therapy, 7,* 47–60.)

Aesthetic Intimacy	Sharing experiences of beauty—music, nature, art, theater, dance, etc.
Communication Intimacy	Connecting through talking. Keeping communication channels open. Listening to and valuing your partner's ideas. Being loving, compassionate, respectful, giving, truthful, and open in your communication.
Conflict Intimacy	Facing and struggling with differences together. Using resolution of conflict to grow closer together.
Creative Intimacy	Experiencing closeness through acts of creating together. Sharing expressions of love in creative ways.
Crisis Intimacy	Developing closeness in dealing with problems and pain. Standing together in tragedies. Responding together in a united way to pressures of life such as working through problems, raising a family, illness, aging, job loss, etc.
Emotional Intimacy	Feeling connected at an emotional level. Being in tune with each other's emotions; being able to share significant meanings and feelings with each other, including negative feelings.
Financial Intimacy	Working together to balance differing attitudes about money. Developing a unified plan for budgeting, spending, and saving. Having shared financial goals.
Forgiveness Intimacy	Apologizing to each other. Asking for forgiveness. Asking your partner, "What can I do to be a better husband/wife?"
Friendship Intimacy	Feeling a close connection and regard for one another as friends.
Humor Intimacy	Sharing through laughing together. Having jokes between the two of you that only you share. Making each other laugh. Enjoying the funny side of life.
Intellectual Intimacy	Experiencing closeness through sharing ideas. Feeling mutual respect for each other's intellectual capacities and viewpoints. Sharing mind-stretching experiences. Reading, discussing, studying together.

(Continued)

Aesthetic Intimacy	Sharing experiences of beauty—music, nature, art, theater, dance, etc.
Parenting Intimacy	Sharing the responsibilities of raising children, including providing for their physical, emotional, and spiritual needs. Includes working together in teaching and disciplining them as well as loving them and worrying about their welfare.
Physical Intimacy	Closeness and sharing through physical touch. Experiencing your physical relationship (including sexual intimacy) with joy, fun, and a sense of becoming one. Being open and honest with each other in terms of desires and responses.
Recreational Intimacy	Experiencing closeness and connection through fun and play. Helping each other rejuvenate through stress-relieving and enjoyable recreation together.
Service Intimacy	Sharing in acts of service together. Growing closer as a couple as you experience the joy that comes from giving to others.
Spiritual Intimacy	Discovering and sharing values, religious views, spiritual feelings, meaning in life, etc.
Work Intimacy	Experiencing closeness through sharing common tasks, such as maintaining a house and yard, raising a family, earning a living, participating in community affairs, etc.
_____ Intimacy	Additional areas of intimacy in your relationship.

31

INTIMACY AND SHARING HURTS

Luciano L'Abate

Purpose: To deepen levels of intimacy through sharing hurts

Introduction

Hurt feelings are a common part of intimate relationships. If they are not expressed and shared with one's partner, they linger within us and produce a number of dysfunctional behaviors at multiple levels in our lives. Intimacy is also an essential part of committed relationships. A number of definitions of intimacy may be found in the family science and marriage and family therapy literature. The author's definition is that intimacy is behaviorally defined as sharing joys, hurts, and fears of hurts (L'Abate, 2011). In intimate relationships, there are three paradoxes inherent in relationships:

- Paradox #1: Vulnerability. We are hurt by and hurt those we love the most because we allow ourselves to be vulnerable due to the intimate nature of the relationship.
- Paradox #2: Neediness. We have a need for connection, and partners must meet the emotional needs of each other in the couple relationship and as individuals. However, in order to be emotionally close, we must also be separate as individuals.
- Paradox #3: Fallibility. We are all fallible human beings. We make mistakes and hurt one another. When we hurt another, we must be able to provide or ask for support, comfort, and forgiveness in order to move past the hurts.

Hurt is therefore an inevitable part of being in an intimate relationship. We consciously or unconsciously hurt the ones we love and are hurt by them. The fact that we experience hurt in intimate relationships is to be expected. What matters is how we deal with the hurt feelings and the ratio of hurt feelings to joys. When hurt feelings outweigh joys, the couple will experience dissatisfaction and dysfunction. On the other hand, when joys outweigh hurts, the couple will be able to experience couple satisfaction and feel intimate with each other. The feeling of hurt may be conscious or unconscious. Hurt feelings may be unspoken, avoided, repressed, or suppressed, and couples presenting for therapy are usually having difficulty sharing their joys and hurts.

Purpose of Sharing Hurts

There is a reciprocal link between intimacy and hurt. Intimacy involves a number of factors, but one of the most important is being able to share hurt feelings. Intimacy involves vulnerability, neediness, and fallibility. These are all part of being ourselves in a close relationship without throwing up walls, presenting a facade, or trying to be exactly what the other person wants. Presenting an inauthentic self is a frequently observed phenomenon among couples seeking therapy. Because partners are not being real with each other, many are not able to experience the full depth of intimacy. The fundamental purpose of this technique is to help couples experience a deeper level of intimacy. Some couples are so fearful and socialized not to discuss hurt that they will substitute other feelings that lead to significant couple conflict, such as anger, rage, criticism, contempt, rejection, and so on. However, when one partner is able to share the hurts they have experienced, and the other provides validation through non-defensive and non-judgmental expressions of empathy, partners will experience increased emotional closeness and connection.

Description and Implementation

There are two ways to share hurts with an intimate partner (L'Abate, 2013). One involves doing a written homework assignment, and the other is done face-to-face in the session. If the therapist chooses to have the couple do the assignment at home through writing, the following instructions are given. If they choose to do it at home in writing first, they then discuss it in the session:

1. Recall a specific painful or hurtful experience that happened between the two of you and how that experience changed how you felt before and after the experience.
2. Write a letter to your partner or have a meeting where you recall a specific event in which your partner felt wounded by you and reassure them that it is important for them to understand that you understand their feelings and you are hurting because you hurt them.

Ask the hurt partner to discuss their hurt and validate it with empathy in the session, whether they started it in writing or in the session.

The second and preferred method is to ask the couple to share their hurt feelings in the session so that the therapist can help the couple process them more fully. The therapist asks the couple to prepare for this experience by facing each other, holding hands and keeping their eyes open or closed (whichever is most comfortable for them). The therapist begins with one partner:

> *This exercise may be hard for you to do, and it will take some time to fully explore all your feelings. I want you to try to get in touch with your feeling of hurt in the relationship (pause). As soon as you have identified an important hurt feeling, let your partner know that you have found a hurt feeling and would like to express it. Start by saying, "I feel hurt because . . ." or "I am hurting because . . ."*

To the other partner, the therapist says, "Please listen to and validate the hurt feeling with empathy and without judgment or defensiveness."

The therapist then helps the couple explore, validate, and resolve the hurt feelings. If they cannot find any hurt feelings, the therapist asks if they are experiencing other feelings and explores those to see if they are covering up hurt feelings.

Contraindications and Safety Procedures

The following rules are used in conducting this exercise: 1) do not proceed until the therapist has a strong bond with the couple and has performed an assessment of the couple; and 2) possible negative consequences of therapy should be discussed and included in an Informed Consent Form administered from the very outset of the therapeutic contract. All parties need to sign the Informed Consent Form prior to proceeding.

Case Example

Josh and Marie had been cohabitating for five years in a volatile relationship. In spite of professing love for each other, they had multiple separations. Marie felt that Josh had a good heart and loved her, but he didn't "know" her. She would try to explain how she felt about various things, and Josh did not know how to validate her feelings and at times looked distracted and disinterested. He appeared to have trouble tracking what she was saying, which meant he was unable to follow her feelings. Over the years, Marie had grown frustrated and angry that he did not appear to care about how she felt, although he provided her with whatever material things she wanted. On entering therapy, Marie was considering leaving the relationship. She had grown so angry and frustrated that whenever they had a fight or she did not feel he was being emotionally attentive, she would become reactive and threaten to leave. Sometimes she would get in her car and just drive around for hours wondering what to do. When Josh was told she was going to leave, he would immediately tell her she was destroying his life, he would never find anyone else, and he would always be alone. He would then shut down, become depressed, and frequently get in bed and not deal with anything. Leading up to the threat to leave, Marie would berate Josh severely by calling him names and telling him about what a cruel person he was. Neither party could express or validate the hurt experienced in the other.

In order to help the couple heal emotional wounds in the relationship and open the door for greater intimacy, the therapist worked with them through a series of exercises in which they identified and shared feelings of hurt with each other. The therapist began by asking Marie to think about one time in their relationship in which she experienced the feeling of hurt. She quickly indicated that she thought of one, and the therapist directed her to share this with Josh. However, before having her begin, the therapist asked Josh to pay attention to the hurt that Marie would express, understand her feeling, and validate the emotion by expressing empathy. Josh had a difficult time with this. The therapist then asked Marie to restate her feeling of hurt, but to break it up into smaller statements so that Josh could attend to each one and respond with empathy. With some coaching, Josh was able to hear and validate her feelings. Following this, the therapist had them switch roles and repeat the exercise. Expressing the hurt they felt opened the door to understanding their difficulties in being able to express this feeling. They could then begin to resolve the barriers to expressing feelings in general, including hurt.

References

L'Abate, L. (2011). *Hurt feelings: Theory, research, and applications in intimate relationships*. New York: Cambridge University Press.

L'Abate, L. (2013). *Research on pre-para-post-therapeutic activities in mental health*. New York: Nova Pub.

32

DEEPENING ATTACHMENT EMOTION IN EMOTIONALLY FOCUSED COUPLE THERAPY (EFT)

Sue Johnson and Lorrie Brubacher

Purpose: To help partners access and express underlying attachment fears and needs

Introduction

The practice of deepening attachment emotion is based on research regarding the nature of couple distress and satisfaction. This research shows that it is the quality of emotional engagement and the expression of clear emotional messages that shifts negative interaction patterns and shapes secure bonding interactions (Johnson, 2004). Nine research studies (Greenman & Johnson, 2012) have found that deepening emotional engagement—especially exploring attachment fears and longings—predicts positive outcome in emotionally focused couple therapy (EFT). Deepening emotional engagement is typical of therapeutic change events, called *softenings*, and has been found to be associated with a positive outcome and reductions in anxious attachment in EFT.

An "emotionally focused" approach (EFT) is based on the powerful role that emotion plays in intimate relationships. The word "emotion" is based on the Latin word *emovere*, "to move," and emotion is recognized for priming key responses (Ekman, 2003) in the dance between partners. Attachment theory (Mikulincer & Shaver, 2008) describes how partners in insecure attachment bonds dismiss or exaggerate emotional cues in themselves and others, deny and fragment emotional experience, and send unclear messages in their best attempts to deal with separation distress and their underlying sense of rejection and abandonment by their partners.

Purpose of Deepening Attachment Emotion

The purpose of deepening attachment emotion is to help partners access, explore, and express their underlying attachment fears and needs in order to send clear messages that will pull their partner closer and foster security. Frequently partners are unaware of the underlying emotions and attachment fears that drive their negative cycles of demand and distance (Johnson, 2013). An angry, critical partner, demanding more attention, at first denies her softer underlying feelings of loneliness and fears of being unloved or even unlovable. A seemingly nonchalant, withdrawn partner is often barely aware of the aching sense of fear that he is failing to measure up in his lover's eyes. After helping partners to access these underlying attachment vulnerabilities, the EFT therapist deepens the present moment of experiencing that emotion, making it more specific, felt, and concrete, in order to help each partner send new signals to the other that evoke new and more compassionate, empathic responses (Johnson et al., 2005).

Description and Implementation

The transformative change events that restructure the attachment bond are created through three D's: "deepening, distilling, and disclosing" primary attachment emotions. "Deepening" emotion means helping a client to get an alive, vivid, concrete, felt sense of this emotion. To deepen attachment emotion, the therapist focuses on the *underlying* emotions that are the gateway to the core attachment needs. Primary interventions used to deepen emotion are reflections and evocative questions that focus in on the cue, the bodily arousal, the perceptions or attachment meanings, and the action tendency of the emotion. Empathic conjectures or hunches of the client's emotional experience are also offered, although an EFT therapist will use reflection, validation, and evocative responding before making a conjecture. It is collaborative and respectful to engage clients in an evocative exploration of their own experience before offering conjectures or empathic interpretations. "Distilling" the emotion means helping the client to specifically recognize and own this as his or her felt experience in the negative cycle. After the emotional experience has become deepened and distilled, the therapist will help the partner to "disclose" this experience to the partner, as in, "So, can you tell her, 'I do shut down and go away (action tendency) when I see your look of disappointment (cue). I just can't bear this dreadful pain (primary emotion) that I am failing to be the husband you need me to be' (attachment meaning)." After directing the disclosing partner to share this message, the therapist checks first what it was like to share this emotional experience and then checks with the listening partner what their in-the-moment experience was in receiving the disclosure. The emotions that emerge from each partner are then focused on (reflected and heightened) to increase engagement within and between partners.

An acronym that guides EFT therapists in this process of focusing and deepening emotion is RISSSC: Repeat, use Images, Simple, Soft, Slow voice, and the Clients' words.

R: The therapist intentionally REPEATS key words and phrases for emphasis. "Emotional handles" are poignant emotion-laden words and phrases such as "crushed" or "feeling disregarded." Repeating an emotional handle deepens the experience: "Crushed. You feel crushed when she says, 'You are perfect is so many ways, but couldn't you just be more romantic?'" Next, the therapist *distills* the deepened emotion in the context of the cycle: "Each time she asks for one more thing, you feel crushed, and it sounds to you that you can just never measure up to what she wants."

I: The therapist uses IMAGES or word pictures that evoke emotions more than abstract labels tend to do. "There is this mountain that you feel you've got to climb to be enough for her. And you want so much to climb this mountain—and you get half way up and you stop." The client responds: "I do—I get half way up and I stop—so certain that I can't make it to the top—afraid that I can never get her approval, so I freeze and stop climbing."

S: The therapist frames responses to clients in SIMPLE and succinct phrases.

S: The therapist speaks in a SLOW pace to deepen the clients' emotional experiencing.

S: The therapist uses a SOFT, low, soothing tone of voice to create safety and encourage the client.

C: The therapist orders, distills, and uses the CLIENTS' words and phrases in a supportive and validating way.

While newly deepened and distilled primary emotion is fully felt and alive in the moment, the therapist helps a partner to share the emotion with the spouse. These emotions are the gateway into core attachment needs, such as the longing for reassurance that the partner is dependably responsive or "there for" another. Deepened emotion disclosed to the partner magnifies the depth of the experience and creates new contact between partners. The expression of fear and vulnerability changes the way a partner is perceived (as in, "He is not cold; he is just scared like me"). It also sends a clear, simple message of primary attachment emotion, which pulls the partner into offering a positive response, initiating a new positive cycle of reaching and responding.

Contraindications

Deepening attachment emotion is contraindicated when a couple is insufficiently de-escalated and thus lacks a safe base to explore and deepen their underlying vulnerable emotional experiences. Negative cycles of pursue-attack/defend-withdraw erupt when partners feel emotionally unsafe. Inviting one partner to deepen their emotional experience before the cycle has de-escalated is likely to trigger the partner and lead to further cycle escalation. Risks must be titrated and emotional balance fostered, so it is only after partners have some awareness of how their negative reactive behaviors trigger and are triggered by the hidden and unexpressed attachment fears that they are ready to deepen their engagement with these emotions and listen to their partner's deepened experience.

Case Example

Kyle and Tara had a familiar pattern of pursue-attack/defend-withdraw. The more she would push him to help around the house, the more he would defend himself and sullenly retreat to his computer, leaving all the tasks he'd promised to do unfinished, after which she would put up a solid wall of anger, and they'd not talk for days. This rapid-fire cycle began to soften as they recognized how they unwittingly triggered a negative cycle, and both deepened their awareness of the more vulnerable emotional music playing in the background. In this case example, the therapist deepens Kyle's engagement with the attachment fears underlying his defensive, withdrawn position.

TARA: When I get angry and start accusing or we start fighting and stuff like that, it's because, yeah, I'm trying to put up walls—to be angry instead of being sad or lonely.

THERAPIST: You put up a wall of anger to protect yourself from feeling sad and missing Kyle (*reflecting, tracking the cyclical pattern, linked to her underlying sadness and loneliness*).

KYLE: And sometimes when she puts up that wall of anger, it triggers my defenses too. And I am trying to be much, much more aware of that and not get so defensive. (*He is aware of how her step in the protective dance triggers his typical step.*)

THERAPIST: You do get scared and know you fire back at her (*reflecting the link between his primary fear and his defensive tendency of firing back*).

K: When we are really upset at each other, she sometimes gets angry with me and that makes me kind of fearful, because it's so powerful. That makes me kind of get scared and defensive, and that makes me argue back.

THERAPIST: So, I wonder if we could just hear a little more about that fear. What is it like on the inside for you when you have this powerful, beautiful person that is obviously so important to you, coming out loud and angry? This is powerful for you—inside what happens? (*evoking, heightening, by replaying the image of the trigger for him in the cycle—to bring his fear alive*).

K: It brings out a lot of insecurity. That I'm not good enough for her. I'm not meeting her needs. It makes me feel like I'm screwing up the relationship. (*The attachment meanings and his negative view of Self emerge.*)

THERAPIST: So, it is really scary (*deepening the fear*). You're saying when you hear Tara angry (*reflecting the trigger for the fear*) that you get very, very scared on the inside, like, "Oh no I could lose her, I'm not good enough. Oh, no I could possibly not meet her needs." And, you get scared you could lose her. What does it feel like in your body? *(deepening fear by replaying the cue and his attachment meanings, and evoking his bodily felt sense of this fear).*

K: I get really tense and anxious.

THERAPIST: Like kind of in your heart or in your gut? *(evoking a more concrete bodily felt sense of this fear).*

K: More like right down in this area.

THERAPIST: Yeah, right in your gut you feel a real tightness. Do you feel any of that now as you are describing it? *(checking if the fear is alive in the moment; if it is alive, therapist will choreograph an enactment).*

K: Um, it's really tense. I'm not able to find words to describe it. Just a real tension, I guess.

THERAPIST: Just this big tense place of, "Oh no, I could lose you!" *(heightening with proxy voice conjecture/reflecting what he has implied earlier).* That is a very scary place. What would it be like to tell her more about how very scary this really is? To think that, "If I can't be good enough for you, I'm so afraid I could lose you. I get so tense inside?" *(heightening, preparing for an enactment by anticipating sharing this with her).*

K: It makes me really nervous when we are arguing that you are going to decide that this is the end of it and you're going to decide that you don't want to be in this relationship anymore.
(*Therapist then invites Kyle to share with Tara this clearly distilled primary attachment fear, and following his disclosure, processes this with him.*) So, what is it like as you are telling her this?

K: I feel like a bit of relief being able to talk to you about this. I don't think I've ever told you how scared I get when we are arguing or when you are upset. It's a relief to let you know inside I get scared of losing you *(owning his primary emotion).*
When the therapist evokes Tara's experience in hearing from Kyle, Tara is clearly moved and expresses her shock and love for Kyle.

Deepening the present-moment experiencing of Kyle's attachment fear made it possible for him to disclose it clearly to Tara, and together they began to create a new positive cycle of reaching and responding that will pull them close and reinforce their bond.

Training resources on the technique of deepening attachment emotion can be found at www.iceeft.com.

References

Ekman, P. (2003/2007). *Emotions revealed: Recognizing faces and feelings to improve communication and emotional life.* New York: St. Martin's Griffin.

Greenman, P. S., & Johnson, S. M. (2012). Process research on emotionally focused therapy (EFT) for couples: Linking theory to practice. *Family Process.* doi: 10.1111/famp.12015

Johnson, S. M. (2004). *Creating connection: The practice of emotionally focused couple therapy* (2nd ed.). New York: Brunner/Routledge.

Johnson, S. M. (2013). *Love sense: The revolutionary new science of romantic relationships.* New York: Little, Brown.

Johnson, S. M., Bradley, B., Furrow, J., Lee, A., Palmer, G., Tilley, D., & Woolley, S. (2005). *Becoming an emotionally focused therapist: The workbook.* New York: Brunner/Routledge.

Mikulincer, M., & Shaver, P. R. (2008). Adult attachment and affect regulation. In J. Cassidy & P. Shaver (Eds.), *Handbook of attachment: Theory, research and clinical applications* (2nd ed., pp. 503–531). New York: Guilford Press.

33

ASKING ABOUT THE ABSENT BUT IMPLICIT IN NARRATIVE THERAPY

Jill Freedman and Gene Combs

Purpose: To help members of a couple speak of what they treasure

Introduction

People make meaning and develop stories from a limited number of life and relationship experiences. Every couple has other experiences, outside of the problematic stories that bring them to therapy, that could offer different meanings and could come to be counted among the important stories of their lives. We can help bring these alternative stories alive in the therapy room by asking about the absent but implicit.

The practice of asking about the absent but implicit was first developed by Michael White (2000, 2003). It is based on the idea that we make meaning of an experience through contrasting it with other experiences, so that in order to distinguish something as a problem, we must be comparing it to some preferred experience (Carey, Walther, & Russell, 2009; Freedman, 2012; White, 2000, 2003). Through what White (2003) has called "double listening," we can hear hints or openings to inquire about what the implied contrasting experience might be. These "implicit" contrasting experiences usually have to do with what people treasure or give value to. When we ask questions about the absent but implicit, we lay the groundwork for meaningful conversation about what the members of the couple care about.

Purpose of Asking About the Absent but Implicit

When we invite the members of a couple to name the implicit or preferred experience they are contrasting the problem with, we offer a new ground for conversation and for meaning-making. A member of a couple who expects to endure blame and conflict in a therapy conversation instead witnesses expressions of what has been important in their relationship or what their partner longs for. The tone of therapy can change from one of tension and dissension to one of enthusiasm and wonder.

Description and Implementation

Asking about the absent but implicit is a collaborative process of puzzling about what members of a couple value that is not being enacted in the relationship. We don't discover the absent but implicit through hypothesizing or suggesting the opposite of what couples find problematic. Instead, we puzzle with them about what is absent in their current experience, but implicit in their description of the problem.

Michael White (2000, p. 38) has suggested the following questions:

- You said that you could no longer continue on. Would it be okay if I asked some questions about your sense of what you had been continuing on with up to this point? Or perhaps about what it was that you had been depending on to see you through up to now?
- You said that you had given up. Could I ask some questions about what it is you are giving up on? Or perhaps about what it is that you are getting separated from, or losing touch with, that had been important to you?
- You said that you can't see a future anymore. Would it be okay for me to ask you what possibilities you had seen for your future? And how, at least to a point, this has been sustaining your life up to this time? Or perhaps about what it was that had made it possible for you, until recently, to keep this future in sight?

Additionally, we have found the following questions to be particularly helpful in beginning this inquiry (Freedman, 2012):

- I'm getting the impression, as you speak of this, that there is something you miss. Is that right? Can you put that into words?
- In saying "no" to this, are you opening the possibility of saying "yes" to something else?
- If this problem is a protest against something, what would you say that something is?
- Has something important been violated? Can you put what has been violated into words?
- Could we say that because you named this as problematic, it means that you don't go along with it? In not going along with it, are you standing for something else?

- Why is it important that you speak of this in front of your partner?
- What does this say about what you treasure?

It is important that the questions we ask are responsive to what the couple brings to therapy. The listed questions are meant to be inspirational rather than prescriptive. We often must persist with a line of questions to reach the absent but implicit.

Once a member of the couple names something that is absent but implicit, we ask questions to experientially engage him or her in developing a rich story that illustrates how it is important. We might ask about events in the history of the couple that fit with this way of being, how this value came to be important, the hopes for the future that fit with this purpose, and so on.

Although this new tone and new subject for conversation is often transformative, sometimes between therapy conversations, people find themselves pulled back into those things that characterize the problems. We think that this is because problematic stories are situated in cultural norms or discourses to which members of a couple compare themselves, their relationships, or their partners. So, although we may be able to enter a different realm of conversation in the therapy room, the operations of these discourses are still at play in the wider world.

However, once we have begun to engage in conversations about what people treasure and prefer, when they are pulled back into problems, we can work to unpack them so that couples have a choice about how to relate to them. The unpacking may be easier at this point in the therapy because the discourses are experience-near; that is, since the couple has felt their pull back into problems, discourses are easier to identify and talk about.

Contraindications

If it is important to the couple or one member of the couple that the problem be more fully talked about and understood before proceeding, we honor that wish. Since we can easily move from working with the absent but implicit into other practices, and since no harm will result from asking a few questions to explore it, there are no serious contraindications.

Case Example

Murray and Belinda consulted me (JF) because of growing distance and dissatisfaction with their relationship. They were considering divorce, but with three young children they decided to at least try therapy. For Belinda, the problem began as she was undergoing treatment for breast cancer. Initially Murray was supportive and took on most of the responsibility for the care of the kids, but later he seemed less and less available for this, and Belinda was left with the bulk of responsibility, even though she was working full time and going through chemotherapy.

When Belinda learned that Murray was using opiates that had been prescribed for back pain as a way of dealing with his fear of her death, she felt deserted. She said Murray had abandoned her at a time she most needed support and the children needed help. Murray, who felt shame about the drug use, also felt anger at Belinda's lack of understanding and support.

At the point they came to therapy, the distrust and disconnection seemed almost insurmountable. When, in order to discover what was absent but implicit, I asked, "What is it that you are disconnected from?" at first they said "from each other." With further thought, Belinda answered, "I think I had a fairytale vision of Murray as strong." I began to explore Belinda's vision of Murray. I asked about experiences that illustrated his strength and what Murray's actions in these memories contributed to Belinda and to the relationship. Murray witnessed these stories and answered similar questions about the understanding he identified as being important.

In a later conversation, I wondered what these visions of each other supported about what they wanted in a relationship. They named "equality and connection" as what they had hoped for. This vision of "equality and connection" was absent but implicit in their finding distance and dissatisfaction so problematic. Further questioning allowed them to relive stories of equality and connection in their relationship.

Once Murray learned that Belinda wanted equality and connection, he apologized for not being fully available during her treatment and tried to live up to his part of a more equal relationship. Once Belinda believed that Murray also wanted equality and connection, she understood that he, too, felt disappointment about his drug use. They began to talk more about struggles and hopes, and less about tasks and shortcomings. There was some fear and distrust along the way, but Belinda and Murray were able to become more connected and to fashion a relationship they both felt good about and could trust.

References

Carey, M., Walther, S., & Russell, S. (2009). The absent but implicit: A map to support therapeutic enquiry. *Family Process*, *48*(3), 319–331.

Freedman, J. (2012). Explorations of the absent but implicit. *The International Journal of Narrative Therapy and Community Work, 4*, 1–10.

White, M. (2000). Re-engaging with history: The absent but implicit. In M. White (Ed.), *Reflections on narrative practice: Essays & interviews* (Chapter 3, pp. 35–58). Adelaide: Dulwich Centre Publications.

White, M. (2003). Narrative practice and community assignments. *International Journal of Narrative Therapy and Community Work, 2*, 17–56.

34

WHAT'S BETTER?

Focusing on Positives

Sara Smock Jordan

Purpose: To co-construct solutions with couples by using solution focused brief therapy (SFBT) language

Description and Implementation of the "What's Better?" Technique

Berg and Reuss (1997) state that the most important things to do in a follow-up solution focused brief therapy (SFBT) session are:

1. Elicit reports of change (e.g., what's better?)
2. Amplify the change (e.g., how did you do that?)
3. Reinforce the change (e.g., so what difference does that make?)
4. Start over (e.g., what else is better?)

The most common way to elicit reports of change at the beginning of a follow-up SFBT session is to ask a version of "What's better?" (de Shazer, Berg, Lipchik, Nunnaly, Molnar, Gingerich, & Weiner-Davis, 1986, de Shazer, Dolan, Korman, McCollum, Trepper, & Berg, 2007). One might ask, "So what has been better since the last time we met?"; "How are things going better for you?"; "What's been better over the course of the last week?" or "So, what is better, even a little bit, since last time we meet?" Using a version of the "What's better?" question is the recommended way to begin a solution-building session. Novice SFBT therapists sometimes will ask, "So has there been anything better this week?"; however, this is advised against (Berg, 1994) because it implies, or presupposes, the therapist's doubt of client improvement. Presuppositions are assumptions that the questioner holds (McGee, Del Vento, & Bavelas, 2005). Since presuppositions are embedded within all questions, SFBT therapists must be extremely careful to craft questions that contain solution-focused assumptions (Bavelas, Smock Jordan, Korman, & De Jong, 2014). When following up with clients, asking "What's been better?" is very useful because it infers that things have gotten better, a key assumption of SFBT.

So, what happens when one or both partners answer the question by saying that nothing has improved or things are worse? One option is to go day-by-day through each partner's week to help them identify any small change that has occurred (Berg, 1994). A therapist might say, "So, you were here last Monday; was Tuesday any better than last Monday afternoon? Even just a little bit better?" A SFBT therapist can go day-by-day to help the client find small, positive change. If one partner is persistent about things staying the same or getting worse, the therapist can ask, "So how did you keep things from getting worse (or much worse)?" The presupposition in this question is that things could have been worse (but weren't), and the client did something to prevent things from getting worse.

In couples work, the challenge can be that each partner holds a slightly different perspective about what is better (or worse). Co-construction of a couple's solution in SFBT begins with the therapist's response to each partner's answers, not the answers themselves. For example, when asking "What's better?", it does not matter how each partner responds (better, the same, or worse) but where the therapist takes the conversation next. If one partner says, "Things are much better" and the other reports that things have gotten worse, the therapist can ask one partner about what's better and the other partner about how they were able to keep things from being worse. The important thing to remember in asking couples "What's better?" is how the therapist responds to their answers. Note: More than one thing could be better, so keep asking "What else has been better?" until all positive changes have been mentioned.

Next, it is important to follow with gathering details about how they *did it* (i.e., made things better) or how they managed to keep things from getting worse. The role of the therapist at this point is to amplify the reported positive change (Berg, 1994). A typical SFBT question to ask at this point would be, "Wow, so how did you do that?" or "That must have taken some hard work; how did you pull that off?" Amplifying change in couples work can also be done by asking relationship questions. For example, "So what did your husband do to make it easier for you to show affection this week?" or "Tracy, what did Jamie do this week that made it easier for you to want to spend time with her?" Once a relationship question is asked of one partner, it is important to check with the other partner by saying something like "Do you agree with that?" If the latter partner does not agree, you can ask them, "What did you do to make it easier, even just a bit easier, for your wife to listen more closely this week?" Co-constructing solutions with couples involves allowing both partners to be heard, having them define their preferred future, and marking progress toward their goals.

Once the change has been amplified, including attempts to keep the problem from getting worse, it is important to ask each partner what difference that change has made. "So Reese, what difference did spending more time with your wife make?" or "Taylor, what difference did it make for you this week that you were able to keep things from getting worse?" Of course, adding a relational component to difference questions is also helpful with couples. For example, "Alex, what difference did Raine's attention to details make for you this week?" or "When Casey came home from work early on Tuesday, what difference did that make for you?" Once the initial difference questions are asked, the therapist can follow with "What else made a difference?" until the couple can't think of additional differences.

After asking the couple "What's better?", amplifying their answers, and asking relational and difference questions, the next step is scaling their progress over the past week and asking the couple a version of, "So, what needs to happen next to continue this positive change?" Scaling and asking "What's next?" can continue throughout the rest of the session until the therapist takes a break, gives compliments, and assigns homework.

Case Example

In the first session with Tyler (the therapist), Molly and Cameron shared that they were seeking therapy for "low relationship satisfaction." At the end of the first session, the couple agreed to set up a follow-up appointment. Tyler begins the second session by asking them, "What's been better during the past week since our first meeting?' Molly and Cameron both report that things have stayed the same over the past week since their last session. Tyler asks, "So, tell me about which days last week were better, even if they were only a bit better?" Cameron attests to feeling a bit more connected to Molly over dinner last Friday night. When asked by Tyler, Molly confirms that she enjoyed their date night. Tyler uses the opportunity to ask the couple one at a time, "So what did you do last Friday night that made it better?" Molly replied by saying that they never go on a date night, so Cameron's suggestion of going out for dinner made a difference. Tyler followed with, "So Cameron, what did Molly do last week that made it easier for you to suggest having a date night?" Cameron described a situation on Thursday night where Molly sat on the couch with him, which she rarely did, and that made a difference for him. Tyler asked Molly, "What did Cameron do to make it easier to sit next to him?" and Molly replied by saying that she didn't know and didn't think much of sitting next to him on the couch. Instead of getting stumped by this, Tyler said to Molly, "So this was different for you to sit by him on the couch?" and Molly confirmed. Tyler summarized by saying, "So sitting together on the couch was different for you, Molly, and made a difference for Cameron—so much of a difference that Cameron suggested going out for dinner on Friday, which was a positive experience for both of you." Tyler then asked what would need to happen to continue the connectedness and enjoyment of each other. The couple responded with several suggestions. Tyler had them scale how confident they were that these suggestions could actually happen in the next few weeks.

References

Bavelas, J. B., Smock Jordan, S., Korman, H., & De Jong, P. (May/June, 2014). Is solution-focused brief therapy different? *Family Therapy Magazine, 13*(3), 19–23.

Berg, I. K. (1994). *Family based services: A solution-based approach*. New York: Norton.

Berg, I. K., & Reuss, N. (1997). *Solutions step by step: A substance abuse treatment manual*. New York: Norton.

de Shazer, S., Berg, I. K., Lipchik, E., Nunnaly, E., Molnar, A., Gingerich, W., & Weiner-Davis, M. (1986). Brief therapy: Focused solution development. *Family Process, 25,* 207–221.

de Shazer, S., Dolan, Y. M., Korman, H., McCollum, E. E., Trepper, T., & Berg, I. K. (2007). *More than miracles: The state of the art of solution-focused brief therapy*. Binghamton, NY: Haworth Press.

McGee, D. R., DelVento, A., & Bavelas, J. B. (2005). An interactional model of questions as therapeutic interventions. *Journal of Marital & Family Therapy, 31,* 371–384.

35

SCALING QUESTIONS WITH COUPLES

Sara Smock Jordan

Purpose: To measure goal progression with couples through the use of solution focused brief therapy (SFBT) scaling questions

Introduction

Beginning clinicians often use scaling with clients because it is an easy way to track progress in treatment. There are three main distinguishing characteristics in solution focused brief therapy (SFBT) scaling questions. First, in therapy models that use scaling questions, each number on the scale has a distinct value and/or meaning. A 5 on a scale of 1 to 10 would represent being in the middle of the scale. The therapist places their value of a 5 onto the client by saying "Your fighting is moderate" or "So you are half way to your goal." Scaling in SFBT is much different. The meaning of the numbers used in scaling are arbitrary (de Shazer, 1994). In SFBT scaling, the clients give their own meaning to their number. SFBT therapists might respond to the client's report of a 5 by saying, "So what does a 5 look like for you?" or "So what lets you know you are at a 5?"

Another main distinction of SFBT scaling is the range, and defining the lower and upper end of that range. Some approaches use a 1 to 100 or a 1 to 10 scale, and may or may not define what a 1 or a 10 represents. A non-SFBT therapist might ask, "If we were going to put this problem on your hierarchy, where would it rank?" A response of 70 or 80 might be given in which the therapist might respond by saying, "Oh, it is up there." SFBT scaling uses either 1 to 10 or 0 to 10 as its range and clearly defines the 1 or 0 and the 10 by asking, "So, on a scale from 1 to 10 where 10 is exactly where you want to be and 1 is furthest from that, where would you say you are today?" The final major difference in SFBT scaling lies in 10 always being the client's desired goal. For example, "So on a scale from 1 to 10 where 10 is the most confident you can be and 1 is furthest from that, where would you say you are today?" Other approaches often indicate the highest number on a scale to represent the absolute worst place a client could rate him/herself, such as, "How bad is the fighting on a scale from 1 to 100?" Overall, SFBT scaling questions use clearly defined scales from 1 or 0 to 10, where 10 represents the client's goal, and the meaning of the client's rating is self-defined.

Purpose of Scaling Questions With Couples

Applying interventions to couples therapy is often challenging, especially for novice clinicians. The purpose of SFBT scaling questions, especially with couples, is to measure the client's progression toward their goal. By examining the work of SFBT experts, therapists can better understand the nuances of SFBT scaling questions.

Description and Implementation

Closely examining SFBT dialogue and describing the therapist's moment-by-moment choices is a helpful way to better understand how to use scaling questions with couples. The following excerpt, from the video *Irreconcilable Differences* (W.W. Norton & Company, 2009), provides an excellent example of a SFBT scaling question by Insoo Kim Berg. Detailed excerpts are given to observe the content of their dialogue as well as reflections on that content.

INSOO: Okay, let me ask you another strange question. I have lots of these strange questions. [Smiles] Okay? Let's say, on a sort of a scale of 1 to 10 . . . Let's say 10 stands for, that you will do just about anything humanly possible to make this marriage work. That stands for 10. Okay, and 1 stands for [puph sound and doing a hand gesture that suggests giving up], you're ready to sort of throw in the towel and you're ready to walk away from this. Where would each of you say you're at on a scale of 1 to 10?

Insoo starts out and mentions that she wants to ask a strange question. This statement is used as a preface for a lot of SFBT questions. When working with couples, there tends to be tension at times, so opening with a clause is often helpful. Next, Insoo defines what each end of the scale stands for. Depending on the type of scaling question you ask a couple, 1 and 10 will stand for different things. Given this couple's current relationship, it was fitting for Insoo to ask about their level of commitment. Let's now look at how each partner answered her question:

LESLIE: [Looks at husband and then looks down; husband chuckles] Honestly?
INSOO: Honestly.

BILL: [Shakes his head] 7.

INSOO: 7, uh huh. How 'bout for you? [Looks at Leslie]

Notice that Insoo just repeats Bill's response and then asks for Leslie's answer.

LESLIE: Well, the past year or so I think I've been at a 10, quite frankly, but . . .

INSOO: Right.

LESLIE: The way I'm feeling now probably [pause] . . . let's put it this way [pause] . . .
      I've talked to a lawyer [looks at husband and nods]. I've talked to a lawyer. I'm
      probably, I'm just, yeah, inquiring about what my rights would be.

INSOO: Uh hmm.

LESLIE: I'm probably about a 5.

INSOO: About a 5.

Again, Insoo just repeats the client's response and continues to listen. She does not
ask any details about Leslie's consultation with an attorney. In SFBT, it is just as
important to note what the therapist is not doing with client responses. Insoo asks
another scaling question to the couple:

INSOO: Okay. Now, uhm, I have another sort of a set of numbers question
      here. Knowing how things are right now [gesturing with her hands]
      between the two, ah, between the two of you, let's say 10 stands for, you
      have every confidence that this marriage is going to survive [pause] . . .
      okay, 10 stands for that [pause], that this marriage has every chance of
      making it, and 1 stands for puh [hand gesture signifying that the marriage
      is over or being washed away], you know it's just the opposite of that,
      there's no chance this marriage is going to make it, where would you say
      things are at right now?

LESLIE: Well, if we worked at it, I could say it would be more than a 5.

INSOO: Really?

LESLIE: If . . . [is cut off by Insoo's next question]

INSOO: So you see a lot of potential in this?

Insoo sees an opportunity and jumps in with the question, "So you see a lot of
potential in this?" for the client. A few moments later, Insoo comes back to the
scaling question to get Bill's perspective.

BILL: I'm just tryin' ta . . .

INSOO: Yeah, what would you say [Bill sighs] the chance is of this marriage
      making it?

BILL: [Long pause, Bill exhales loudly and Leslie touches his arm] Huh, uhm
      [pause], I would really say an 8 [looks at Leslie].

INSOO: 8.

Again, Insoo just repeats the client's response but does not ask them to elaborate.

BILL: Because you know, uhm, I want this to work.
LESLIE: Hmm,
BILL: You know I'm willing to try to make it work.

Insoo then continues the dialogue by asking both Leslie and Bill what it would take to go up one point on the last scale. By looking at a few minutes of dialogue, including two scaling questions, one can see a pattern of inquiry and response from an SFBT expert.

Application and Self-Examination of SFBT Scaling Questions

In order to develop their proficiency at using SFBT scaling questions, therapists can compare their scaling questions with couples to Insoo's dialogue above. A helpful tool in examining the moment-by-moment therapeutic dialogue is a free software program called ELAN (can be downloaded at http://www.mpi.nl/tools/). This program allows for MPEG files to be played in micro-segments for moment-by-moment observations (e.g., Smock, 2010). First, find a segment of a couple's session that utilizes scaling questions. On a secure computer, download ELAN and open the scaling example. Next, type up a rough transcript of the dialogue to better recognize and track micro-interactions. Compare phrasing of an SFBT scaling question with the comparison clip. Note specific instances when the selected clip follows the standards of SFBT scaling. Using the detailed annotation of Insoo's questions and responses above as a guide, compare the scaling questions and answers from the selected clip. This comparison to an SFBT expert can be repeated with different SFBT couple sessions. Additional expert SFBT sessions can be purchased from www.sfbta.org.

References

de Shazer, S. (1994). *Words were originally magic*. New York: W. W. Norton.

Smock, S. A. (2010). Evidence-based supervision: Identifying successful moments of SFBT. In T. S. Nelson (Ed.), *Doing something different: Solution-focused brief therapy practices* (pp. 197–200). New York: Routledge.

W. W. Norton & Company, Berg, I. K., Brief Family Therapy Center, Psychotherapy.net, Alexander Street Press, & Counseling and Therapy in Video (2009). *Irreconcilable differences: A solution-focused approach to marital therapy* [S.l.] Alexandria, VA: Alexander Street Press.

36

SUPPORT TALK

Intervention for Enhancing Social Support Based on PREP (Prevention and Relationship Education Program)[1]

Lane L. Ritchie, Aleja M. Parsons, and Howard J. Markman

Purpose: To help couples strengthen the positive aspects of their relationship

Introduction

In addition to decreasing negative aspects of relationships (i.e., reducing harmful and unproductive conflict), the field of couples research has increasingly focused on the importance of also protecting, preserving, and enhancing positive aspects of relationships (i.e., strengthening constructive interactions, such as support and friendship, between partners; e.g., Cordova, 2009). In fact, studies have found that it takes several positives to outweigh the harmful effects of one negative (Markman, Stanley, & Blumberg, 2010). Thus, research-based clinical interventions promoting relationship health now include strategies for deepening positive connections in addition to strategies for reducing harmful conflict.

Especially as problems develop within a relationship, it is common for couples to focus on those problems and neglect to seek support from one another about external stressors outside the relationship. Often, partners want to be supportive of one another, but lack information about what type of support would be helpful to their partner (e.g., advice-giving, empathetic listening, physical touch). In fact, there is a common tendency for both men and women to provide support by giving advice; unfortunately, this often leads to frustration, as advice is not typically the preferred type of support one is hoping to receive (Markman, Stanley, & Blumberg, 2010). The Support Talk skill, described in this chapter, provides an opportunity for partners to share their needs and preferences, and to be able to provide effective support to each other, without giving advice. Rather than discussing problems within the relationship, the focus of Support Talk is to discuss problems that cause distress *outside* of the relationship. This technique is a valuable opportunity for partners to show that they care about one another and desire to grow closer together. Notarius & Markman (1993) describe such positive interactions as "deposits" that couples add to their relationship bank account that help to protect the relationship from emotional "bankruptcy."

Several evidence-based strategies for decreasing negative experiences in relationships have been developed and implemented, but interventions for increasing positives remain sparse and under-researched, with a few exceptions. The Prevention and Relationship Education Program (PREP; Markman, et al., 2010) is a skills-based relationship education curriculum designed to promote effective communication and healthy relationships. In addition to strategies for reducing negative conflict, PREP also contains interventions for increasing support in romantic relationships and activities for helping partners identify the types of support that are most important for each of them. Here we focus on emotional and physical support.

The Support Talk skill described here provides an opportunity for partners to support one another surrounding a topic outside of the relationship. Such support within couples is associated with increased closeness, resilience, and sustained relationship satisfaction over time for both partners (Halford, Markman, Kline, & Stanley, 2003).

Purpose of Support Talk

The purpose of Support Talk is to create a space for one partner to share a concern outside the relationship while the other partner listens. It allows partners to provide and receive support without disruption from other types of talk (e.g., talking about a conflict within the relationship). There is some evidence that simply perceiving support to be available is more important than the amount of support that is actually utilized (Dehle, Larsen, & Landers, 2001). Thus, just by checking in with one another and scheduling times for Support Talks, couples are likely to see positive results because they are reminded that their partners desire to be supportive.

Description and Implementation

The first step in Support Talk is making time to have a conversation. If a person knows their partner is upset about a topic outside of the relationship (e.g., a problem at work or with a friend) or is going through a difficult time (e.g., job loss, illness), they could make an effort to check in with her/him regularly. In so doing, the person ought to avoid making assumptions about how the partner may be feeling (e.g., "You've been upset lately"); instead, the person should speak from their own perspective (e.g., "It seems to me like work may be frustrating for you right now"). It also may be helpful to ask a partner how he/she is feeling (e.g., "Has work been frustrating for you this week?"). Partners may check in face-to-face or via telephone, email, text, or another method. When the partner is receptive to engaging in Support Talk, the partner in the supportive role should plan a time either immediately (e.g., "Do you have a few minutes to talk about this now?") or in the future (e.g., "Let's talk Sunday morning about your frustrations at work"). It should be clear to both partners that this time is intended to discuss difficulties *outside* of the relationship, rather than issues within the relationship. During the Support Talk, couples should not talk about topics of conflict between them. Instead, they should remain focused on providing and receiving support. If a couple-related conflict emerges, partners should make a conscious choice to either pause the Support Talk in order to discuss that conflict or call a "time-out" (i.e., save the conflict topic for another time) and return to the Support Talk topic.

While engaging in Support Talk, the partner receiving support is responsible for describing the distressing situation and their feelings associated with it. The partner providing support is responsible for listening carefully and empathetically, without providing advice unless it is specifically requested. Below are some strategies for providing support, although it is important to remember that each strategy may not be appropriate in all situations. Couples ought to try various strategies in order to learn what works best for each partner in various contexts.

- *Active Listening.* While the partner receiving support is speaking about their concerns, it is important for the partner providing support to communicate that they are listening and attempting to empathize. The supportive partner may periodically respond with phrases of understanding and validation (e.g., "That must be so upsetting") or questions ("How were you feeling when you finished the phone call with your sister?"). During Support Talk, it is best to refrain from multitasking (e.g., texting, answering the phone).
- *Physical Touch.* Various types of physical touch can be used on their own in order to increase intimacy and convey support in a relationship. However, here we discuss touch as a way to complement Support Talk. For example, holding one's partner's hand when he/she is talking about something upsetting sends the message of being there through difficult times. Other types of supportive touch include placing a hand on the partner's arm or leg in a comforting way and putting an arm around the partner.
- *XYZ Statements* ("When you do X in situation Y, I feel Z"). The structure of XYZ statements helps to communicate a feeling that arises in a specific situation. These statements can be used to express concerns, but they can also be used to express gratitude for support and intimacy that is being provided or has been provided in the past. For example, after engaging in Support Talk, the person who received support might say, "When you listened to my frustrations at breakfast this morning, I felt loved." In addition, the person who provided support might say, "When you shared your sadness about your father last night, I felt close to you." XYZ statements can also be used to elicit specific types of support. For example, a partner seeking physical touch during Support Talk might say, "When you hold my hand while we talk, I feel close to you."

Case Example

Riley and Sam have been in a relationship for 11 years and have two young children. Throughout the years, they have had a very good relationship in a variety of domains—romantically, sexually, domestically, and as co-parents. They care deeply for one another, but they have been so busy that they have not connected to talk about much besides daily tasks, such as picking the children up from school and making dinner. Recently, Riley has noticed that Sam has been stressed about work and worried about his mother's declining health. Sam visits his mother in the hospital daily after work, leaving little time for him to relax and get adequate sleep. Riley already helps to relieve this burden on Sam by cleaning the house and giving him back massages most evenings.

Riley has decided to initiate Support Talk as an additional strategy to support Sam. Because of their busy schedules, Riley scheduled a time in advance by texting Sam, "Thinking of you. It seems like you have been stressed lately. Could we talk on Saturday after the children go to bed about how you are doing and how I might be able to help?" Sam responded positively to this suggestion, so they planned to talk Saturday evening. During the Support Talk, Riley asked Sam to speak about the difficulties he had been experiencing at work and to share his feelings about his mother's health. Sam described his feelings of helplessness, as he has multiple competing responsibilities. Riley listened carefully, asking questions in order to better understand Sam's experience. Riley held Sam's hand as Sam described his fear of losing his mother. During the conversation, Sam expressed gratitude for the support by saying, "When I got your text about having dinner together, I felt so thankful to have you as a partner."

In summary, this case example shows how Support Talk can be used effectively to help couples increase a positive aspect of their relationship that is often neglected by couples as well as by many couple intervention approaches.

Note

1. Preparation of this chapter was supported in part by grant 5R01HD053314-26 from the National Institute of Child Health and Human Development (NICHD), awarded to Howard J. Markman, Galena K. Rhoades, and Scott M. Stanley. The contents are solely the responsibility of the authors and do not necessarily represent the official views of NIH or NICHD.

References

Cordova, J.V. (2009). *The marriage checkup: A scientific program for sustaining and strengthening marital health.* Lanham, MD: Jason Aronson.
Dehle, C., Larsen, D., & Landers, J. E. (2001). Social support in marriage. *American Journal of Family Therapy, 29*(4), 307–324. doi: 10.1080/01926180126500

Halford, W. K., Markman, H. J., Kline, G. H., & Stanley, S. M. (2003). Best practice in couple relationship education. *Journal of Marital and Family Therapy, 29*(3), 385–406. doi: 10.1111/j.1752–0606.2003.tb01214.x

Markman, H. J., Stanley, S. M., & Blumberg, S. L. (2010). *Fighting for your marriage: A deluxe revised edition of the classic best-seller for enhancing marriage and preventing divorce.* New York: Wiley.

Notarius, C., & Markman, H. J. (1993). *We can work it out: How to solve conflicts, save your marriage, and strengthen your love for each other.* New York: Putnam.

37

HUGGING, HOLDING, HUDDLING, AND CUDDLING (3HC)

Luciano L'Abate

Purpose: To help couples be emotionally and physically present through touch

Introduction

The cornerstone of love and intimacy is being emotionally available and physically present through prolonged physical contact. These activities have been grossly underemphasized in the clinical literature. This technique is designed to stress the importance of extensive, non-erotic affectionate hugging, holding, huddling, and cuddling (aka, 3HC) (L'Abate, 2013).

Purpose of Hugging, Holding, Huddling, and Cuddling (3HC)

Therapists seem to agree that couples need to be emotionally available and physically present to one another through affectional, sensual, and sexual ways. The purpose of this technique is to provide the couple with several ways of connecting with each other in non-sexual ways that will enhance feelings (and perceptions) of love and intimacy. The four activities that are part of this intervention can be expressed and perceived along a variety of dimensions and levels, including:

- The recipient of this exercise or activity;
- Intensity (enthusiasm, excitement, etc.);
- Degrees of anticipated duration;
- Frequency;
- Goal or intent of the experience (affection, manipulation, seduction, validation, etc.);
- Context (immediate, delayed, public/private).

Unfortunately, hugging has become so commonplace in our society that it has lost much of its meaning with regard to the goal of this activity. Hugging used to be reserved for people in very close relationships and held special meaning. Today, hugging is much more common among friends who aren't in a close relationship. For couples, the hug must be more than a brief encounter but a more sustained experience showing a feeling of wanting to be with the other person. Holding each other in whatever manner is comfortable usually lasts from a few seconds to a few minutes. The only difference between huddling and cuddling is the duration of the experience. Huddling with each other can last from 5 to 15 minutes, and cuddling may last for a few minutes to hours. For the purpose of these interventions, these activities are intended to help couples communicate their love and desire for physical closeness through nonverbal means. The emphasis is on being together and doing something with each other that is not goal- or outcome-oriented.

Description and Implementation

The therapist would ask the couple what these terms mean to them; how often, if at all, they use any of them, and whether they feel interested in connecting with each other in these ways. Additionally, the therapist might want to inquire about touching in the family-of-origin in order to gain some insight about their views regarding expressions of and comfort with physical contact. Each of the four activities requires progressively more physical contact and potentially more emotional vulnerability and intimacy. Therapists should ascertain which level both partners are comfortable with and begin with this activity. If they agree they are ready, they can be given a handout describing the steps or verbal instructions in the sessions. L'Abate (2001) pointed out the rules appear very simple, but getting the couple to actually carry them out may prove to be difficult. The rules are:

- Decide on which activity to do and make an appointment.
- Make sure there will be no distractions or interruptions.
- Find a place that is comfortable, usually not the bedroom unless the activity is cuddling.
- Agree on the duration of the activity.
- Allow yourself to feel whatever you feel without judgment (a mindfulness approach).
- If sexual feelings overpower the situation, the couple has to delicately discontinue the exercise to avoid feelings of sexual objectification by one partner and talk about it with each other and the therapist in the next session. The partners need to understand this feeling might occur, and they need to stop the exercise without engendering a feeling of rejection in the other.
- Describe the experience to the partner in positive terms: what they liked and what they might do next time to make it more enjoyable.

We have noted that men usually have more difficulty with these activities than women. Men tend to sexualize touching activities, which can lead the female partner to think she is just a sexual object. On the other hand, women more frequently desire affection in order to feel love and intimacy without the demand for sex. Thus, this particular set of activities may be targeted toward specific non-erotic relational problems, such as recovering from trauma; increasing feelings of trust, reliance, commitment, and confidence; or simply strengthening the couple's bond.

Contraindications and Provisos

The most obvious contraindication is when the couple says they are not yet ready to engage in any touching. For a variety of reasons, some couples enter therapy without having touched each other for months or years. The therapist should not prescribe any of these activities until she/he has assessed the couple and believes they are open to and ready for physical closeness. Accordingly, predictors of successful implementation of those activities are reciprocated levels of partner involvement and jointly identifying what they would like and not like. The therapist should stress that these activities are a start to becoming physically and emotionally connected, and the couple is likely to encounter some difficulties along the way. For example, some impediments can provide valuable feedback regarding why they have had trouble with emotional closeness. The partners should take note when they are having negative thoughts, unpleasant feelings, or find themselves avoiding or sabotaging the activity. These findings are brought to the session for thorough processing.

Case Example

Marsha and Jim had been married for over 30 years. During most of their marriage, they had what they considered a highly functional and satisfying relationship. They both had what they considered a normal sexual relationship. They had both worked in high-level jobs with tremendous responsibility. They decided to retire early and work part-time. Throughout their marriage, Marsha always kept herself extremely busy. After her retirement, she began having flashbacks of being sexually abused from an early age until she was a teenager by both her mother and father at the same time. The reason for her delayed recollection of these memories was a mystery. Her sexual abuse was among the most severe and persistent this therapist had ever seen. When they entered couple therapy, Marsha had already been in individual therapy for several years. She had been diagnosed and was being treated for dissociative identity disorder (DID), post-traumatic stress disorder (PTSD), depression, and sexual trauma. She was taking multiple medications and getting therapy twice a week. She was often scattered, unfocused, depressed, and anxious in the couple sessions. Her partner had become her caretaker, which had changed their dynamics significantly. He was able to put his needs aside, make no demands of her, and do whatever necessary to help her get through the day in many instances. When he touched her after the flashbacks began, she would recoil and go into a fetal position. She felt guilty and responsible, but helpless, that she was depriving him of a sexual relationship. He was afraid that touching her would lead to a psychological setback.

For Marsha, individual therapy had to precede couple therapy in order to deal with the trauma. Once she was functioning better, especially after the resolution of the DID, they began couple therapy where their counselor introduced the 3HC exercise, beginning with simple hand- holding and hugs, and then gradually progressing to the more advanced exercises. The process was slow and tedious, sometimes reigniting her trauma, which meant she needed to do more individual work. They both developed the attitude that they could re-establish their physical bond in spite of her earlier trauma and were persistent in their efforts to keep the process moving forward.

References

L'Abate, L. (2001). Hugging, holding, hudding, and cuddling (3HC): A task prescription in couple and family therapy. *The Journal of Clinical Activities, Assignment, and Handouts in Psychotherapy Practice, 1*, 5–18.

L'Abate, L. (2013). *Research on pre-para-post-therapeutic activities in mental health.* New York: Nova.

38

"YOUR CYBERPLACE OR MINE?"

Electronic Fantasy Dates

Katherine M. Hertlein

Purpose: To use technology to enhance intimacy in couple relationships

Introduction

Technology is a method by which therapists can effectively intervene in relationships. The Internet and other media technologies support relationship intimacy and development in key ways. Previous research has supported the notion that people who communicate via technology (i.e., text messaging, social networking, email) develop relationships characterized by higher levels of commitment and intimacy in the earlier phases of the relationship as compared to those relationships developed offline (McKenna, Green, & Gleason, 2002; Yum & Hara, 2006). The Electronic Fantasy Date is one method by which therapists can assist couples with navigating greater degrees of intimacy in their relationships.

Purpose of Electronic Fantasy Dates

The purpose of the Electronic Fantasy Date is to utilize media (specifically texting) to augment and support intimacy enhancement in a couple's relationship. The intimacy-enhancing characteristics of technologically mediated communication are based on the ecological elements or "Seven A's" (Hertlein & Stevenson, 2010) that are unique to the Internet and new media: accessibility, anonymity, affordability, approximation, acceptability, ambiguity, and accommodation. In other words, the Internet is highly accessible and affordable. Users have a certain degree of anonymity in their interactions with one another in that they can hide non-verbal communications as a way to create a more desirable emotional or physical setting. Through speed of response and thick, rich description, users can approximate real world settings. They can also use technology to accommodate behaviors in which they would not normally participate. Finally, with the lack of non-verbal communication and ambiguity surrounding technology usage, users may feel more freedom in interpreting events in a positive way.

Description and Implementation

While there are many techniques grounded in technology a therapist can offer to a couple, the one presented in this chapter is designed to use the Seven A's to augment the relationship. This technique, the Electronic Fantasy Date, makes use of the accessibility and affordability characteristics to create a date experience that lasts throughout the day for little to no cost. Such accessibility provides a sense of immediacy in relationships, which has resulted in people reporting a greater sense of connection, thus forging a stronger relationship (Bargh & McKenna, 2004). The thick, rich description of the date provides approximation of the date setting and accommodating one's desires with ambiguity, allowing the recipient room to use their imagination. There may also be a positive end of anticipation built up in the expectation of a message being received, providing a more positive feeling about one another throughout the day.

To begin this intervention, the therapist assigns the couple to take one another on an "Electronic Fantasy Date." The therapist or couple, depending on the treatment goals, can decide who will be the first person to initiate the date (known as the sender). The therapist may assign one individual to take their partner on a date one week, and the other partner to initiate the date the next week, or even assign two dates in one week. This technique is to be done on the couple's own time as homework. There are three phases in this intervention—the introduction to the date, the date itself, and then termination of the date. Each phase will be described in detail below.

Phase 1: Introduction to the Date

The initial message sent should occur early in the day (even on a workday) and continue periodically throughout the day (predicated on the assumption that both the sender and the receiver will have the ability to send and receive messages periodically throughout the day). On the day selected for the intervention, the sender will begin by sending a rich, detailed description to portray the beginning of the date. This could include picking up the sender at their location and describing the process of taking them on this particular date. When describing the location, setting, or environment, the sender is to describe a situation as if the receiver is already there. In other words, instead of saying, "I want to take you to a waterfall", the partner types, "We are at a waterfall. . . ." This type of texting imagery can be augmented by sending photos of places being described, thus playing into the quality of approximation described earlier.

Phase 2: Date Activity

Once at the date location, the descriptions transition into the next phase, where the activity for the date is portrayed. Common activities to be portrayed in detail include picnicking, hiking, swimming, taking a walk in a certain place, etc. Over the course of the day, the sender should continue to send no fewer than eight total messages to the receiver describing the date. Like the initial scene-setting messages, date activity messages should provide a detailed description of the environment and how it has changed as the date has progressed. For example, as the sender describes the process of getting to the date location, the setting and scenery is likely to change. The changes should be described in enough detail that the receiver is able to follow the changes and have a continuous image of the date. Senders can focus on describing what might be noted in the environment, such as the temperature, smells, what can be viewed, etc. The sender also describes the activity or what they are doing during the different messages in as much detail as possible.

Phase 3: Termination

Once the sender describes the activity, the sender will portray the conclusion of the date. This might include how the sender drops the respondent off at work again, or at home, or another conclusion. Again, the sender provides a rich, detailed description to portray how the scenery changes as the date moves toward termination. After this activity, the couple can choose to actually live out the fantasy date on a specific day or time. They could also extend the date to when they reunite. Finally, the couple may then switch places—the sender becomes the receiver and the receiver becomes the sender—and repeats the intervention.

Contraindications

The contraindications for this technique will be contextually dependent. For example, in cases where the couple has experienced some infidelity related to the Internet, the partners may experience a heightened level of anxiety when assigned to use the Internet or new media to develop a more solid relationship. Issues regarding Internet infidelity or Internet sex addiction should be processed to the point where use of technology is not a trigger prior to beginning the activity.

Brief Case Example

Courtney and J.T. came to therapy citing communication issues. The couple had been married for 15 years, and both had professional jobs. Courtney reported that she frequently felt criticized by J.T. with regard to how she handled situations in the home and with their daughter; J.T. stated he felt as if he could not provide feedback about his experiences in the relationship for fear of Courtney feeling criticized. The level of intimacy and positive interactions had suffered as a result of these problems. The therapist assigned J.T. the task of initiating the Electronic Fantasy Date by texting Courtney in the next week on a day when she would be at work. J.T. completed the assignment by texting Courtney every hour on the top of the hour and describing a date at a local nature preserve (a place they have enjoyed going together). With each text, J.T. focused on describing the surroundings as well as their activities—hiking up a walk to a clearing where they had a picnic, talking about their favorite memories together, then heading back down to the car and him dropping her back off at the house and asking for a second date. During the messages, J.T. described the temperature as mid-seventies and pointed out how the breeze felt on Courtney's face. Also during his description, J.T. focused on specific details and even texted about how Courtney stumbled at one point and how she fell onto his arm and he held her up, and they continued to hold hands throughout the hike. Once they hiked up to the top of the clearing, J.T. described how they could hear the waterfall and a bit of an echo in the area. Courtney enjoyed this imagery and began looking forward to the texts on the hour. Toward the middle of the day, Courtney began writing back and filling in some of the areas of imagery as well, also providing rich, detailed descriptions of events and surroundings.

Both Courtney and J.T. reported feeling closer after the participation in the Electronic Fantasy Dates. Courtney indicated that she was surprised at how creative J.T. could be, and noted it was more difficult to see him as a person who was critical of her when he was mapping out such a nice picture for the two of them. After participating in the Electronic Fantasy Dates, the couple reported that they instituted a new routine on Fridays during their lunch breaks—texting love notes to one another.

Electronic Fantasy Dates can be processed in session. Attention is paid to the initiation of the date and what elements about the date were enjoyed by the couple. The couple also discusses whether it would be useful to keep this as part of their dating practices in the event that they are unable to spend time together.

References

Bargh, J.A., & McKenna, K.A. (2004). The Internet and social life. *Annual Review of Psychology, 55*(1), 573–590. doi:10.1146/annurev.psych.55.090902.141922

Hertlein, K. M., & Stevenson, A. J. (2010). The seven "As" contributing to Internet-related intimacy problems: A literature review. *Cyberpsychology: Journal of Psychosocial Research on Cyberspace, 4*(1), article 1. Retrieved from http://www.cyberpsychology.eu/view.php?cisloclanku=2010050202

McKenna, K.Y., Green, A., & Gleason, M. (2002). Relationship formation on the Internet: What's the big attraction? *Journal of Social Issues, 58,* 9–31.

Yum, Y. O., & Hara, K. (2006). Computer-mediated relationship development: A cross-cultural comparison. *Journal of Computer-Mediated Communication, 11*(1), 133–152.

39

FORGIVENESS IN COUPLES THERAPY

Expanding Compassion, Responsibility, and Apology

Miyoung Yoon Hammer and Terry D. Hargrave

Purpose: To help couples restore love and trust

Introduction

Forgiveness work with couples can take on many forms, depending upon the circumstances of the violating event(s) as well as the availability and willingness of one or both partners to participate in this work. Although forgiveness work can be effective when working with individuals alone, we have found that it is most effective when both partners are committed to the process. The procedures described in this chapter are based mostly on conjoint work. The techniques of expanding compassion, responsibility, and apology in the work of forgiveness with couples are based on the Restoration Therapy (RT) model developed by Terry Hargrave (Hargrave, 2000; Hargrave & Pfitzer, 2011). The RT model is a family systems model that assumes all pain results from violations of identity (i.e., being loved, valued, and known) and/or safety (i.e., trustworthiness). According to this assumption, people cope with the pain by being destructive toward others by blaming or controlling and/or by being destructive toward themselves by shaming and escaping.

In the RT model, forgiveness work focuses on understanding pain and restoring love and trust where violations of identity and/or safety have damaged the couple's relationship (Hargrave, 2001). There are two broad categories of forgiveness work, as seen in Table 39.1. The first category is called Salvage because partners salvage their agency to be loving and trustworthy in relating to one another. Salvage is possible when partners gain *insight* about their power to stop committing destructive harm toward others or allowing it upon themselves, and when they *understand* one another by gaining clarity and compassion for self and also

TABLE 39.1 The Four Stations of Forgiveness.

The Work of Forgiveness			
Salvage		*Restoration*	
Insight	**Understanding**	**Giving Opportunity for Compensation**	**Overt Forgiving**

through connection of story and shared humanity. The second broad category of forgiveness work is called Restoration, where couples restore trustworthiness to their relationship by the stations of *giving the opportunity for compensation* (predictable and dependable giving and receiving from one another) and *overt forgiveness* (the violator initiating responsibility for wrongdoing and intending to do differently in the future). Couples may work through forgiveness issues by any of the four stations and strategies outlined here depending on their abilities and the severity of the violation between them. It is important to note here that there are four stations that couples work through in sequence as described in Table 39.1.

Purpose of Expanding Compassion, Responsibility, and Apology

The purpose of expanding the couple's capacity for compassion, responsibility, and apology is to restore love and trust by re-establishing their connection to each other, restoring hope and trust, and making their commitment to build a new relationship explicit. The techniques are also like the nails that reinforce and strengthen the legs of a three-legged stool upon which forgiveness rests. The three legs are love, power, and justice, and all three must be in sturdy balance in order for forgiveness to have integrity. If any one of the legs break, the stool cannot support forgiveness, and the relationship continues to be in danger of further violation. Therefore, expanding compassion engenders love, an essential for maintaining genuine care and connection. Expanding responsibility stabilizes power by promoting action and agency. Finally, expanding apology promotes justice as the couple attempts to heal from the past and step toward a better future.

Description and Implementation

When working through a relationship violation and seeking forgiveness, couples may do so in conjoint sessions or, depending on the severity of the violation and potential issues of safety, the couple may begin with individual sessions and come together later in the process, possibly for the first time at the Overt Forgiving station.

Expanding Compassion

Expanding the couple's capacity for compassion and love for themselves as well as for each other begins in the first two stations of Insight and Understanding. As victims gain insight about the root of their pain and how their identity and/or safety has been violated, they realize the impact of the violation on their self-construal. They also begin understanding how their emotional reactivity stemming from the violation seeps into other relationships. This insight enables victims to have compassion for themselves by removing displaced, undeserved self-blame, empowering them to protect themselves from future violations in the relationship, and ensuring they do not perpetuate their pain in future relationships. At the same time, as victims gain greater insight about the violator's pain and why they violated, their compassion for their partner increases. Understanding allows the victim to join the violator in the shared human experience of pain. Victims may even begin to understand their own tendencies to violate, further expanding their compassion for the violator.

Violators expand their compassion through insight and understanding as well. Violators gain awareness about how their actions result in violations of identity and safety in their partner when they explore their own pain. As violators delve into their stories of pain, compassion for themselves (and possibly their own violators) expands, and their own humanity is restored. Understanding does not eliminate taking responsibility for their actions, but rather rebuilds the compassion of both the violator and the victim and facilitates greater responsibility for them to make healthier choices about their interactions.

Expanding Responsibility

The stations of Insight and Understanding lay the groundwork for expanding responsibility, which is the heart of the work in the third station of forgiveness: Giving Opportunity for Compensation. This is also where there is opportunity to restore balanced power in the relationship. For the victim, withholding forgiveness and denying any chance for compensation gives the victim power in a relationship where he or she was once violated and disempowered. In this station, victims must take a risk by giving violators the opportunity to prove they are reliable. Violators, too, must attempt to demonstrate their trustworthiness, while knowing their efforts might be rejected or go unacknowledged. They cannot expect anything in return. When violators are able to take responsibility for their actions and demonstrate loving and honest, trustworthy acts—time and time again, without any obligations or expectations—and victims receive these acts of compensation, the possibility of healing the relationship emerges. Depending on the severity of the damage, the couple may remain in this station for a long time. However, if the violator is able to prove himself/herself to be emotionally and physically safe by patiently and consistently demonstrating love and trustworthiness, it becomes possible for a new relationship to supersede the old one, illuminating a clear pathway to apology.

Expanding Apology

The final station in forgiveness work is Overt Forgiving, and this is where apology is possible. This station's task expands the couple's ability to apologize and to complete the forgiveness process. It is here that justice, the third critical component of forgiveness, is restored. In Overt Forgiving, both partners must be present, either in a session or at a meeting at home. For some couples, this is the first time in the forgiveness process that they are meeting together. Therefore, preparing the couple for this transition is important. This station involves the couple jointly dealing with the past violation and eventually making an overt, explicit commitment to move forward in their relationship, free of the harmful emotions of the past. The violator, who by this time has proven to be loving and trustworthy, commits to taking responsibility for his/her actions and to continuing to be trustworthy. The victim makes a commitment to genuinely release the resentment and pain from the past and live fully in the relationship, while continuing to apply the insight and understanding they have about each other.

Contraindications

When only one partner is committed to forgiveness work, the Restoration stations cannot be pursued nor completed successfully. Other contraindications include situations where one or both partners are actively abusive toward one another, mood-altering substances are currently being used, or other violating behaviors persist (i.e., infidelity). In these cases, the work of forgiveness and couples therapy, in general, cannot be successful.

References

Hargrave, T. D. (2000). *The essential humility of marriage: Honoring the third identity in couple therapy.* Phoenix, AZ: Zeig, Tucker, & Thiesen, Inc.

Hargrave, T. D. (2001). *Forgiving the devil: Coming to terms with damaged relationships.* Phoenix, AZ: Zeig, Tucker, & Thiesen, Inc.

Hargrave, T. D., & Pfitzer, F. (2011). *Restoration therapy: Understanding and guiding healing in marriage and family therapy.* New York: Routledge.

40

RESTORATION OF RELATIONSHIPS AFTER AFFAIRS

Terry D. Hargrave and Miyoung Yoon Hammer

Purpose: To help couples recover after infidelity

Introduction

While infidelity is certainly not the norm in coupling, it does represent a major reason that couples seek therapy (Blow & Hartnett, 2005). Laumann, Paik, and Rosen (1999) basically confirm our best research that puts infidelity rates around 21% for men and around 12% for women. We also know that the majority (56%) of couples that experience an infidelity in their relationship stay married (Hargrave, 2000). While infidelity rates are not as high as one might suspect and survival rates of relationships are relatively high, couples do report an enormous amount of emotional and relational distress when a partner is unfaithful in a committed relationship. Of course, this makes perfect sense when one considers that the heart of a committed relationship is based on mutual giving and receiving, openness and intimacy, and trustworthy predictability. Infidelity strikes at the heart of trustworthiness and calls into question the ability of partners to be committed, giving, and open in their relationship.

Our purpose here is to describe a process by which a couple can restore their relationship after an occurrence of infidelity with one of the partners, and how therapy can be of best assistance. It is important to note here that not all therapists or professional organizations agree that the revelation of an infidelity is best in couple therapy. For our purposes, however, our assumption is that a couple seeks therapy because of the revelation or discovery of an infidelity, and that it has caused significant relational distress. Although couples differ widely in their ability to restore their relationship after infidelity, we find that there are typically three phases in which we work therapeutically with a couple in seeking to stabilize and heal the relationship after an affair. These three phases are: 1) crisis stabilization, 2) rebuilding of trustworthiness, and 3) couple improvement therapy.

Purpose of Restoring Relationships After an Affair

In traditional systemic therapy, infidelity in a couple relationship was simply seen as a symptom of an unhappy couple relationship. As a result, many therapists saw infidelity within the context that both partners were responsible because they both contributed to a problem in the health of the relationship. Therapy, therefore, most often took the perspective of the therapist engaging in couple therapy instead of directly addressing the issues and violations of trustworthiness connected with the infidelity (Hargrave, 2000). We not only see this perspective as unproductive in assisting a couple in recovering from an infidelity, we see it as damaging because the victim of the infidelity is made to feel responsible or even blamed for the partner's affair.

Most couples that experience an infidelity and come to therapy are seeking to repair the relationship from the violation of trustworthiness. Some couples come to therapy after a discovered or revealed infidelity where the unfaithful partner intends to carry on the extra-marital relationship or is unsure about cutting the infidelity off. In these cases, however, we would argue that reconciliation of the couple and that restoring their relationship is not the focus of therapy. Most couples that experience an infidelity desire to move away from the damage of the affair and heal their openness, intimacy, and trustworthiness.

Description and Implementation

It is imperative that the therapist sees the initial phase of infidelity treatment as being about *crisis stabilization* (Hargrave, 2001) and not so much being about *couple therapy*. There are significant challenges a couple faces with an infidelity. A victim of the infidelity must confront the realization that much of the relationship has been characterized as deceitful and must acknowledge the breaking of commitment and reliability. The resulting feelings of anger and hurt are consistently contrasted with the emotions of care and regard for the partner that have resulted in closeness and intimacy in the past. As a result, the victim of the infidelity often is on a roller coaster of emotion, where one moment they despise and even hate their partner, and the next they have compassion and care for the victimizer. The therapist must be patient in hearing this pain and allowing the emotions—both positive and negative—to be expressed. The victimizer, or unfaithful partner, also has substantial variance in emotions. It is usual for this partner to feel a terrible sense of guilt and regret, as well as often dealing with much ambiguity over emotions felt toward the other person involved in the affair. Again, the therapist must listen in a non-judgmental and accepting fashion as both partners express these painful emotions. If allowed to express this pain, usually in three to five weeks, the emotional extremes stabilize and constructive recovery can begin.

The other factor that is important during this crisis stabilization phase is cutting off contact and involvement with the other person with whom the infidelity was committed. Repeated return of the unfaithful partner to the other person continues to be victimizing to the partner and is ill advised to be accommodated in therapy, the same way that a therapist would not continue to see a couple if domestic violence or abuse occurred. We usually recommend that the therapist discuss this openly with the couple and go into great detail about how the relationship with the third party ended. To consolidate this work, we often recommend that the couple construct a two-paragraph letter to the third party indicating that any contact will be reported to the partner and that the relationship is over permanently—even if the couple therapy is unsuccessful at restoring the relationship. This action assures the couple that they will work together to repair the relationship.

The second phase of the work with a couple in restoring their relationship after an infidelity is to *rebuild trustworthiness*, which is most often crushed by infidelity. Trustworthiness is built on the foundation of predictability of behavior, fairness of give and take, and openness or transparency. In order to address this, reconciliation, or restoration of the relationship, is most often built by a station of forgiveness that Hargrave (2001) calls *giving opportunity for compensation*. In this station of restoring the relationship, the therapist helps the victim specify clear behaviors the victimizer can perform that are based on justice and that restore trustworthiness. If the unfaithful partner performs the behavior consistently and reliably, then predictability and fairness will be built over a period of time. For instance, if the victim asks for the victimizer to call hourly when out of town and the victimizer complies reliably, fear and anxiety caused by the violation of trust can be ameliorated over time. Trustworthiness and restoration in this station of forgiveness are built a little at a time over a long period of time.

In this case, the therapist is actually asking the victimizer to willingly engage in a *one down* position, or actively engage in more giving to the injured party than what is reciprocated back in the way of giving. This is intentional and is designed to provide the victim with compensation for the wrong that has been inflicted. We believe that the work of forgiveness does not just involve a victim letting go of hurt, anger, and wrong, but also involves the victimizer addressing the imbalance of justice and the pain by changed behavior. In this phase of giving opportunity for compensation, the victimizer demonstrates changed behavior, and gives the victim reason to trust once more and reason to forgive the wrongdoing. It is important to note, however, that the relationship cannot bear this phase of therapy and inequality of give and take permanently. We recommend that this phase of therapy last only three to nine weeks as the couple learns how to stabilize trust and consolidate new patterns. It is then important to restore the relational partnership to relational equals. This also signals the time for the third phase of recovery where the couple engages in *couple therapy*. Like all effective couple therapy, the concentration of recovery is now focused on identifying mutual couple weaknesses and helping the partners head toward more loving and trustworthy behaviors. Although we are offering little direction here in the third phase of affair recovery because of space limitations, it is important to note that this phase is a legitimate need; a couple has to seek improvement in the relationship and reach a deeper level of satisfaction in order to enhance commitment and intimacy.

Contraindications

As mentioned before, it is difficult for a couple to restore any sense of relationship after the revelation of an infidelity if the unfaithful partner is unwilling to give up the additional relationship. In addition, addictions of any type make the restoration of trustworthiness difficult and sometimes impossible. Additional contraindications would include diagnosis of one of the partners with a personality disorder or for there to be the presence of couple violence.

Recovery and restoring couple relationships are possible, and in many cases, desirable. Using the methodology outlined above, most couples not only recover from an infidelity but also describe their relationship as stronger as a result of working through their issues.

References

Blow, A. J., & Hartnett, K. (2005). Infidelity in committed relationships II: A substantive review. *Journal of Marital and Family Therapy, 31*(2), 217–233.

Hargrave, T. D. (2000). *The essential humility of marriage: Honoring the third identity in couple therapy.* Phoenix, AZ: Zeig, Tucker, & Theisen.

Hargrave, T. D. (2001). *Forgiving the devil: Coming to terms with damaged relationships.* Phoenix, AZ: Zeig, Tucker, & Theisen.

Laumann, E. O., Paik, A., & Rosen, R. C. (1999). Sexual dysfunction in the United States: Prevalence and predictors. *Journal of Family Psychology, 22*(1), 41–50.

41

MYTHS ABOUT MARRIAGE

Jeffry H. Larson

Purpose: To help couples identify myths about marriage that may lead to relationship distress

Introduction

Myths are defined as widely-held beliefs we hold as true that have no basis in reality or scientific evidence. They help sustain and sometimes create marriage problems. They are often stated as expectations or maxims for our partner or relationship, e.g., "Couples should never quarrel" or "Don't ever go to bed when angry!" Many of these myths are passed down through generations in families as well-meaning advice. Unfortunately, believing in them creates marital problems (Larson, 2003). The technique described below is based on cognitive-behavioral couple therapy principles.

Expectations are crucial to assess and modify in couple therapy, as they are the standards by which marriage is judged as satisfying or dissatisfying. Some call these myths or faulty expectations "irrational thoughts or dysfunctional beliefs" (Baucom et al., 2008). Thus, changing one's mythical expectations of a partner, self, or marriage may be more fruitful in marital therapy than trying to convince a partner to change to meet mythical expectations.

Purpose of the Myths About Marriage Technique

The following are eight common myths about marriage that have been identified in couple therapy and couple education settings. The therapist can assess a couple's belief in these myths in two ways: 1) the therapist will likely hear a partner state one of these myths or expectations in a therapy session; in that case, the therapist must challenge the belief in the myth; or 2) the therapist can give a couple a quiz on the myths and score it with them (e.g., see Larson, 2003), followed by debunking the myths. Debunking involves providing an alternative, more realistic belief for each myth. Debunking encourages the couple to discuss the myth's validity, better understand its truth, and see the benefits of substituting an alternative for the myth. This will invite the couple to be more realistic in what they expect for themselves and their partner in marriage. Thus, this process is similar to the gentle challenging through Socratic questioning used in cognitive-behavioral couple therapy (e.g., Baucom et al., 2008). In cognitive-behavioral therapy, this type of questioning is designed to help couples examine the evidence for their beliefs and challenge irrational or unrealistic beliefs.

Description and Implementation

Here are the myths, explanations of why the myth is untrue, and alternative beliefs or expectations partners can substitute for the myths.

1. *Myth #1: If my partner really loves me, he/she should instinctively know what I want and need to be happy* (Larson, 2003). This is referred to as the ESP (extrasensory perception) or mind-reading myth. Research shows, instead, that even spouses married for a long time do not necessarily know or understand each other as well as they say they do! The point is partners have to communicate clearly about their needs, wants, and expectations for their partner to have any chance of fulfilling them. So, the reality (debunking the myth) is: If partners really love each other, they will openly and respectfully tell each other what they want and need and not expect the other to be able to read their minds (Larson, 2003).

2. *Myth #2: I can change my partner by pointing out his/her inadequacies, errors, and other faults.* Such blaming, especially if it rises to the level of criticism, has been shown to predict divorce (Gottman, 1994); no one likes to feel they are being criticized or controlled by their partner. Nagging can lead to power struggles. The reality is: You can positively influence your partner's behavior if you know how, and that can be learned (e.g., catch him/her doing something good)—but nagging never works.

3. *Myth #3: My partner either loves me or doesn't love me; nothing I do will affect the way he/she feels about me.* This is similar to the "I'm good enough just as I am" myth. However, if one partner exhibits loving behaviors, the other partner's love for him/her will likely increase in a reciprocal way. And both partners can control their own behavior. The reality is: If you behave more lovingly, your partner will love you more in return.

4. *Myth #4: I must feel better about my partner before I can change my behavior toward him/her.* It *will* be easier for partners to be positive around each other if they feel love for each other, but how do they change their feelings first? Where

is the magic potion? The reality is: Part of being married is learning you sometimes have to do things for your partner that you would rather not do, *simply to please your partner.* Your partner's happiness will likely reciprocate with pleasing behaviors from him/her, too. So don't wait around for your feelings to change, but get to work changing yourself, first. Positive feelings result from positive behaviors, not vice versa.

5. *Myth #5: Marriage is a 50–50 partnership.* Unfortunately, circumstances and individuals are too complicated to assume that spouses can always maintain equal inputs into their marriage (Larson, 2003). Some days a spouse may have to put in 100% while the other spouse puts in 20% due to illness, stress, fatigue, etc. Only *unhappy* couples worry about "who is doing more in this marriage." The reality is: Your marriage will be stronger if you focus on pleasing your partner and not keeping a tally in your mind of who is contributing the most.

6. *Myth #6: Marriage can fulfill all of my needs and dreams.* Newlyweds may believe this! But over time, married couples discover that marriage cannot meet ALL of their needs. Nor should it. Married people still need friendships, clubs, joint activities with others, fulfilling work, healthy recreation, etc., to make life full. The same principle applies to "downloading a miserable, frustrating day" to your spouse. Doing so may build some closeness, for sure, but a spouse can sometimes download negativity instead on a best friend, favorite sister, or mom instead of his/her partner. The reality is: Marriage can fulfill many of your needs, and the others can be fulfilled by other appropriate people in your life.

7. *Myth #7: The more my spouse discloses positive and negative information to me, the closer I will feel toward her and the greater our marital satisfaction.* So, spouses should tell their partner whatever is on their mind, positive or negative, right? This was a motto of the 1960s: With people you love, "Let it all hang out!" Now we know that disclosing too much negative information (especially if it applies to your spouse) can harm a marriage (Gottman, 1994). The reality: The expression of positive thoughts and feelings increases intimacy in marriage. If you have something negative to say, watch how you say it in order to avoid offending your spouse.

8. *Myth #8: Couples should keep their problems to themselves and solve them alone.* This is referred to as the "intermarriage taboo" (Mace, 1979). It is based on American privacy values. Unfortunately, too many unhappy couples keep their problems to themselves, don't seek advice, or go to therapy, and hence, their relationship dies. Close, trusted friends or relatives, clergy, couple educators, and therapists can help. The reality is: Keeping your problems quiet and going at it alone often leads to marital failure. Get trusted others to help you. *One warning:* Before you share private couple information, with a family member especially, it is best to first get the permission of your spouse. Men, especially, can be embarrassed if they find out their wives have been discussing marriage problems without their knowledge.

Contraindications

The only contraindication of using this approach is to first consider a couple's ethnic group or cultural expectations. For example, in some cultures, it may be taboo to share marriage problems with others. In others, it may be expected (collectivistic societies like those in Asia). So, be careful. Also, you do not want to infer that the couple is just plain ignorant if they believe in some myths; reassure them that these are commonly held beliefs in most of the U.S., and the goal is not to make them look foolish, but to challenge myths that may hurt their relationship.

Case Example and Guidelines

I regularly use these myths as a quiz in a marriage enhancement workshop that I teach. People generally love the challenge of a quiz; it gets them thinking harder. This quiz can also be used early in couple therapy and discussed in a session. Each couple will have their unique set of beliefs and expectations regarding these myths. Once each partner's beliefs are identified, the therapist can help the couple discuss and challenge the mythical beliefs or unrealistic expectations through questions that invite the couple to reflect on the possible inaccuracies or downsides to the beliefs they hold (long sentence). It is also helpful to trace the origin of a client's belief in a myth, like, "My grandmother always taught me that_____." What may have worked in Grandma's day may not work in modern marriage!

References

Baucom, D. H., Epstein, N. B., LaTaillade, J. J., & Kirby, J. S. (2008). Cognitive-behavioral couple therapy. In A. S. Gurman (Ed.), *Clinical handbook of couple therapy* (4th ed., pp. 31–72). New York: Guilford Press.

Gottman, J. (1994). *Why marriages succeed or fail.* New York: Simon & Schuster.

Larson, J. H. (2003). *The great marriage tune-up book.* San Francisco, CA: Jossey-Bass.

Mace, D. (1979). Marriage and family enrichment: A new field? *Family Coordinator, 28,* 409–419.

42

DEVELOPMENTAL TASKS IN THE CRITICAL FIRST YEAR OF MARRIAGE

Clinical Guidelines

Jeffry H. Larson

Purpose: To help recently married couples begin to complete "developmental tasks" that should be accomplished in the early year(s) of marriage to improve their chances of good marital adjustment and satisfaction

Introduction

Developmental tasks in the first year of marriage refer to aspects or dimensions of a couple's early marital relationship that should be discussed, decisions that should be made, and skills that should be learned early in the marriage in order to increase the couple's current and future marital adjustment. Simply put, they are topics that are important to a couple that ought to be discussed and decided on by mutual consent. These tasks are based on the theoretical work of David Mace, founder of the marriage enrichment field in the U.S. and Great Britain, and the theory and research of Around and Pauker (1987) and others. The process of helping a couple accomplish these tasks is mainly *preventive* in nature, i.e., couples who accomplish these tasks early in their marriage lower their risks of developing problems later. Thus, the population of couples this technique applies to is early-married couples up through the second year of marriage or so.

Purpose of Developmental Tasks in the First Year of Marriage

The purpose of this technique is to help couples get a better start to their marriage by accomplishing early marriage developmental tasks that make them less at-risk for future marital problems. The clinician's aims are to structure several therapy sessions to discuss with the couple the *definition* of early marriage developmental tasks, and a *description* of each, to help the couple *assess* if they have accomplished each task, and to have a *clinician-guided discussion* of the topics that make up the tasks if the couple has not accomplished them. Some of the topics may be difficult for couples to address due to the anxiety related to them (e.g., sex and money). Therefore, some couples may need help communicating about these topics in a functional way. In such cases, the clinician may need to teach them how to use good communication and problem-solving skills.

Description and Implementation

The developmental tasks were first described by Mace (1982) as part of the stages of early marriage. They should be accomplished in the *mutual adjustment stage* of early marriage and include competently dealing with seven important issues. Spouses should discuss these issues thoroughly and reach a consensus. They are as follows:

1. *Psychological separation from the family of origin (FOO) and reprioritizing one's allegiance to the new couple relationship.* This involves creating secure attachment in the couple relationship, which is difficult to do if a partner has not yet conceptualized his/her new marriage as *the primary relationship* in life. Problems in separating from the FOO are exemplified by disagreements about celebrating holidays (e.g., whose family do we visit during Christmas?), disagreements about couple rules regarding boundaries between the couple relationship and each person's FOO (e.g., privacy issues; i.e., what couple-related topics are taboo for sharing with one's FOO), and struggles with developing the couple's own new traditions for holidays, birthdays, vacations, etc. Clinicians assist couples with having constructive conversations and coming to agreements on each of these topics. Often, it is necessary to teach couples negotiation and compromising skills.
2. *Power issues* confront every couple in early marriage (Around & Pauker, 1987; Markman, Stanley, & Blumberg, 2010). Power in marriage is often reflected in *how* important decisions are made. Are they made as equals in the marriage, often with compromises? Couples also have to decide whether to have a traditional marriage, a more egalitarian marriage, or their own hybrid model. Most research shows an egalitarian relationship is best for most partners (e.g., Christensen & Jacobson, 2000). Clinicians help couples decide how to share power in marriage.
3. *Communication and conflict resolution styles.* In early marriage, the patterns of communication and problem-solving for an entire marriage are built. Many couples lack effective speaking and listening skills. Most do not have a constructive model of conflict resolution to follow. Assessing skills, and then teaching empathy, clear speaking, and conflict resolution skills, are important interventions for the clinician to implement.

4. *Husband and wife roles* should be discussed and settled-on *before marriage,* ideally. But early in marriage they need to be specifically defined and agreed-on. This includes power-sharing issues described above, as well as responsibilities such as: Who will be the major breadwinner? How will we divide up the housework? Who does the cooking? Who initiates sex? What are each partner's roles in child care and child rearing? Who manages the money? Again, the clinician can guide the couple through discussions on each of these important topics.

5. *Closeness-distance issues.* This refers to time spent alone versus time spent together as a couple. Every couple must address this issue and come to an agreement that works for both partners. Likely, one of the partners prefers alone time more than the other; this can hurt the feelings of the more-time-together partner. Thus, this usually has to be negotiated with the clinician's assistance.

6. *Money management.* If a couple does not come to a workable and realistic agreement on how to create a budget, who pays the bills, who keeps the checkbook, how to set spending priorities, and how to decide on saving and retirement, financial stress can eat away at their marriage. Arguments about how to spend, who manages the funds, etc., are common. Few individuals have ever been taught when growing up how to budget money, invest, save, etc. And the way their parents managed money is often what couples fall back on as a solution. The problem is, their parents may have had radically different styles. The clinician can assist the couple in discussions about these topics and recommend good books/websites for developing money-management skills.

7. *Sexual adjustments* take most couples over a year to find comfort and agreement on preferred lovemaking styles, family planning, and the frequency of sex (Around & Pauker, 1987; Markman et al., 2010), especially if they have little or no sexual experience before marriage. The same communication and negotiation principles and techniques described above should be used by the therapist to help the couple come to agreements on the various aspects of their sex life. For those with little sexual experience, referring them to good self-help books may also be helpful.

The final stage of the critical first year of marriage Mace (1982) calls *mutual fulfillment.* Part of the feeling of fulfillment comes from the result of partners having equal input, making fair decisions about all the topics presented above, and having done it in a mutually satisfying way.

Contraindications

The only contraindication for using these techniques is if a spouse is suffering from a mental disorder, an addiction, or if there is violence in the marriage. In these cases, those issues must be resolved first. Furthermore, depending on the couple's ethnicity and cultural background, some subjects (e.g., sex) may be considered too private to discuss with an outsider. Therefore, be sure to inquire about this before launching into these discussions.

Case Example

I am currently working with a couple married less than a year who presented with high conflict over boundaries between them as a couple and his family of origin. His family of origin believed in openly sharing marital problems with each other; her family believed that what happens in one's marriage is private and should never be disclosed to others. She felt betrayed by him for talking about their conflicts to his mother, whom he claimed gave excellent marital advice. She felt "ganged-up on" by his mother, sister, and even a cousin. By teaching them couple communication skills and focusing on coming to a compromise, the couple came up with a "Marriage Rule" that fairly represented both their opinions and needs. Emphasizing that all couples have to do this "task" helped normalize the situation for them and lowered their anxiety and distress.

References

Around, M., & Pauker, S. L. (1987). *The first year of marriage: What to expect, what to accept, and what you can change*. New York: Warner Books.

Christensen, A., & Jacobson, N. S. (2000). *Reconcilable differences*. New York: Guilford Press.

Mace, D. R. (1982). *Close companions*. New York: Continuum.

Markman, H. J., Stanley, S. M., & Blumberg, S. L. (2010). *Fighting for your marriage*. San Francisco, CA: Jossey-Bass.

43

THE USE OF THE SEXUAL GENOGRAM

Nancy Gambescia

Purpose: To help couples discuss sexual intimacy

Introduction

Sexual intimacy is a common theme in couples therapy; yet, many clients are too embarrassed or unable to communicate about sexual preferences or concerns. Moreover, many therapists feel unqualified or inexperienced in facilitating dialogues about sex and weaving sexual topics into the overall assessment; thus, discussion of sex is circumvented due to therapist and client discomfort. This fact is particularly disturbing since sexual dynamics are embedded in the couple's partnership, and relationship patterns are reflected in sex. The two are inseparable.

We have found in clinical practice that communication is an area of difficulty for most of our clients. This is unfortunate because communication is the mediating factor between sexual and relational satisfaction. Discussing sexual issues enhances relational happiness, and vice versa. There is a dearth of empirical literature about techniques that promote communication about sexual issues. While the clinical literature is rich with examples of sexual problems and solutions, little attention has been given to the use of the sexual genogram as a technique for assessment and treatment.

Purpose of the Sexual Genogram

Frequently when couples present with sexual issues, they are caught in a cycle of blame, disappointment, helplessness, and pessimism. The sexual genogram is a therapeutic tool that illuminates the bigger picture in understanding the intergenerational forces behind the existing couple concern. Expanding the focus helps to reduce criticism, blame, anger, and other elements that can be destructive to the couple's relationship. The sexual genogram provides opportunities for continual exploration of sexual behavior, attraction, self-identification, preferences, and historical information. Additionally, it allows the partners to reflect on sexual topics as a way to begin discussing them. When the couple identifies problems, the therapist helps to reframe them as challenges to be discussed and understood rather than obstacles or impediments. This systemic technique fosters motivation to work, empathy, and optimism.

Description and Implementation

A genogram is a graphic illustration of a family map or tree portraying relationships among family members. Typically, the diagram involves three or four generations and uses symbols and other codes to depict domestic patterns and relationships. Specifically, the genogram tracks the intergenerational transmission of relationship themes.

The sexual genogram is a focused version of the genogram that relates to gender, romantic love, attachment, intimacy, and other themes associated with sexuality. These topics are viewed within the larger contexts of the couple's relationship, families of origin, previous relationships, and so on. Often, family secrets such as hidden pregnancies, affairs, abortions, sexual trauma, and sexual compulsivity are chronicled. Additionally, children from the present or prior partnerships are included with a concentration on how intergenerational legacies can affect them.

Questions used in a traditional sex history are comingled with an open-ended, storytelling approach to promote communication about sexual themes in one's life. In Hof & Berman's (1986) original conceptualization, several areas of concentration were included, such as the transmission of overt and covert messages regarding sex, gender roles, and intimacy. The therapist observes how partners communicate about intimacy and sex, and facilitates discussions with open-ended questions. Partners are encouraged to discuss their reactions to the other's portion of the genogram or to embellish or refine the final product—although it is never really finished, because people change, sexual preferences fluctuate over time, and desired physical and emotional stimulation varies throughout the lifespan. Lastly, the genogram allows clients to explore wishes about how their sexual relationship could be different.

Belous, Timm, Chee, and Whitehead (2012) expanded the scope of the sexual genogram to incorporate more contemporary issues about the diversity of gender expression, sexual attraction, and sexual orientation; the privilege of one group over another; and gay, lesbian, bisexual, and transgender issues. Additionally, they emphasize the use of a sexual timeline in order to track consistencies and changes in sexual development over time.

The well-thought-out use of open-ended questions is the essential component of the sexual genogram. A few examples are offered below, although most questions should flow from the material of the session.

- What does the term "sex" mean to you?
- How would you define intimacy?
- How would you define affection?
- Did you see affection demonstrated in your family? How?
- How was sex talked about in your family?
- How did you learn about sex?
- From whom did you learn about sex (e.g., parents, siblings, friends, school, media, Internet)?
- When do you remember first learning about sex?
- What did you learn about sex?
- When did you begin to explore your own body in a sexual way?
- How did you feel about self-exploration?
- What are your feelings now about solo sexual activity?
- What does the term "gender" mean to you?
- How do you self-identify in terms of gender?
- How do you perceive sexual attraction? Sexual desire?
- Is your sexual attraction or interest consistent with the way in which you see yourself?
- What messages did you receive about masturbation within your family? From friends?
- What role did religion/culture play in shaping your sexual values?
- Were there any "secrets" in your family about sex?
- Were these secrets quiet or open to family discussion?
- Who knew the "secrets?"
- Do you still have secrets as an adult?
- Does anyone in your family have a history of sex abuse or compulsivity?
- Were there any stillbirths, abortions, deaths, affairs, etc., in your family?
- Were you ever touched in a way that seemed inappropriate?
- Did you see sexual scenes or materials that made you uncomfortable?
- Were you told things you should not have known?
- How did you react to your first wet dream? Menses?
- Do you have information or events about yourself sexually that you have not told anyone about?
- Are you ashamed of who or what you are attracted to? If so, what? When did this begin? Have you ever talked to someone close to you about it before?
- How has aging affected your sexuality?
- How do you anticipate your own sexuality in the future?

Case Example

Ted and Sally, in their mid-50s, sought treatment because they had not had sexual relations for over a year. She was a busy attorney, and he was a physician. They shared a similar world view about politics, finances, and religion. Additionally, they hardly ever quarreled; in fact, the relationship was very flat. Sally felt she should leave the marriage because she was not interested in sex. Ted was very concerned but unable to express fears about separation or sexual desires. The topic of sex was off-limits. Through the use of the sexual genogram, written and physical homework assignments, and focused discussions in session, the couple gradually experienced a new level of intimacy and closeness. They learned about how emotional and sexual intimacy were never discussed or demonstrated in their families of origin, and that they were perpetuating a legacy of sexual silence. With this new awareness, they steadily reintroduced sex into their lives, and they enjoyed new forms of talking about their wishes and preferences. After six months of treatment, they considered themselves "experts" in sex and continued to work on their sexual genogram to keep the momentum alive.

References

Belous, C. R., Timm, T. A., Chee, G., & Whitehead, M. R. (2012). Revisiting the sexual genogram. *American Journal of Family Therapy, 40*(4), 281–296.

Hof, L., & Berman, E. (1986). The sexual genogram. *The Journal of Marital and Family Therapy, 12,* 39–47.

44

A SYSTEMIC APPROACH TO SENSATE FOCUS

Gerald R. Weeks and Nancy Gambescia

Purpose: To help couples reconnect physically and emotionally

Introduction

Sensate focus (SF) is a behavioral technique developed by Masters and Johnson (1970) as a part of treating a wide range of sexual dysfunctions. Although this method is widely employed in sex therapy, couple therapists can use SF principles to help partners become more intimate. SF was traditionally conceptualized as a series of touching exercises designed to lower anxiety over sex. Originally, SF involved two levels of touch (Masters & Johnson, 1970). The first level (SF I) involved sensual touching while avoiding breasts and genitals. The next level (SF II) involved both whole-body touching and genital touching or stimulation for the purpose of pleasure and not performance. Additionally, sexual intercourse was prohibited because SF was viewed as a non-demand or non-performance based exercise. There was no expectation of orgasm, but only a greater awareness of sensual and sexual sensations and improved communication. Originally the exercise was one-sided; the partner with the sexual problem was the focus of treatment, while the "asymptomatic" partner acted as a surrogate therapist who performed certain exercises at home to help the symptomatic partner overcome their sexual problem. This treatment was originally non-systemic.

Our approach to SF is quite different. We believe that most sexual problems are systemic in nature; that is, both partners are a part of the origin or continuation of the problem. Thus, SF is a shared exercise in which partners contribute equally in giving and receiving sensual/sexual touch. The graduated incremental SF exercises are started in the early phases of treatment, thereby rendering a more accurate diagnostic picture of how the couple functions in a physical interaction.

The sensual, intimate nature of SF promotes management of sexual difficulties as well as other relational problems. It can provide a form of joining, both physically and emotionally, and promote communication of feelings and desires. For instance, a couple may have experienced conflict over a period of time and lost physical contact with each other. Additionally, when sexual relationships become problematic, all other forms of sensual and affectional contact can cease. Although SF continues to be an important element of sex therapy, there are no uniform sets of practices. Further, we have not seen many articles in the couple therapy literature about using SF.

Purpose of Sensate Focus

Weeks and Gambescia (2009) published the first extensive chapter about the systemic use of SF. With a systemic focus, the couple is the unit of treatment rather than the symptomatic partner. Weeks and Gambescia (2009) demonstrated that SF could serve at least nine different functions or purposes for the relationship. These included: (1) helping each partner become more aware of their bodily sensations; (2) learning to focus on one's own pleasure without worrying about the other partner; (3) learning to communicate one's own affectional, sensual, and sexual needs, wishes, and desires; (4) gaining an increased awareness of their partner's likes; (5) expanding their repertoire of pleasurable touch; (6) learning to enjoy touch for the sake of touch without it leading to sex; (7) creating a positive relational experience; (8) building a physical and emotional connection; and (9) enhancing the level of love, caring, commitment, intimacy, cooperation, and perhaps sexual desire.

The therapist can choose to stress different functions of the SF experience at different points in its implementation. For example, when the process first begins, the focus might be on individual awareness of what one wants and being able to express those wants clearly and consistently. Once this foundation has been established, the therapist could proceed to build in other functions, such as connecting the experience to feelings of affection, love, or sexual desire.

Description and Implementation

The traditional description and implementation of SF is filled with problems. The idea that SF involved only two levels of stimulation without a more gradual and incremental approach is contrary to the whole concept of systematic desensitization. Rather than SF I and II, we think of it more in terms of SF 1.1, 1.2, 1.3, and so on for the non-genital touching, and then SF 2.1, 2.2, 2.3, and so on for sexual touching. We assess how much and what kind of touching is currently taking place, and generally use that as a starting point. If they haven't done any touching in years, we suggest a very slow and conservative approach. The exercise is described in a general way as involving taking turns touching each other in a safe environment, free from any sexual expectation or pressure, and for a specified period of time, usually starting with just a few minutes each. The therapist and couple then decide what kind of touching will take place, for how long, what parts will be touched, and where the exercise will take place. As we mentioned above, certain aspects of the touching will be emphasized, and they are to keep good mental and/or written notes on their experiences. It is best to prescribe the exercise a minimum of three times and for the couple to decide whether they need to take turns initiating, put it on the calendar, and so on. After the first round of exercises, the therapist can assess how the assignment is working.

Contraindications

Some couples will not be ready to start the SF exercises from the beginning of treatment. In order to be successful in doing the exercise, the couple must desire a physical connection with each other, be willing to work cooperatively, and be relatively free of relational conflict, anger, and other issues that might get in the way of doing the homework. Even though one or both partners believe they are ready to have sex, we frequently see couples who have a host of individual/ relational problems that might preclude SF exercises. For instance, if they are experiencing intense, hurtful conflict throughout the week, they may not want to connect physically. If there has been partner violence that is unresolved, then at least one partner will be afraid of physical contact. If one partner has an addiction such as alcoholism, they are not ready to begin SF. In fact, in all these cases mentioned above, the couple is not ready to begin a course of sex therapy, but must first work out their individual and relational issues. As a rule of thumb, sex therapy is only undertaken after major individual and relational issues are resolved. These certainly include major psychopathology, addictions, secrets (e.g., affairs), partner violence, and anything else that would impede the progress of couple therapy, not to mention sex therapy.

Sometimes it appears the couple is ready to begin the SF exercises, but after the first trial the therapist realizes they need something even more conservative or that both partners need to work through some individual issue first. For example, Tom and Mary had not touched for several years but had a non-conflicted relationship built strictly on companionship. They believed they were ready to begin some form of touching. The original assignment was to sit in the living room just holding hands for 5 to 10 minutes while watching TV. They were successful the first time they did the exercise, but the second time Mary decided to interweave her fingers with Tom's. He reacted to this change with shock, jumped up, and said he needed to leave the room. He clearly was not ready for the SF exercise, even in a basic format. Rather than press for SF, we decided to discuss his aversion to touching. This discussion revealed that when they were first married, Mary had a variety of psychological problems. Whenever he touched her, she immediately recoiled. Tom did not want to make her uncomfortable to the point of tears. At first he was angry with her, but that only made matters worse. He then began to suppress his sexual feelings, stay disconnected physically, and only connect emotionally at a superficial level. While it appeared they got along as companions, he carried a great deal of resentment over the fact that their relationship lacked emotional depth, affection, and sexuality.

Case Example

In order to discuss the implementation of SF, we use the example of Chuck and Marie, who had been dating for several months. Chuck had experienced sexual difficulties and disapproval for many years in his first marriage of 18 years. Also, his mother was extremely critical of him while he was growing up. Chuck's assumption about women was that he would be criticized and no one would consider his needs; therefore, he suppressed most of his wishes and did "what he was supposed to do." In the current relationship, there was very little touching and kissing, although he was still attracted to Marie. Additionally, he was fearful of physical touch with her. Touching meant he was opening the door for criticism. Moreover, he has no sense of awareness of what he might like or what his partner might like.

We view systemic SF as a collaboratively designed exercise involving both partners and the therapist that focuses on different aspects of the nine functions as the exercises proceed. The general instructions given to Chuck and Marie were something like: "If you feel you are ready to begin reconnecting physically, we can work on designing exercises for you to do at home about three times per week. We will start slow and build from there. The exercise must be within the comfort range of both of you. I will give you the general idea, and you can fill in the gaps. The purpose of the exercise to help you engage in physical touch again and to gradually create a physical and emotional connection with each other. The exercise is not intended to lead to intercourse. So, let's take intercourse off the table for now so you don't have to worry about this. The exercise involves doing some touching three times a week, beginning with about 5 to 10 minutes with each of you being the giver and receiver. As the giver, you want to gently touch/caress your partner's body in a manner that feels good to him or her. When you are on the receiving end of being touched, you need to focus on what feels good, briefly communicate what feels good, and communicate what you desire in order for it to continue to feel good. Each partner will take a turn at being the giver and receiver. You will want to be careful to set aside time for the exercise, and you will probably find that, although it sounds easy, it is not. Most couples have trouble with communicating what feels good and/or what they want. Over time, we will gradually increase the exercise according to your comfort level and desire. I may suggest certain types of touch depending on my sense of what would help, and you can ask each other for whatever you want as long as the partner agrees and it does not involve sex. This does not have to be a cold, clinical exercise. Feel free to use dim light, candles, music, lotions, and anything else to spice it up. Any questions? Where do you think you could start?"

In the first exercise, Chuck and Marie sat on the couch, fully clothed and holding hands; that was as much as he could tolerate. They proceeded very slowly, but eventually they were able to enjoy a full range of touching and sexual activity with pleasure. It took several months and numerous iterations and adjustments before his fears dissipated, and eventually they were able to enjoy affection, sensuality, and sexuality. Along the way, the couple was encouraged to communicate preferences, likes, and dislikes regarding physical touch. Additionally, they were provided with psychoeducational reading material that the therapist reviewed with them.

References

Masters, W., & Johnson, V. (1970). *Human sexual inadequacy.* Boston: Little, Brown.
Weeks, G., & Gambescia, N. (2009). A systemic approach to sensate focus. In K. Hertlein, G. Weeks, & N. Gambescia (Eds.), *Systemic sex therapy* (pp. 341–362). New York: Routledge.

PART F

Health and Wellness

45

A BIOPSYCHOSOCIAL-SPIRITUAL ASSESSMENT IN BRIEF OR EXTENDED COUPLE THERAPY FORMATS

Jennifer L. Hodgson, Angela L. Lamson, and Irina Kolobova

Purpose: To gather biopsychosocial-spiritual information for providing comprehensive care

Introduction

The Biopsychosocial-Spiritual (BPSS) Interview Method, first published in 2007 (Hodgson, Lamson, & Reese, 2007), is grounded in the work of Engel (1977, 1980), who brought the biopsychosocial model to the attention of medicine; and by Wright, Watson, and Bell (1996), who advocated for the addition of a spiritual dimension. The BPSS interview was developed to help family therapists extend their assessment beyond common mental health or relational questions and explore how clients' physical health history and spiritual beliefs influence psychosocial well-being, and vice versa. Furthermore, it was designed to help health care providers incorporate more psychosocial and spiritual questions into their patient interactions. Ultimately, the BPSS interview has been cited by many medical family therapists (as noted in Hodgson, Lamson, Mendenhall, & Crane, 2014), who endorse it as a guide to maximizing clinicians' and providers' recognition of the interconnectedness of BPSS health, illness, trauma, and loss.

The use of a BPSS assessment has become more important than ever due to the growth of integrated care (IC). IC is a model of care whereby mental or behavioral health providers work alongside other health care providers simultaneously, in brief therapy or health care visits (Doherty, McDaniel, & Baird, 1996), to provide one to three sessions that are, on average, 15 to 20 minutes in length. The depth of the provider's questioning and the consistency of using the BPSS assessment is influenced most by the provider's training in BPSS health along with the level of integration within the care context (Hodgson et al., 2014). This assessment method is valuable for clinicians working with couples in traditional therapy formats as well as brief IC visits.

Purpose of the Biopsychosocial-Spiritual Assessment Interview

The four assessment dimensions of the BPSS interview method include: 1) *biomedical*—physical history and current health concerns, 2) *psychological*—emotional, cognitive, and behavioral patterns and current states, 3) *social*—individual and couple relational history and existing support systems, and 4) *spiritual*—beliefs and meaning attributed to the current challenges (see Table 45.1 for examples of BPSS interview questions). Each segment of the BPSS interview format can be tailored to fit a 15 or 50+ minute therapeutic encounter. If done in a brief IC format, the types of questions may be more targeted to the identified patient's chief complaint (e.g., new diagnosis of diabetes). If done as part of a traditional 50-minute therapy session, the couple therapist can gather information across several sessions (e.g., how depression and hypertension influence the patient's relationships and work productivity) to develop a comprehensive treatment plan. In both instances, collaboration with health providers is essential for the best BPSS health outcomes.

TABLE 45.1 Examples of BPSS Interview Questions.

Dimension	Example Questions
Biomedical	1. How does your body, and your partner's, react when stressed? 2. What physical symptoms concern each of you the most right now? 3. What medications do each of you take and for what reasons?
Psychological	1. How do you and your partner show feelings similarly and differently? 2. What thoughts do you each experience when you are feeling stressed about your relationship (e.g., hopeful, defeated)? 3. What behaviors/coping mechanisms do you turn to when feeling stressed (e.g., increase/decrease exercise, drink/smoke more, isolate, pursue/distance from partner)?
Social	1. How do you let one another know when you need support from one another? 2. Who in your support system is most encouraging of your relationship and what do they do to support you? 3. Who do each of you talk to when you need relationship advice?
Spiritual	1. Why do you believe your relationship is functioning the way it is now? 2. What does it mean to you to seek support for your relationship? 3. What guides your beliefs about your relationship and its purpose?

Description and Implementation

After obtaining consent, a couple therapist should introduce the BPSS interview method and its purpose to the couple. Whether in a traditional or IC session, the couple therapist should leave the session knowing at least one factoid for each BPSS dimension at the initial encounter. Regardless of time, it is important that the questions asked extend a respect for the social location (e.g., economic climate, interracial, and/or interfaith differences) that the couple resides in and how sociocultural factors may be a source of strength or stress to the couple relationship.

Contraindications

While the belief behind capturing BPSS information is that it strengthens the therapist's understanding of the couple's overall health, there are a few contraindications. First, the BPSS assessment should not be done at the expense of the couple's urgent issues or concerns. Collecting BPSS data can be done over time if the therapeutic relationship is ongoing. If not, collecting the most pertinent information about the couple for the health care team (e.g., the partner's role in dispensing medications) should be the focus of the assessment. Second, therapists may collect biomedical and spiritual information, but they should not operate outside of their scope of practice and hypothesize causes or treatments for physical symptoms or offer spiritual/religious counseling unless trained in this area. Operating outside of one's scope could unintentionally harm a patient and cause a therapist to lose the ability to practice. Third, obtaining BPSS information for each partner is critical or the therapeutic alliance may be unbalanced. A concerted effort should be made to ask each partner the same questions.

Case Examples

Two brief case examples are presented to help illustrate how the BPSS interview method may be used with couples during a brief 15-minute IC visit and a 50-minute session. Sensitive information has been changed to protect the patients' information.

Integrated Care (15-Minute) Visit

The patient is a 58- year-old, married, African-American male, accompanied by his wife, who is addressing his hypertension, diabetes, obesity, and depression concerns. This is a follow-up visit with his primary care provider (PCP) after starting a new medication regimen. The PCP requested that the therapist meet with the couple to check on the patient's health status prior to her entering the room. After introductions, the therapist asked the patient and his wife which of the patient's current medical illnesses was most concerning to them. The wife reported that the patient's blood pressure was too high because he forgets to take his medication. The husband expressed concerns with medication side effects from his antidepressant (e.g., low libido).

The therapist asked the couple how these medical issues have impacted their relationship. The patient reported that he thinks his wife worries too much. The wife reported that she gets very frustrated that her husband does not take better care of himself. The therapist asked how they let each another know when they need support. The wife reported that she tries to talk to her husband, but he is not very responsive so she seeks support from her sisters. The patient reported that he does not like asking for support, particularly about his "manhood," and instead keeps things to himself. The therapist proceeded to ask if the couple relied on any other forms of support, such as spirituality or religion, in relation to their concerns. The patient said that he made a promise to God to take care of his wife until his last day and he had no intention of going back on his promise. She stated she prays daily for his health to improve. Together, each dimension completes a powerful composite of what is going on for the couple across dimensions.

Traditional Session

The clients are a white, non-Hispanic same-sex couple in their mid-twenties who want to work on communication issues. The therapist initiated the BPSS interview by asking how each partner notices when her partner is stressed. Partner A reported that her partner is very talkative, while Partner B stated that her partner has frivolous spending habits when stressed. Partner A reported that she holds back her emotions and tends to disengage when she feels tension in her relationship. When asked about their support system, the couple reported that both of their families are very supportive and that they belong to a very supportive church community. With regard to medical health, Partner A reported no current or past medical issues, and Partner B reported having leukemia as a child. As a result of the BPSS interview, the therapist began to identify strengths and potential areas for intervention, while also integrating pertinent collaborators into their care.

References

Doherty, W. J., McDaniel, S. H., & Baird, M. A. (1996). Five levels of primary care/behavioral healthcare collaboration. *Behavioral Healthcare Tomorrow*, October 1996.

Engel, G. (1977). The need for a new medical model: A challenge for biomedicine. *Science, 196*, 129–136.

Engel, G. L. (1980). The clinical application of the biopsychosocial model. *American Journal of Psychiatry, 137*, 535–543.

Hodgson, J., Lamson, A., Mendenhall, T., & Crane, R. (2014). *Medical family therapy: Advanced applications*. New York: Springer International Publishing Co.

Hodgson, J., Lamson, A., & Reese, L. (2007). The biopsychosocial–spiritual interview method. In D. Linville, D. Lusterman, & K. Hertlein (Eds.), *Therapist notebook for family healthcare* (pp. 3–12). New York: Hayworth Press.

Wright, L. M., Watson, W. L., & Bell, J. M. (1996). *Beliefs: The heart of healing in families and illness.* New York: Basic Books.

46

USING THE WELLNESS WHEEL WITH COUPLES

Toni Schindler Zimmerman and Shelley A. Haddock

Purpose: To help couples identify strengths and areas for growth along eight dimensions of their relationship

Introduction

A Wellness Wheel is a simple drawing of a circle divided up into sections, similar to a pizza, in which each section (or slice of the pizza) represents an aspect or dimension of a person's life. The underlying premise of the Wellness Wheel is that personal wellness is achieved when an individual attends positively to each dimension of his or her life (Myers, Sweeney, & Witmer, 2011), thereby achieving balance. When one dimension of an individual's life is neglected, the wheel is thrown out of balance and wellness is compromised. Therapists can use the Wellness Wheel to help individual clients assess their lives along each dimension and to set goals that may help them achieve more balance. Although other dimensions can be used, some dimensions of a Wellness Wheel might include:

- *Intellectual*: Investing in lifelong learning, maintaining curiosity, or investing in creative endeavors.
- *Social*: Investing in relationships with family and friends, developing a sense of belonging to one's communities, or feeling connected to others.
- *Emotional*: Maintaining awareness of one's feelings, effectively managing one's emotions through life's challenges, or appropriately sharing one's feelings with others.
- *Occupational*: Investing in a profession, job, or education; volunteering; or maintaining work-life balance.
- *Spiritual*: Investing in one's spirituality through mediation; worship; or finding inspiration, purpose, and meaning in life.

- *Environmental*: Having a healthy and safe living space and environment.
- *Physical*: Investing in physical health through exercising, eating well, and practicing healthy habits.

The Wellness Wheel is more frequently used with individual clients, but it can also be used with couples in therapy. Because being one's best as an individual is an important contribution to a healthy couple relationship, the Wellness Wheel might be used in a couple's therapy to assess each partner's level of personal wellness and how this wellness might affect the couple relationship. Additionally, the Wellness Wheel can be used with couples to explore aspects or dimensions of their relationships. For instance, when using the wheel with couples, dimensions of the Wellness Wheel might be adapted as follows:

- *Intellectual*: Sharing or producing creative ideas together, or engaging in learning about something together.
- *Social*: Spending time with family and friends as a couple, or feeling connected to one another.
- *Emotional*: Being in tune with one another's feelings; being able to help support one another with emotions through life's challenges.
- *Occupational*: Managing work-life balance in a way that maximizes couple time; volunteering together; supporting one another with occupational demands and stressors.
- *Spiritual*: Engaging in mediation, worship, or finding inspiration, purpose, and meaning in life as a couple.
- *Environment*: Creating and maintaining a healthy and safe living space and environment to share as a couple.
- *Physical*: Exercising, eating well, and maintaining healthy habits as a couple; enjoying a satisfying sexual relationship.

Purpose of the Couple Wellness Wheel

The purpose of the Wellness Wheel is to provide a visual tool to help couples evaluate the individual well-being of each partner, as well as the well-being of the couple relationship along various dimensions. The Wellness Wheel also is intended to help clients set treatment goals based on this evaluation.

Description and Implementation

When a couple comes to therapy for an intake, the Wellness Wheel can be a tool to have them evaluate and communicate about the areas of their relationship that are flourishing as well as those that need attention. The Wellness Wheel offers a framework to discuss strengths and areas for growth in a more structured way. The therapist can place a large piece of paper on the table on which the wheel is drawn and the dimensions labeled. The therapist can introduce the

Wellness Wheel by explaining that she or he would like to inquire about each dimension of their relationship. The therapist can first inquire about the couples' strengths in each area. For example, in talking about the occupation dimension, the couple may report that they are happy with their jobs and income, they rarely argue about money, and they have similar spending habits. The therapist can write these strengths next to a plus (+) sign on the wheel. After discussion strengths in each area, the therapist can inquire about the dimensions that the couple is struggling with or has brought them into therapy. For example, a couple might respond that they are struggling to find enough time with one another because of work demands. In this case, the therapist could write "challenges with work-life balance" next to a minus (-) sign in the "occupational" dimension.

Through this process, the couple gains a visual representation of their relationship. Many couples discover that not all dimensions of the relationship are in need of work. A couple might discover that they are having trouble in two dimensions that are connected, such as social and occupational. For instance, they may report that they are frustrated with their third-shift work hours, which has led to them feeling isolated from friends who work different hours from them. The therapist and couple can explore how these two dimensions may create a cycle that needs to be interrupted or adjusted. For example, the couple may decide that one option for staying connected with friends is to get together with them for breakfast instead of dinner, since they work in the evening.

Contraindications

Some couples may feel confined by using the Wellness Wheel in their intake session. If they prefer to tell their story and their reasons for seeking therapy in a less structured way, the therapist can simply take notes on the wheel as clients explain their situation. This may allow the couple to benefit from the visual representation of their relationship without confining them in how they communicate their situation and needs to the therapist.

Case Example

In Jenny and Jose's intake session, the therapist placed a large piece of paper on the table in front of them. On the paper was drawn a large circle, and the circle was divided into dimensions (like a pizza). Each dimension was labeled (e.g., social, emotional, occupational, spiritual, environmental, and physical); see Figure 46.1.

The therapists explained that, as a couple, they share many dimensions of life with one another, and that this diagram can give them a structured way to assess how well each of these areas is functioning in their relationship. The therapist introduced each dimension of the Wellness Wheel, providing examples of life elements that might be included in each dimension. The therapist invited Jenny and

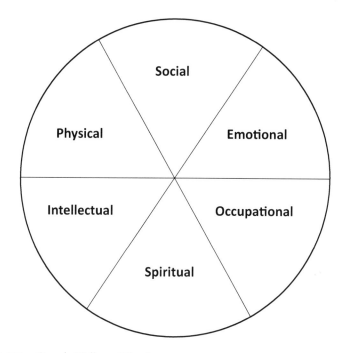

FIGURE 46.1   Couple Wellness Wheel.

Jose to reflect on their life together in each of these areas, including the strengths and frustrations in each area.

Jenny and Jose wanted to begin with the area of "occupation." They reported that they were both in satisfying jobs and, although money was tight, they were good at budgeting. They reported that they experienced no difficulties in this dimension of their lives together. Next, they talked about the "environment" dimension. They reported that they were living with Jose's family right now while they were looking for a house. They went on to describe that living with Jose's family was creating many stressors for them, and, as a result, they had been fighting more frequently. In the "emotion" dimension, the couple reported they were having different experiences in living with Jose's family, and they were struggling to understand one another's feelings. Whereas Jose was not finding it stressful to live with his family, Jenny was highly stressed in this situation. They reported that when Jenny would communicate her stress to Jose, he would respond by saying that she was ungrateful to his family for letting them stay at their house. As the couple discussed this situation, it became clear to the therapist that part of the treatment plan and goals for therapy would involve helping the couple develop tools in the dimension of "emotion," such as learning to listen and validate one another's feelings. The therapist guided the couple in discussing each dimension of the Wellness Wheel in this way. At the conclusion of this process, the couple was able to look together at the visual representation of their relationship. The therapists asked the couple what they noticed in examining the Wellness Wheel, and both reported that it helped them see the many areas of strength they have in their relationship. They also noted how this new living situation had thrown their Wellness Wheel out of balance, and they were able to establish goals for obtaining balance once again.

Reference

Myers, J. E., Sweeney, T. J., & Witmer, J. M. (2011). The wheel of wellness counseling for wellness: A holistic model for treatment planning. *Journal of Counseling & Development, 78*(3), 251–266.

47

IDENTIFYING AND REDUCING STRESS THAT INFLUENCES RELATIONAL HEALTH

Angela L. Lamson, Jennifer L. Hodgson, and Amelia R. Muse

Purpose: To reduce indicators of stress in the context of couples' relational health

Introduction

Physiological Stress Response

A physiological stress response occurs when a person recognizes a stressor (i.e., a benign or chronic threat to the mind, body, or spirit) that activates the autonomic nervous system (ANS) (Raff & Levitzky, 2011). The ANS is comprised of the parasympathetic nervous system (PNS) and the sympathetic nervous system (SNS). The PNS is active in the absence of a stressor and is responsible for "rest and digest" activity, while the SNS is activated in response to a stressor and contributes to a physiological "fight or flight" response, such as dilating pupils, increasing heart rate, and increasing blood pressure (Raff & Levitzky, 2011). The SNS response is critical for responding to and surviving stressful or life-threatening events.

A significant period of physiological stress can take a toll on the body physically, mentally, and emotionally. Chronic physiological stress can strain the cardiovascular system, dysregulate stress hormones, and prevent normal parasympathetic activity from occurring (McEwen, 2007). These long-term effects can contribute to the development of chronic medical conditions such as hypertension, obesity, or diabetes; impair cognitive functioning; contribute to anxiety and depressive disorders; and endanger relational health (McEwen, 2007).

Given the deleterious effects of chronic physiological stress, it is of little surprise that when one partner is experiencing a prolonged elevated stress response, it affects the stress response of his/her partner. These bidirectional effects have been observed in several studies examining the stress hormone cortisol in couples (Laws, 2014). Given the bidirectional influences partners have on one another's physiological stress, it is important to utilize the couple dyad in intervention when targeting physiological stress.

Purpose and Description of Identifying and Reducing Stress in Couples

Diaphragmatic Breathing (DB) (Hance, 1917)

Diaphragmatic breathing (DB) is a technique that focuses on helping couples breath in a way that strengthens their respiratory muscular system. It changes their physiological activity by slowing their heart rate and breathing frequency while increasing ventilation and oxygen saturation. It also improves their ability to think through stressors apart from crisis mode. The therapist begins with teaching the couple to breath from their diaphragm (aka, belly breathing) instead of their upper chest, where full breaths are not possible. They are taught to uncross legs, arms, and hands, then to draw in air through their nose until their belly is bloated (i.e., full like a balloon) and then blow the air out slowly and steadily out their mouth, bringing the bellybutton back toward the spine. This exercise can be paired with having them imagine their favorite color as they breathe in, and their least favorite color being blown out as they exhale. It is best done in session with the therapist modeling the correct breathing pattern. The process can be repeated several times in a day.

Visual (Guided) Imagery (VI) (Utay & Miller, 2006)

Visual, or guided, imagery (VI) is a technique designed to help individuals reduce the noise from their current stress load and focus on an image that brings them calm and peace. Couples will not likely share the same image in their VI experience. The therapist who is guiding the process can allot 5 to 30 minutes to this activity, depending on the availability of time. Each therapist will have his/her own approach to transitioning the couple into the relaxation process, but it is important that whatever method is used to transition them into the visualization is the same one used to transition them out.

One approach is to have the couple close their eyes and imagine walking down a hallway where the lights dim slowly as each person approaches a door. Have them stop and imagine that beyond the door is a place that they each equate with calm, peace, and feeling stress-free. Encourage them to confirm that they have a place in mind before opening the door. If the therapist needs to offer examples, she/he may, but keep them generic (e.g., a beach with soft sand or a grassy meadow). As they enter their place of peace, they are asked to experience it with all five of their senses (imagine what they would see, hear, touch, taste, and smell). It is important that the couple is allowed quiet time to experience the place they choose without the therapist's voice. The couple should be told that if external noises occur (e.g., phone rings, ambulance passes by) they can place the sound on a cloud, leaf, etc., and watch it float away. As the exercise concludes, the therapist gently encourages the clients to turn toward the door they initially stepped through into their place of peace. Before they exit the door, the therapist asks them to turn back around and thank the place for what it means to them and to their well-being. The therapist then has them open the door and proceed down the hallway slowly until the light becomes brighter, and eventually becomes the light within the therapy room. Then, the therapist asks them to open their eyes and process their experiences with one another. This technique can be used as often as needed. Some clients find it helpful before bedtime or even in the middle of a stressful day.

Progressive Muscle Relaxation (PMR) (Jacobson, 1938)

Progressive muscle relaxation (PMR) is a technique used to help clients create awareness of tension and relaxation in their bodies. Progressive muscle relaxation is termed "progressive" because it proceeds through all major muscle groups, relaxing them one at a time until total muscular relaxation is achieved. The exercise allows couples to work together and arrive at a calmer physiological state simultaneously. It begins by asking the couple to find a place to sit where they are most comfortable and uncross their legs, arms, and hands. Begin with asking them to squeeze their toes as much as they can comfortably, and to hold the squeezed position to the count of 10. At the end of the 10-count, have them squeeze even harder once more and then quickly release. Encourage them to feel the blood flow through their toes and feet as a sense of calm takes over that region of the body. Encourage them to proceed up the legs, squeezing various leg muscle groups one at a time (e.g., calves, quadriceps, hamstrings). Then, have them progress to the lower back, abdomen, middle back, upper back, chest, shoulders, neck, shoulders, arms, and end with the hands. Ask them to then do a full-body muscular contraction, hold, and release, like they did for the other muscle groups.

Upon the conclusion of any of these exercises, ask the couple to debrief how they felt individually. Let the couple know that these exercises should not cause discomfort, and that they should stop any exercise that does not feel physically or emotionally comfortable. Any discomforts should be reported back to their therapist or primary care provider.

Contraindications

DB should not be used with people who have breathing complications, because it may increase the effort it takes to breathe or cause shortness of breath. Therapists using VI should be aware of each client's trauma history to ensure that this technique is indicated as part of their treatment. PMR should be used with caution with those who have chronic pain or high blood pressure. The contract-relax method may aggravate sensitive pain areas for those with chronic pain, or cause a temporary increase in blood pressure, which could be harmful to those with hypertension. If clients are interested in trying these techniques but have either breathing complications, chronic pain, or high blood pressure, then they should consult with their primary health care provider to see if the exercises are appropriate for their condition.

Case Example

A couple presented for therapy due to an increased frequency in escalating arguments. The couple had a difficult time starting the sessions, often interrupting one another, and showed obvious signs of physiological stress. The therapist decided that diaphragmatic breathing followed by progressive muscle relaxation would be used for the first five to eight minutes of every session. Over time, the couple's debriefing about the techniques (i.e., the discussion between the couple and the therapist related to the use of DB and PMR in session) indicated that both partners were able to focus more on listening to their partner when the other was talking rather than feeling the need to interrupt their partner. The partners also described how their bodies felt more relaxed compared to how they used to feel when they disagreed or argued (e.g., heart pounding, upset stomach, headaches).

References

Hance, I. W. (1917). Diaphragmatic breathing. *Transactions of the American Clinical and Climatological Association, 33*, 52–58.

Jacobson, E. (1938). *Progressive relaxation*. Chicago: University of Chicago Press.

Laws, H. (2014). *Modeling dyadic attunement: Physiological concordance in newly married couples and alliance similarity in patient-therapist dyads* (Order No. 3615428, University of Massachusetts Amherst). ProQuest Dissertations and Theses, 147. Retrieved from http://search.proquest.com.jproxy.lib.ecu.edu/docview/1523951356?accountid=10639 (1523951356)

McEwen, B. S. (2007). Physiology and neurobiology of stress and adaptation: Central role of the brain. *Physiological Reviews, 87*(3), 873–904. doi: 10.1152/physrev.00041.2006

Raff, H., & Levitzky, M. G. (2011). *Medical physiology: A systems approach*. New York: McGraw-Hill Professional Publishing. Retrieved from http://www.ebrary.com

Utay, J., & Miller, M. (2006). Guided imagery as an effective therapeutic technique: A brief review of its history and efficacy research. *Journal of Instructional Psychology, 33*(1), 40–43.

48

PSYCHOEDUCATION ON THE INFLUENCE OF STRESS ON COUPLES

Anne Milek and Guy Bodenmann

Purpose: To help couples be aware and identify the influence of external stressors

Introduction

Based on stress research in couples (for a review, see Randall & Bodenmann, 2009), two therapeutic elements in coping-oriented couple interventions have been proposed: (1) *psychoeducation*, explaining to couples how external daily stress impinges on the couple's life and how they can protect the relationship against the negative impact of stress; and (2) teaching couples how to *cope together effectively* with stressful encounters by means of the 3-phase method aiming to enhance dyadic coping and mutual understanding of each other's functioning (see Chapter 49).

Psychoeducation is intended to help couples be aware and identify the influence external minor stressors (e.g., having a bad day at work, annoyance with neighbors, having problems with extended family members, financial strain, etc.) can have on their lives and their functioning as a couple. A number of studies show that chronic daily stress may erode the foundation of close relationships slowly, and over time unnoticed daily hassles may have a subtle but significant negative impact on relationships (e.g., Karney, Story, & Bradbury, 2005; Randall & Bodenmann, 2009). The impact of everyday stress on couples' lives (e.g., their communication, time spent together, personality and emotional well-being) is not instantly evident but unfolds over time.

Purpose of Psychoeducation on the Influence of Stress on Couples

Psychoeducation on external stress has two major goals: (1) to increase couples' awareness of how external minor chronic stress impacts their relationship and raises the likelihood for arguments, alienation, and dissatisfaction; and (2) to increase mutual understanding and acceptance by explaining how partners may differentially react to stress based on individual factors (e.g., personality, prior experiences, personal schemata, etc.).

Description and Implementation

The therapist should explain how external stress (i.e., stress that initially has nothing to do with the close relationship) affects the couple by (1) reducing the time that partners spend together, (2) deteriorating the communication quality (more withdrawal, less positivity, more negativity), (3) making difficult personality traits of the partners more evident, (4) decreasing their general well-being and quality of life, (5) triggering dysfunctional attributions, as well as by (6) negatively impacting sexual intimacy.

Effects on Time

Stress reduces time that partners spend together in a harmonious context and leads to fewer shared experiences, fewer joint leisure activities, fewer opportunities for emotional self-disclosure, and fewer possibilities to cope together with adversities and daily hassles. Stress may lead partners to withdraw more into their individual lives (personal recreation) or spend their free time fulfilling work demands. Reduced time for the partner gives him/her a feeling of being neglected, and of being less important than other things.

Effects on Communication

Stress brought home from outside in general has an impact on daily couple interactions by reducing partners' positivity (a decrease of compliments, caring, openness with the partner, interest in the partner, and affection). At the same time, stress increases negativity toward the partner (an increase of criticism, defensiveness, contempt, and belligerence). Additionally, emotional self-disclosure is reduced, and partners interact more superficially and are more solution-focused, with the intention to resolve problems as quickly as possible. This leads to fewer shared emotions and less personal and intimate exchanges, increasing emotional distance between partners.

Effects on Personality

External minor stressors trigger personal vulnerabilities (i.e., personal schema, see also Chapter 49) and increase unpleasant partner behavior, such as rigidity, dominance, stubbornness, anxiety, or insecurity. These are traits that may be less obvious in normal or relaxed life conditions but can be exacerbated in stressful times. Once activated, these behaviors and attitudes are perceived as annoying and bothersome, disturb dyadic interactions, and tend to increase dissatisfaction with the other partner.

Effects on Well-Being

It is well known that stress has, in the long term, a negative impact on psychological well-being (tension, nervousness, anxiety, depression, sleep problems) and physical health (heart problems, digestion problems, etc.) (e.g., Graham, Christian, & Kiecolt-Glaser, 2006). Within a couple, the health problems of one partner affect the other one significantly by means of a disturbed equilibrium among partners (e.g., affecting role division), by necessity of additional support and caring, by worries about the partner, as well as by reduced free-time activities and effects on a couple's sexuality.

Effects on Attribution

Another goal of psychoeducation is to create awareness of dysfunctional attribution processes. When one partner often comes home stressed out and in a bad mood, showing withdrawal or angry, hostile behavior, the other partner might interpret these behaviors as a sign that (1) the partner no longer loves him/her, or (2) the partner has become a grumpy person. He or she might attribute these negative behaviors to the disadvantage of the close relationship, not realizing that external stress could have caused the negative behavior.

Effects on Sexuality

A number of studies indicate that external stress also has a deleterious impact on a partner's libido (especially female sexual desire), sexual activity, and sexual pleasure, hence increasing sexual problems. The more stress one or both partners experience during the day, the less sexual activity the couple shows in the evening or night, and the more problems are reported (e.g., sexual arousal problems, and in men, erection problems or premature ejaculation). As physical intimacy and sexuality are important indicators of couples' functioning, the impact of stress on sexuality is considerable.

Practical Therapist's Behavior

The therapist introduces the negative impacts of external stressors to the couple either by teaching (theoretical input) or by exploring these effects with the couple using the Socratic dialogue technique. Using this technique, the partners talk with each other in order to gain a deeper understanding of the stressors. The element of psychoeducation can be used at any stage in therapy whenever the therapist feels a need to explain to the couple that their negative interactions or feelings of alienation may be due to external stressors rather than being solely a consequence of their close relationship. This externalized focus of the problem can encourage the couple to fight together against the demands and adversities of their life and may help build and strengthen their motivation for dyadic coping.

Case Example

In the therapy session, Mary complains that Kim has no time for her, that all other things are more important to him. Kim defends himself and explains that his work life is hard and that he does not have the resources to be open to his wife's needs when he comes home. She does not believe him and takes his behavior as proof of his lack of love and commitment for her and their relationship.

The therapist validates both partners' perceptions of the situation and then explores with the couple why their life is currently unpleasant and what conditions led to this situation. When it becomes clear that Kim's work stress and other minor daily hassles spill over into the couple relationship, the therapist talks about the detrimental effects of external stressors (theoretical input). He discusses with Mary and Kim whether and how these theoretical findings fit with their reality. This leads Mary and Kim to realize that the effects of various stressors in their lives are having a greater negative effect on their relationship than they realized. This prompted them to reevaluate their outside commitments and create firmer boundaries around their relationship.

References

Karney, B. R., Story, L. B., & Bradbury, T. N. (2005). Marriages in context: Interactions between chronic an acute stress among newlyweds. In T. A. Revenson, K. Kayser, & G. Bodenmann (Eds.), *Couples coping with stress: Emerging perspectives on dyadic coping* (pp. 13–32). Washington, DC: American Psychological Association.

Graham, J. E., Christian, L. M., & Kiecolt-Glaser J. K. (2006). Stress, age, and immune function: Toward a lifespan approach. *Journal of Behavioral Medicine, 29,* 389–400.

Randall, A. K., & Bodenmann, G. (2009). The role of stress on close relationships and marital satisfaction. *Clinical Psychology Review, 29*(2), 105–115. doi: 10.1016/j.cpr.2008.10.004

49

3-PHASE METHOD OF DYADIC COPING

Guy Bodenmann and Anne Milek

Purpose: To help couples cope with external stress together and prevent negative spillover effects

Introduction

The 3-phase method of dyadic coping was developed by Bodenmann (2005, 2007) to help couples prevent external stressors from deteriorating their intimate relationship (see Chapter 48) by strengthening their dyadic coping skills. Research findings on stress and coping in couples suggest that this is a promising avenue for improving the outcomes of couple's therapy. The 3-phase method is based on the systemic transactional model (STM) of dyadic coping (Bodenmann, 2005) and integrates methods from behavioral marital therapy, cognitive therapy, and classical communication trainings. Both partners are invited to engage in the dyadic coping process, but roles are clearly defined: One partner is the speaker, nonverbally and verbally communicating his/ her stress, and the other partner is the listener, providing support. The speaker learns to talk about his/her stressful experiences in a more explicit and emotionally self-disclosing way to facilitate mutual understanding; the listener learns that understanding his/her partner's stress experiences is a prerequisite to providing adequate support and to appropriately responding to the partner's needs. In total, a 3-phase method sequence takes approximately 45 minutes per partner (see Table 49.1).

Purpose of the 3-Phase Method of Dyadic Coping

The 3-phase method aims to enhance mutual dyadic coping by (a) enhancing partners' ability to communicate their stress to their partners in a deeper,

TABLE 49.1 3-Phase Method of Dyadic Coping. Reprinted with permission from Bodenmann, G. (2012). *Verhaltenstherapie mit Paaren [Behavioral therapy with couples].* (2nd ed.). Bern: Huber.

1. Phase (30 minutes)	2. Phase (10 minutes)	3. Phase (5 minutes)
Emotional stress exploration by partner A:	**Provision of dyadic coping by partner B:**	**Feedback from partner A about his or her experience of dyadic coping received from partner B:**
He/she tells the partner about a stressful experience that happened outside the close relationship (i.e., external stress) and what was emotionally relevant. Speaker rules: • Be specific • Be self-focused ("I") • Share emotions Listener rules: • Active listening • Summarize • Open-ended questions	He/she is invited to support the partner on the level of emotional engagement that matches the level of intimate emotional disclosure on the part of partner A in the first phase.	Partner A tells partner B: • How satisfied he/she was with the dyadic coping. • How helpful this support was. • What else he/she would have needed to feel better and to cope more effectively with the stressful situation.

self-disclosing way (phase 1); (b) fostering empathy and adapting their support to the specific needs of the other (phase 2); and (c) refining their ability to offer dyadic support based on the partner's feedback (phase 3).

Description and Implementation

Setting and coaching behavior: Partner A and partner B are asked to sit on two chairs directly facing each other (dyadic setting; see Figure 49.1), while the couple therapist is positioned to the side equidistant from both persons. The therapist briefly explains the 3-phase method (speaker and listener rules; see Table 49.1) and asks the couple who wants to go first in being the speaker and telling the partner about an (emotionally relevant) external stress event that happened outside the close relationship. To keep the conversation between the two partners, the couple therapist stays in the background as much as possible by (a) not focusing on one partner, but looking back and forth between both partners attentively; (b) using a soft voice; (c) keeping phrases very short when intervening (e.g., "How did you feel?"; "What did that mean to you?"; "Is there anything else you felt?"; "Are you anxious, and if so, why?"; "What are you angry about?"); (d) reinforcing desirable nonverbal and verbal behaviors with positive feedback-channeling (e.g., when partner A talks about feelings or

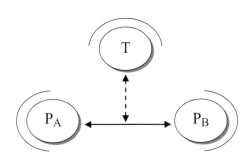

The couple sits face to face and the therapist is positioned to the side, equidistant from both persons. The partners speak to each other, with one as the speaker, and the other as the listener in Phase 1. The therapist gently facilitates the process and prompts both partners. The speaker does not speak with the therapist but only with the partner. The therapist is active but in a very discrete and unobtrusive way.

FIGURE 49.1   Setting During 3-Phase Method. Reprinted with permission from Bodenmann, G. (2012). *Verhaltenstherapie mit Paaren [Behavioral therapy with couples]* (2nd ed.). Bern: Huber. Note: In the figure, T = Therapist; P_A = Partner A; P_B = Partner B; the solid arrow indicates direct interaction between partners; and the dotted arrow suggests discrete, unobtrusive interaction from the therapist.

partner B summarizes partner A's feelings, then the therapist could say "mmhh," "good," "keep going").

Description of the 3-Phase Method

Phase 1: The stressed partner A (speaker) is guided by the therapist to explore his/her emotional stress with the main goal to gain deeper insights into emotions, cognitions, physiological sensations, and images that are related to the stressful situation. Concurrently, the therapist prompts partner B (listener) to actively listen and summarize important aspects of partner A's self-disclosure. By switching back and forth between partner A (disclosing) and partner B (summarizing what he/she understood), the therapist helps both partners to mutually deepen their understanding of partner A's stress.

   At the beginning, the speaker is asked to start with a brief narrative description of a specific stressful event, and is then guided by the therapist to further explore deeper cognitive and emotional aspects of the stressful event (funnel method). By reflecting on open-ended questions (e.g., How did you feel? What did this mean to you? Why was this so stressful?), the speaker emotionally revives the stressful experience and the fundamental personal schema that was triggered by the situation (e.g., not being worthy to receive attention from others). By sharing an intensive emotional experience and discovering the reason (personal schema) underlying the stress reaction, couples experience a feeling of "we-ness" and intimacy. At the same time, partner B, learning more about reasons for partner A's strong stress reaction, develops a deepened understanding, acceptance, and tolerance and is enabled to provide appropriate support fitting partner A's needs later in phase 2. During phase 1, the listening partner should only try to understand empathically what the speaker is experiencing.

Phase 2: Partner B is invited by the therapist to provide positive emotion-focused support while partner A is primarily listening. The therapist ensures that partner B provides support corresponding to the level of emotional self-disclosure of partner A, and prompts emotion-focused support when necessary. However, being aware of the significance of the stressful experience by partner A, partner B is likely to be emotionally involved, and experience and show authentic empathy and interest. After expressing his/her empathy and understanding, partner B may also provide other forms of dyadic coping, such as reframing the situation, helping to actively resolve the problem, etc.

Phase 3: Partner A evaluates partner B's support and tells him/her which aspects of the provided support were most helpful and what else he/she would have needed to feel better and to cope more effectively with the stressful situation. The feedback phase is important to enhance the couple's skills to mutually support each other adequately.

Afterwards, partners change roles in order for both partners to experience deepened stress-related self-disclosure as well as support-giving and support-receiving. In each session, both partners should be in both roles.

Contraindications

As this method requires mutual trust, commitment, and engagement, the therapist should not apply this method when one or both partners do not intend to maintain the relationship. It is important to ensure that both partners are able and willing to symmetrically engage in the disclosing process: One-sided emotional self-disclosure without a validating corresponding (coping) reaction from the partner is detrimental and must be avoided by all means.

Furthermore, the 3-phase method is not indicated if one partner: (a) displays anti-social personality traits (e.g., is not able to feel empathy), or (b) has severe psychological disorders (e.g., psychotic disorders). However, in the context of treating affective, anxiety, or sexual functioning disorders, the 3-phase method has been shown to be suitable and helpful for couples.

Case Example

In one session, Sue told Tom about a situation when she was late for an important appointment. At first she reported more easily accessible emotions, such as a more general arousal that goes along with nervousness and embarrassment. But by further exploring this event, Sue touched upon beliefs such as being perceived by others as unreliable, untrustworthy, or incompetent. This led to activation of deeper emotions, such as disappointment, guilt, shame, anxiety, and sadness, and revealed a personal schema (not being accepted by others the way she was). Through this process, Sue and Tom had a clearer understanding of the reasons why the "apparently" minor matter of being late was so stressful for her.

References

Bodenmann, G. (2005). Dyadic coping and its significance for marital functioning. In T. Revenson, K. Kayser, & G. Bodenmann (Eds.), *Couples coping with stress: Emerging perspectives on dyadic coping* (pp. 33–49). Washington, DC: American Psychological Association.

Bodenmann, G. (2007). Dyadic coping and the 3-phase-method in working with couples. In L. VandeCreek & J. B. Allen (Eds.), *Innovations in clinical practice: Focus on group and family therapy* (pp. 235–252). Sarasota: Professional Resources Press.

Bodenmann, G. (2012). *Verhaltenstherapie mit Paaren [Behavioral therapy with couples]* (2nd ed.). Bern: Huber.

PART G

Intimate Partner Violence

50

CLINICAL ASSESSMENT INTERVIEW FOR INTIMATE PARTNER VIOLENCE

Douglas B. Smith and Jason B. Whiting

Purpose: To identify physical and psychological violence in couple relationships

Introduction

Physical and psychological violence are not uncommon in intimate relationships. Conservative estimates for the rates of intimate partner violence (IPV) consistently indicate that physical violence will occur in 20–25% of all intimate partnerships. In clinical settings, the number of couples affected by violence is considerably higher. However, very few couples identify violence as a presenting problem when entering therapy. In our clinic at Texas Tech University, intake data indicate that at least one partner reports physical violence in slightly over 50% of couples seeking treatment, which is consistent with research findings. The implication is that family therapists working with intimate partners, whether in couples therapy or in the context of family therapy, are dealing with IPV whether they are aware of it or not. Unfortunately, many clinicians lack the training and feel unprepared to assess for or address IPV in relationships. Because systemic treatment and intervention have the potential to increase tension and/or conflict in relational systems, working with undisclosed IPV is a roadblock to change and a safety risk.

Purpose of the Clinical Assessment Interview for Intimate Partner Violence

The main objective of this technique is to identify the presence of physical and/or psychological violence in couple relationships through a series of questions in cases in which violence is not specifically identified by the clients as the problem, or to assess the severity of violence if violence is identified by the clients as a clinical concern. Given the frequency with which IPV is found in intimate partners seeking therapy, it is essential that every couple be assessed for IPV at the outset of treatment. This will help increase safety both in the relationship and in the therapeutic environment, and allow therapists to develop appropriate treatment goals early on with their clients. For example, in our brief IPV intervention, intimate partners reporting IPV are required to complete no-violence contracts, individual safety plans, and develop negotiated time-out plans (for an excellent discussion of some of these elements, see Davies, Lyon, & Monti-Catania, 1998; Rosen, Matheson, Stith, McCollum, & Locke, 2003; Stith & McCollum, 2011). A thorough IPV assessment also aids the treatment team in determining whether conjoint therapy is appropriate.

Description and Implementation: Assessment for IPV

Conducting a clinical interview assessment for IPV with a couple or family requires safety considerations that may not be needed when working with an individual. We recommend that the evaluation be conducted separately with each member of the intimate partnership. Asking questions about violence in the presence of both partners before obtaining a clear picture of the nature of the power differential and conflict in the relationship could place one or both partners at risk for serious harm.

While the assessment will be most effective if the questions take place conversationally, it is important that answers to certain structured questions are obtained. We recommend that the therapist begin by asking a general question about "conflict" in the relationship. For example, the therapist may say, "*When working with couples, there is always the potential for therapy to bring up sensitive topics. So, it is useful for me to know what conflict looks like in your relationship.*" Because the assessment is taking place at the beginning of the first session, asking directly about physical violence may seem irrelevant to the clients' stated goals for therapy. Clients will often freely volunteer information about IPV when asked about conflict. However, if clients do not identify IPV, it is important for the therapist to ask directly about the occurrence of physical and psychological violence in the relationship. Each question should be asked in reference to both the partner's behavior and the behavior of the individual answering the question.

"*Have you (or your partner) ever been physically violent toward your partner (or you)? For example, have you ever grabbed, pushed, slapped, hit, physically restrained, or prevented your partner from leaving a space? Have you ever done anything else that might make your partner feel physically threatened?*" The therapists should use clear and specific language (e.g., physical violence), offer some concrete examples of what defines violent behavior, and ask for specific descriptions of violent behavior in order to avoid minimization of violence or misunderstandings due to differing cultural narratives.

"*Have you ever been verbally aggressive toward your partner? For example, have you ever yelled at your partner, called them names, said things to make them feel stupid, or tried to control them?"* Questions about verbal/psychological violence can be skipped during the initial assessment (and revisited later) if the client(s) report physical violence, because psychological violence almost always accompanies physical violence.

"How often does the physical/psychological violence occur? When was the last time the violence occurred?" Answers to these questions begin to provide a picture of the cycle of violence in the relationship and where in the cycle the clients are currently.

"Has a weapon ever been used as part of the violence? Have you ever been injured as a result of the violence in your relationship? For example, have you ever had bruises, cuts, sprains, or broken bones? Have you ever sought or should you have sought medical attention as a result of violence in the relationship? What is the worst episode of violence that has ever happened between you and your partner?" These questions provide information about the severity of violence and identify crossed boundaries. Previously crossed boundaries may provide an indication of the potential severity of future episodes of violence. The answers should be taken seriously because once a boundary has been crossed, it is easier to cross again.

"Who do you think is most responsible for the violence in your relationship?" Asking about responsibility serves two purposes. First, if a perpetrator of violence is unable to take any responsibility for their behavior, conjoint therapy is not recommended. Second, understanding the degree to which victims blame themselves for the violence is clinically relevant.

Another unique challenge of conducting a clinical interview assessment for IPV with couples or families is answering the question, *"Who should be assessed first?"* Having multiple forms of assessment data can help. In general, we recommend that if another source of assessment data indicates the IPV is unidirectional or if one partner is reporting they are the victim of more violent behaviors, the partner experiencing the greatest level of violence should be interviewed first. If assessment data is lacking or inconclusive, we recommend that female partners in heterosexual relationships be interviewed first. Women are far more likely to be injured or killed by an intimate partner than are men, and they are more likely to be coerced and controlled. Because of this, the assessment itself may increase the risks to a victim. Conducting the assessment first with the partner who is at the greatest risk allows the therapist to take steps to mitigate the danger.

Three additional questions are necessary when conducting violence assessments with adult partners in couples or families. *"I was planning on asking your partner the same set of questions I just asked you. It is likely they will guess that I asked you these questions. Do you feel safe if I bring up the same questions to your partner?"* If the first partner indicates they feel unsafe, the therapist should meet individually with the other partner, but refrain from asking about violence. If the second partner interviewed feels unsafe, the therapist will have to take additional steps to manage the safety of the clients. This may include increasing the session length to develop safety plans or arranging for alternate transportation for one of the partners. Client safety must always be the main priority. *"Do you feel safe if we discuss the violence you reported with your partner as part of therapy? Are you willing to sign an agreement to not engage in physical violence?"* If either adult partner answers "no," conjoint therapy is not appropriate until such time as both partners feel safe and are willing to commit to a violence-free relationship.

Contraindications

We strongly believe that a violence assessment should be conducted at the beginning of therapy with every intimate partnership. While we do recognize and have alluded to the safety considerations the assessment can create, we believe engaging a couple or family system with undisclosed violence in therapy is potentially far more dangerous. However, identifying IPV is only the first step. The safety of the clients should be the primary consideration when deciding how to proceed with therapy, especially if conjoint therapy is requested. Therapists who work with IPV need specialized training and connections to community support services, such as women's shelters and anger management groups. The process or procedures of therapy should never take precedence over the safety of the clients.

References

Davies, J., Lyon, E., & Monti-Catania, D. (1998). *Safety planning with battered women: Complex lives/difficult choices.* Thousand Oaks, CA: Sage Publications.

Rosen, K. H., Matheson, J. L., Stith, S., McCollum, E. E., & Locke, L. D. (2003). Negotiated time-out: A de-escalation tool for couples. *Journal of Marital and Family Therapy, 29*(3), 291–298.

Stith, S. M., & McCollum, E. E. (2011). Conjoint treatment of couples who have experienced intimate partner violence. *Aggression and Violent Behavior, 16*(4), 312–318.

51

"I DIDN'T HURT YOU, BUT IF I DID I HAD A GOOD REASON!"

Denial and Distortion in Abusive Couples

Jason B. Whiting and Douglas B. Smith

Purpose: To help therapists reduce denial, blame, and distortion in high-conflict and violent couples

Introduction: Violence and Distortion

Brittany and Brian were experts at annoying each other. He would criticize how she put their son to bed or her social skills. She would fume, cry, and claim that he didn't appreciate all she did for him. He would blow her off and imply that she was a lazy TV addict. He would get in her space, and smirk as she became emotional. She would explode and call him names, and sometimes push or slap. When they entered therapy, Brian suggested that Brittany had the problem, saying that she was "ridiculous" and "way too emotional." Brittany claimed persecution from him and said that she couldn't live this way any longer. Neither took any responsibility for the failures in their relationship.

If you have worked with couples who have high conflict, you have seen denial and distortion. This includes minimizing, exaggerating, rationalizing, or misrepresenting what happens in the relationship. Distortion usually happens as emotions escalate, and it is always present when conflict deteriorates into abuse and violence. When both partners are abusive, they may use similar types of distortion and blame. For example, they might excuse their behavior by blaming the other ("I wouldn't have called you an idiot if you didn't miss that turn"). Or they might exaggerate details or ascribe negative motives to behavior ("You are just trying to annoy me by not making the bed").

However, when violence is part of a coercive controlling pattern (usually male to female in straight couples), the distortions are more extreme from the perpetrator. This happens as the victim is blamed ("You knew I would lose it, but you just kept nagging"), threats made ("I know you are talking to guys on Facebook without me knowing"), or outright lies are told ("I haven't used meth in months"). This kind of controlling abuse (called intimate terrorism) is severe, and has the effect of causing self-doubt and self-blame in the victim (Whiting, Oka, & Fife, 2012). In other words, in typical intimate terrorism, the controller blames and excuses his behavior, and the victim buys into these distortions at some level and blames herself or doubts her own perceptions. His distortions excuse his behavior, and confuse and control her. She may also be rationalizing and minimizing things, but it is a way to cope with a traumatic situation where she may feel trapped and scared. Although both parties in this dynamic have distorted perceptions, we are not suggesting that victims have equal responsibility in perpetuating abusive dynamics. However, all distortions keep couples from changing their patterns. For abuse to stop, partners must face the reality of the situation and take responsibility for their behavior (and in the case of intimate terrorism, the male must acknowledge his greater responsibility for the control and increased capacity to hurt). Generally, this is more likely to happen in non-controlling violence.

Description and Implementation

At Texas Tech University, we have a standard protocol that is implemented when physical violence or psychological abuse has occurred (see Chapter 50). In the second half of the intervention, there is an exercise designed to help couples see their distortions and take ownership for them. The goal is to reduce blame, denial, and rationalization, which can help to eliminate conflict and violence. This portion of the intervention comes after the couple has been separately assessed and the protocol has progressed through several components, including defining their cycles of escalation and externalizing the violence (using standard narrative therapy guidelines). At this point, the therapist discusses the idea of distortion. This is introduced with a script about how perception becomes distorted during fights. For example, the clients are told something like: "When people fight, they almost always have distorted perceptions and reactions. They often blame each other for the problems, and minimize their own contributions to them. When behavior becomes aggressive or abusive, partners usually accuse each other of things that aren't accurate, and make excuses." The therapist then gives specific definitions and examples that the couple may relate to, including the following:

> *Blame:* Accusing your partner of causing the problem ("You are destroying this relationship"; "You make me scream at the kids").
> *Rationalization:* Giving an excuse for your behavior ("I was tired"; "You set me off"; "If you wouldn't have left it so messy").
> *Minimization/Exaggeration:* Claiming something is better or worse than it was ("It wasn't that bad"; "I barely touched you"; "You *always* ignore me").

Victimization: Playing up how bad things are because of your partner ("I am trying so hard to help, but you don't appreciate me"; "No one else knows how bad my life is").

Denial: Claiming innocence or not acknowledging something ("You didn't say it like that"; "I didn't mean any harm"; "That never happened").

Deception: Lying or misleading ("I don't know why our money is gone"; "I was late because I got delayed").

After reviewing the examples, the therapist invites the couple to reflect upon times that he or she (not their partner) has engaged in distortion or denial. They are asked about excuses they may have used, things they exaggerated, or any other time they may have distorted the truth of the situation. Most couples are able to identify with some of these examples, and if calm, they can usually share ways that they have done similar things. After this discussion, the therapist reads a vignette:

> *Chuck and Mary are fighting because Mary came home late from work and Chuck is suspicious. Although Mary previously had been involved emotionally with a co-worker, she denies that she has done anything wrong, which frustrates Chuck further. She tells him that he is stupid and stomps off to another room. Chuck follows her, accusing her of cheating, and she pushes past him and he slaps her and shoves her to the couch. After the incident, Chuck is angry and Mary is crying. He says that if she wouldn't have called him a name and pushed him, he wouldn't have hit her. He also tells her that it wasn't that bad, and that it wasn't like he punched her face. He tells Mary that he is sorry, but that she is overreacting. She accuses him of jealousy and says that she called him names because of his suspicions.*

Again, the clients are invited to reflect first about the story and then apply it to their own situation. They are asked about various ways they might distort, including minimizing or downplaying the impact of their own actions, or claiming that they are innocent. They are asked questions like, "Can you share examples when you have blamed your partner for your own hurtful choices?" They are also asked solution-oriented questions regarding how things might improve if there were less blame, accusation, and exaggeration in their relationship, or what things they could do to reduce distortion.

Contraindications and Outcomes

As discussed in Chapter 50, couple interventions are not appropriate where coercive control is ongoing in the relationship. Indeed, one of the ways to know if couples are ready for this intervention is if they can see their own distortions and take a basic level of responsibility for them. All couples distort at times, but male perpetrators who are unwilling to admit this may well fit in the controlling typology and should be referred to batterer intervention programs, and female partners referred to women's protective services. Those who are experiencing non-controlling, situational violence (for more information on these typologies, see Johnson, 2008) can benefit from couples therapy if the clinician has an understanding of violence and abuse (see Stith, McCollum, Rosen, 2011). Our brief intervention provides a structured way to engage and help those who have violence in their relationship (Pettigrew, Whiting, & Smith, in press).

Therapists should make sure that both parties are engaged in this discussion and not putting the blame inappropriately on the other. If things become heated, then the therapist should back off of their line of questioning, address the emotion, and help partners self-soothe and feel heard. This is particularly important if things become escalated because this is likely to generate distortion during that discussion. When things are heated, people often don't realize they are distorting, but they usually can see it when they are calm. It is the therapist's job to help them get to a calm and reflective place to explore their contributions to the relationship deterioration. Even high-conflict and violent couples can generally admit and see their own distortions when they have participated in this exercise.

Case Example

Brittany and Brian reluctantly agreed to participate in the intervention. He continued to assert that Brittany needed the help, but he came because she threatened to leave if he didn't. When the idea of distortion was introduced, Brian surprised the therapists by volunteering examples of rationalizations and excuses that he had seen his father use. This set the stage for them to hear the definitions and case study with an open mind, and prompted some interesting discussion. Brittany recognized that she often exaggerated how hard she was working at home, and suggested that her overreactions were a way to get Brian's attention. Brian realized that he liked provoking Brittany because it helped him feel in control, and it made it easy to blame her for their problems. He still would make excuses for some of his mean comments, but he eventually realized that he enjoyed the peace at home that came when he was nicer to her. Although they still yelled at times or said rude things, they did reduce the blatant blame and victimization that was occurring. Brian stopped getting in Brittany's space and calling her names. She had no further incidents of pushing or slapping, and they both improved in their ability to share their concerns without exaggeration and blame.

References

Johnson, M. (2008). *A typology of domestic violence: Intimate terrorism, violent resistance, and situational couple violence.* Boston: Northeastern University Press.

Pettigrew, H., Whiting, J. B., & Smith, D. B. (in press). Experiences of couples in a brief intimate partner violence intervention: A grounded theory. Manuscript in preparation.

Stith, S. M., McCollum, E. E., Rosen, K. H. (2011). *Couples therapy for domestic violence: Finding safe solutions.* Washington, DC: American Psychological Association.

Whiting, J. B., Oka, M., & Fife, S. T. (2012). Appraisal distortions and intimate partner violence: Gender, power, and interaction. *Journal of Marital and Family Therapy, 38,* 133–149.

PART H

Addressing Childhood Sexual Abuse in Couple Therapy

52

USING PSYCHOEDUCATION WHEN ASSESSING AND TREATING THE EFFECTS OF CHILDHOOD SEXUAL ABUSE (CSA) IN COUPLE RELATIONSHIPS

Colleen M. Peterson and Laura S. Smedley

Purpose: To provide psychoeducation to promote understanding, facilitate couple coping, and treat the effects of CSA where one partner is a CSA survivor

Introduction

Although there is a widely recognized body of literature regarding the known effects of childhood sexual abuse on CSA survivors, most survivors and their partners are unaware that these effects are common to survivors. In therapy, psychoeducation is recognized as an effective treatment intervention through organizing and normalizing symptoms and experiences related to a specific diagnosis or presenting problem. Often clients and their partners experience distress believing that their symptoms are a result of their own flaws, character weaknesses, or "craziness." When clients are provided psychoeducation regarding the common effects of CSA, they are relieved to learn that their experiences are not unique to them. Thus, it is vital for therapists working with CSA survivors and their partners to have a solid working knowledge of the effects of CSA and a framework for naming, organizing, presenting, and identifying the specific effects that are currently impacting the survivor and the couple relationship. The effects associated with CSA fall into the major categories of intrapersonal and interpersonal (Peterson, Fife, & Smedley, 2013).

Purpose of Technique

The purpose of this technique is to help couples become educated regarding the effects of CSA and to normalize the struggles that couples experience related to the CSA. During the discussion of the common effects of CSA, the couple identifies the challenges specific to their relationship. This provides the couple the opportunity to work together around the issues, validates the survivor's struggle, and increases the partner's understanding, empathy, and compassion. The discussion also validates and increases awareness of the partner's corresponding experience. Often the partner's experience includes confusion, alienation, guilt, rejection, and a sense of powerlessness related to the survivor's distress.

The process of discussing common CSA effects and identifying effects specific to the survivor and their couple relationship allows the couple to view their problems in a new light. Rather than assigning blame to the survivor or the partner, the couple is able to view the problems as a result of the abuse. In essence, it externalizes the problems, assigning them to the childhood abuse rather than to individual weakness or relationship failure. This can unite the couple in their efforts to combat the effects. The psychoeducation technique decreases the confusion, anxiety, tension, and blame for the survivor, the partner, and their relationship, thus creating an empowering sense of cognitive, emotional, and relational freedom to explore new solutions.

Description of Technique and Pertinent Background

Research on childhood sexual abuse indicates that there are predictable effects associated with being a CSA survivor, including individual effects on the survivor (intrapersonal) and effects on relationships (interpersonal) (Kuyken, 1995). With the couple, the therapist introduces research related to the effects of CSA on survivors and their relationships and suggests that it is often helpful to explore and discuss those effects. The therapist then describes the effects as falling into two broad areas: intrapersonal and interpersonal. The therapist presents and discusses the different effects in each of the areas. The first task is to explain the effects that CSA has on the individual (see Table 52.1). The second task is to help the couple identify how CSA is impacting their relationship (see Table 52.2). This knowledge and awareness helps the couple understand that their problems are not the result of some character defect or a lack of love or commitment to the marriage. Rather, their problems are a direct result of CSA and are common to many survivors of CSA. This usually creates a collective "sigh of relief," as it were, that they are not inherently flawed or culpable. It greatly reduces the blame and shame that they may have internalized and allows them to externalize the problem(s) and develop a plan to address the challenges together.

It is important that the therapist recognize significant factors that impact the severity of the CSA effects. These factors include: the age of the victim at the time of the abuse, how many perpetrators were involved, the child's relationship to the perpetrator, the exact form and intensity of the abuse, its duration and frequency, and the circumstances surrounding the disclosure of the abuse and the subsequent response of family members. Research has shown that whether or not there was sexual penetration, the use of force, violence, or threats; a high frequency and

TABLE 52.1 Intrapersonal Impact of CSA.

Psychological Distress	depression, anxiety, fatigue, post-traumatic stress, dissociation, personality disorders, somatization, sensory memories, eating disorders and substance abuse
Emotional Distress	shock, confusion, pain, emotional flooding, guilt, shame, fear, anger, rage, blame, depression, anxiety, loss and hopelessness
Emotional Dysregulation	excessive emotional reactivity, hypervigilance, hostility, flashbacks, social anxiety, mistrust, numbing, sleep disturbances, irritability, nightmares, self-harm, and suicidality
Cognitive Disruption	difficulties maintaining concentration, intrusive thoughts, irrational beliefs, cognitive distortions, denial
Disruption in Sense of Self	confusion surrounding one's identity, low self-esteem, worthlessness, unlovability, feeling flawed, broken or dirty, powerlessness, sexual identity confusion, personal boundary confusion, distorted body image, feelings of stigmatization, self-blame, self-loathing
Maladaptive Coping Strategies	physical or emotional numbing, depersonalization, dissociation, isolation, addictions, obsessions and compulsions, eating disorders, overwork, escapism, sexual promiscuity, and seeking unhealthy relationships

TABLE 52.2 Interpersonal Impact of CSA.

Ambivalence Toward Relationships	torn between wanting and avoiding relationships; not knowing how to be in a healthy relationship/what it looks like
Difficulty with Fear and Trust	decreased ability to love and trust others, fear to love or trust others, fear of abandonment, fear of rejection, increased need for love and approval, fear of being trapped, commitment volatility, need for sense of power/control
Difficulty with Intimacy: Emotional	emotional cutoff, commitment volatility, numbing, anxious-avoidant attachment styles, avoidance of vulnerability, difficulty accessing and expressing emotion, exaggeration of personal defenses and conflicts, emotional reactivity
Difficulty with Intimacy: Physical	sensory memories/triggers, lack of boundaries, freezing, dissociation, hypersensitivity, sensitivity to encroachment on personal space
Difficulty with Intimacy: Sexual	sexual confusion, fear of being sexual, inhibited or hypoactive sexual desire, dichotomous view of sexual connection—either sexually submissive or aggressive, promiscuity, perceived lack of knowledge/ability to be a good sexual partner, dissociation with sexual contact, negative associations with past sexual abuse (ideas such as sex = pain, sex = badness, sex = victimization, sex = love, sex = power, sex = personal value/validation, "everyone wants sex from me", "I am my body"), sexual and emotional disconnect

intensity of abuse; a younger age for the onset of victimization; a close family member as perpetrator(s); and an extended time period of abuse all serve to increase the degree of trauma to the survivor (Kuyken, 1995). The combination of these factors generally influences the subjective severity of the trauma and the nature of the psychological and emotional sequelae.

Partners may suffer secondary trauma as a result of being exposed to the traumatic material and distressing symptoms associated with the survivor's trauma. When awareness and healing of a survivor begins, it often results in the systemic upheaval of the relationship. The couple may have difficulty negotiating a new way of being in the marriage. Partners may also experience symptoms similar to those of a survivor, including emotional, physical, and spiritual fatigue; victimization; sleep disturbances; hypervigilance; nightmares; denial; emotional withdrawal; depression; low self-esteem; and secondary shame.

Contraindications

Active abuse within the relationship would prohibit the formation of the trust needed to explore CSA issues. Likewise, if the partner denies the reality of the abuse or minimizes or disbelieves its impact on the survivor, the survivor may not experience the requisite safety or commitment in the relationship to warrant open dialogue about these deeply painful experiences.

Case Example

Bill and Kara presented for counseling with regard to emotional volatility and problems with sexual intimacy. They had been married for two years and had no children. During assessment and creation of a therapeutic alliance, Bill expressed his hurt and frustration with the frequency and nature of their sexual relationship. Bill complained that Kara was never interested in sex, and that when he approached her, she was aloof and unresponsive. When he tried to talk about it with her, she became irritable and distant and refused to talk about it. Before their marriage, she was affectionate and sexually flirtatious, but now she seemed to "freeze up" on the rare occasion that they were sexually intimate. Bill reported symptoms of depression and verbalized feeling hurt, confused, and rejected. Bill expressed a desire to know why his wife had changed and what he could do to renew intimacy in their marriage. He reported that they had not been intimate for four months.

Kara stated that it's not that she doesn't love Bill, it's just that she "doesn't like" sex. She stated that she feels guilty and bad for Bill, but when she tries to be sexual, it's like her body "shuts down" and she just can't go there. During the assessment, Kara revealed that she has a history of childhood sexual abuse.

As part of couple therapy, the therapist used the psychoeducational technique described to educate, validate, and empathize with Bill and Kara and to provide them with contextual understanding of their difficulties with intimacy. They also discussed the impact that the CSA effects were having on their relationship and on themselves personally. The therapist validated their distress and externalized their struggles as relating to the deep wounds Kara experienced in childhood. During the course of the discussion, Bill and Kara recognized several effects that were playing out with Kara and their relationship. Bill expressed relief when he realized that Kara's lack of sexual expression was not because she didn't love him. He turned to her and took her hand, demonstrating decreased guardedness and increased compassion toward Kara. Kara acknowledged fear and discomfort surrounding sexual intimacy and was relieved to know that there was a reason for her feelings. Bill and Kara identified several goals for couples therapy based on the couple's symptoms with regards to the effects of CSA and their sexual and emotional intimacy. With insights from this intervention, the therapist worked with Bill and Kara to create coping strategies and formed a treatment plan based on the symptoms the couple was experiencing. This increased awareness helped Bill and Kara identify times of fear and distress for Kara. Kara was able to incorporate breathing techniques, mindfulness, and sharing her feelings with Bill to help her reduce her symptoms of CSA. Bill was able to be more patient and compassionate with Kara and not take her intimacy difficulties personally. They were able to talk about what she needed from Bill to feel more calm and present with him as they gradually increased the degree of intimacy in their marriage. These tools helped decrease the anxiety and stress in the relationship and allowed Bill and Kara to work together on their problems, thus strengthening their relationship.

References

Kuyken, W. (1995). The psychological sequelae of childhood sexual abuse: A review of the literature and implications for treatment. *Clinical Psychology and Psychotherapy, 2*(2), 108–121.

Peterson, C., Fife, S. T., & Smedley, L. (2013, November). *Childhood sexual abuse survivors and sexual intimacy: What heals or hurts the couple relationship*. Paper presented at the annual conference of the National Council on Family Relations, San Antonio, TX.

53

PROMOTING HEALING OF CHILDHOOD SEXUAL ABUSE (CSA) SURVIVORS WITHIN THE COUPLE RELATIONSHIP

Laura S. Smedley and Colleen M. Peterson

Purpose: To identify and facilitate relational behaviors that promote healing from childhood sexual abuse (CSA)

Introduction

This psychoeducational technique builds on Chapter 52 wherein the effects of CSA on survivors and their partners were identified. The literature indicates that partners of CSA survivors often feel at a loss as to what they can do to support and help their partners (MacIntosh & Johnson, 2008). In this chapter, partner behaviors that promote healing, and behaviors that hinder healing for CSA survivors, will be presented. Instructions for helping couples identify and facilitate healing behaviors and eliminate harmful behaviors will be given. This technique helps distressed couples identify specific relational dynamics that may be hindering the survivor's healing. In addition, partner behaviors that facilitate the survivor's healing are identified, taught, and incorporated into the couple relationship.

Purpose of Promoting Healing of CSA Survivors Within the Couple Relationship

The purpose of this technique is for the therapist to provide psychoeducation regarding specific relationship behaviors that perpetuate the effects of CSA trauma and those that promote healing, safety, and trust in the relationship. This technique facilitates a couple approach to helping the individual survivor to heal from the effects of CSA. It also helps the couple identify relationship behaviors that will enhance a healthy and secure bond within the couple relationship. This technique is implemented within the context of the couple's interactions and enables the therapist working with the couple to identify those relational interactions that trigger the painful effects of the partner's unique trauma. The therapist also helps the couple identify specific partner behaviors that soothe painful emotions and establish new, healthy relational boundaries and interactions. This tangible, behavioral map will help to counter feelings of anxiety and helplessness that are common to couples dealing with past trauma (MacIntosh & Johnson, 2008). It is often difficult for couples to know how to fight "ghosts from the past," and having a road map to healing will empower the couple with specific, effective tools to create the type of relationship that they desire. This will allow them to reclaim their relationship and make it their own, throwing off the shadow of those persons and events that came before.

Description and Implementation

In this technique, the therapist builds upon the previously identified intrapersonal and interpersonal effects of CSA that the couple is experiencing (see Chapter 52). The therapist first suggests exploring and discussing how these research findings pertain to the couple. Current research has provided knowledge and insight into how specific behaviors within relational couple dynamics affect a CSA survivor and what partners do to hinder or help their companions heal from the abuse (Smedley, 2012). Based on the specific CSA effects that the survivor is experiencing, the therapist helps the couple identify how those effects are influenced by their relational interactions.

For example, when discussing what happens when Kara "freezes up" in response to Bill's attempt to initiate sexual intimacy (see the case example in Chapter 52), the therapist and couple are able to discover that Kara feels more anxious about sexuality when Bill's advances seem aggressive, or when she is not asked beforehand if she is open to sexual intimacy. The therapist uses the list of behaviors that can be hindrances to healing (see Table 53.1) to help the couple identify problem areas that are negatively affecting healing and healthy marital intimacy. The therapist then presents the research on what partners do to help healing (see Table 53.2) and engages the couple in a discussion of how these principles can be applied in their relationship.

Based on this evaluation, the therapist helps the couple set specific goals for change that address the needs of both the survivor and the partner. The therapist assists the couple to further explore these principles in detail and identify what these changes will look like for the couple. The therapist then integrates this information into the working treatment plan with the couple. Once the areas for improvement/strengthening have been identified, the therapist supports these behavioral changes through a written behavioral plan, role-playing, modeling, displacement stories, and positive feedback.

TABLE 53.1 What Partners do to Hinder Healing.

Criticism and Rejection	Blame, shame, judgment, "not good enough," withholding love/ attention, lack of responsiveness, lack of affirmation, lack of understanding, lack of support, lack of touch, lack of empathy, decreased personal responsibility, unrealistic expectations, sexual rejection
Betrayal	Physical or emotional affairs, disloyalty, lies, pretense, disingenuousness, breach of confidence/trust
Disrespect of Personhood	Minimizing impact of abuse, disrespecting boundaries, taking boundaries as a personal offense, other things matter more than me, greater concern for outward appearances, partner's needs take precedence, sex when anxious or distraught
Lack of Choice	Opinions ignored, pressure to change thoughts/feelings/ behaviors, guilt-tripping, controlling in the relationship, pressure for sex
Lack of Communication	Decreased responsiveness, avoiding subjects, lack of safety in relationship
Partner Mistrust	Jealousy, suspicion
Lack of Growth	Resistance to partner's growth and change, unwillingness to change/grow with survivor

Contraindications

This technique assumes that both partners are committed to the relationship and are willing to work together to help promote growth and healing. Ongoing abuse or minimization by the partner regarding the effects of CSA might interfere with the safety necessary to address these difficult issues.

Case Example

As described in the case example in Chapter 52, Bill and Kara presented for counseling, and during the assessment Kara revealed a history of childhood sexual abuse. As part of couple therapy, the therapist used the psychoeducational technique described in Chapter 52 to educate, validate, and empathize with Bill and Kara and to provide them with contextual understanding of their difficulties with intimacy. They also discussed the impact that the CSA effects were having on their relationship and on themselves personally. The therapist validated their distress and externalized their struggles as relating to the deep wounds experienced in childhood. During the course of the discussion, Bill and Kara recognized several CSA effects that were playing out with Kara and their relationship. This increased awareness helped Bill and Kara identify times of fear and distress for both Kara and Bill.

TABLE 53.2 What Partners do to Help Healing.

Safety and Trust	Open communication, honesty, loyalty, commitment, no shaming, no criticism, respect for feelings, respect for wishes, sense of protection, physical proximity, value personhood, survivor's needs take precedence before partner's needs
Acceptance and Validation	No blaming, no shaming, no judgment, responsiveness, interest, belief in abuse story, verbal affirmations of acceptance/validation, understanding, forgiveness, respect for feelings
Open Communication	Open discussion on any topic, sense of safety and trust, lots of time spent talking, listening, full disclosure, mutual disclosure, negotiation of needs
Emotional Connectedness/ Intimacy—Perception of Being Loved	Mutuality, emotionally responsive and aware, verbal expressions of love, non-sexual physical touch, thoughtful service, kindness, friendship, sexual intimacy with emotional connectedness and perception of freedom
Support	Listening, understanding, quality time, verbal affirmations of support, commitment, encouragement, reassurance, service, generosity, non-sexual physical touch, financial support
Empathy	Expressions of sorrow/sadness, expressions of care and concern for partner, tears, indignation, compassion
Freedom of Choice	Patience, personal boundaries honored, respect opinions/ voice, support sense of personal control, no pressure for sex, no pressure for change of feelings/behaviors
Positive Growth	Modeling, encouragement, perception of successful relationship

With insights gained from using the psychoeducational intervention, the therapist utilized the information in Tables 53.1 and 53.2 to explore with Bill and Kara the patterns and behaviors in their relationship that either help or hinder healing for Kara. Based on the symptoms the couple was experiencing and the information from the tables, the couple and therapist worked together to create coping strategies and form a treatment plan. Kara and Bill identified safety and trust, open communication, emotional connectedness, and freedom of choice as areas that they wanted to improve in their marriage. They worked with their therapist to develop a behavioral plan specific to: 1) their sexual relationship; 2) non-sexual physical touch in their marriage; and 3) increased open communication between the two of them.

Kara and Bill agreed to hold off on their sexual relationship temporarily until safety and trust could be increased through open communication and increased emotional connectedness. When the time came, they agreed that they would negotiate sexual boundaries together and commit to honoring those boundaries.

Bill and Kara decided to give up watching an hour of TV in the evenings in order to spend time talking together. They agreed that they would start by holding hands and facing each other, taking turns sharing their thoughts and feelings about any subject, with the exception of sex and Kara's abuse, for the first couple of weeks. Then Kara thought that she might be ready to talk about some of her childhood experiences and how she felt about and experienced sexuality. She thought it would be nice if Bill spooned her or sat behind her and held her during those conversations. They agreed that it would be a good idea for Bill to also share some of his experiences, thoughts, and feelings surrounding sexuality. The therapist suggested that they use a 1–10 scaling technique to help their partner understand their level of anxiety or intensity of feeling surrounding any given topic of discussion. The therapist helped Bill and Kara practice reflective listening, open-ended questions, and messages of acceptance and validation to help prepare them to succeed in this process of increased sharing and vulnerability.

Another part of Bill and Kara's plan to increase safety, communication, and emotional connectedness was to begin giving positive affirmations and expressions of gratitude to one another. They agreed to give each other at least five positive messages a day, either written or verbally. The therapist helped them understand that these new skills and new ways of being in the relationship would take time to shape and practice. Bill and Kara agreed to continue to meet with their therapist in order to evaluate their progress and adjust their treatment plan and relational goals as the need arose. Bill and Kara were relieved, excited, and hopeful to have a tangible plan in place to improve their marriage.

References

MacIntosh, H. B., & Johnson, S. (2008). Emotionally focused therapy for couples and childhood sexual abuse survivors. *Journal of Marital and Family Therapy, 34*(3), 298–315.

Smedley, L. (2012). *CSA survivors: What heals and what hurts in a couple relationship.* Retrieved from digitalscholarship.unlv.edu